Archaeological
Theory and Practice

Archaeological Theory and Practice

edited by D E STRONG
Institute of Archaeology
University of London

1973

SEMINAR PRESS
London · New York

Seminar Press Limited
24/28 Oval Road, London NW1

U.S. edition published by

SEMINAR PRESS INC.
111 Fifth Avenue,
New York, New York 10003

Library of Congress Catalog Card Number: 73-7042
ISBN: 0 12 914050 3

PRINTED IN GREAT BRITAIN
BY WILLMER BROTHERS LIMITED, BIRKENHEAD

Essays presented to

Professor William Francis Grimes
C.B.E. D.Litt. F.S.A. F.M.A.

by his colleagues in the Institute of Archaeology
University of London
at
his retirement Summer 1973

PROFESSOR W. F. GRIMES C.B.E. D.Litt. F.S.A. F.M.A.

Photograph: Richard Hubbard

Contributors

J. A. ALEXANDER — *Extra-Mural Studies, University of London*
DEPARTMENT WITHIN INSTITUTE
OF ARCHAEOLOGY

WARWICK BRAY — *Prehistoric Archaeology*
V. M. CONLON — *Archaeological Photography*
I. W. CORNWALL — *Human Environment*
G. W. DIMBLEBY — *Human Environment*
P. G. DORRELL — *Archaeological Photography*
J. D. EVANS — *Prehistoric Archaeology*
I. GLOVER — *Prehistoric Archaeology*
M. W. C. HASSALL — *Archaeology of the Roman Provinces*
H. W. M. HODGES — *Conservation of Archaeological Materials*
F. R. HODSON — *Prehistoric Archaeology*
J. G. NANDRIS — *Prehistoric Archaeology*
M. NEWCOMER — *Prehistoric Archaeology*
JAMES MELLAART — *Western Asiatic Archaeology*
DAVID OATES — *Western Asiatic Archaeology*
P. J. PARR — *Western Asiatic Archaeology*
D. PRICE WILLIAMS — *Western Asiatic Archaeology*
RICHARD REECE — *Archaeology of the Roman Provinces*
JOAN M. SHELDON — *Human Environment*
H. M. STEWART — *Archaeological Drawing and Surveying*
D. E. STRONG — *Archaeology of the Roman Provinces*
D. STURDY — *Mediaeval Russia and Eastern Europe*
J. d'A. WAECHTER — *Prehistoric Archaeology*

Foreword

This volume of essays has been written by a number of colleagues of Professor Grimes, and is dedicated to him on the occasion of his retirement as Director of the Institute of Archaeology. The list of the contributors to this volume and the wide variety of the subjects covered are in themselves a striking tribute to the high renown and esteem which Professor Grimes enjoys in the realm of Archaeology. Past and present members of the staff and students at the Institute have testified how much they owe to the Director by reason of the breadth of his interests and the encouragement he has unsparingly given to the particular work or research on which they have been engaged .

Professor Grimes graduated in the University of Wales, and after an apprenticeship in Archaeology and Museum work at the National Museum of Wales, eventually in 1945 succeeded Sir Mortimer Wheeler as Director of the London Museum, a post which he held until 1956. For a year or so prior to the outbreak of the 1939 war he was on the staff of the Ordnance Survey at Southampton, and during the war he was seconded to the Ministry of Works, where he rendered valuable service in excavating monuments threatened with destruction on defence sites. One volume of his reports on this work has already appeared and others are expected to follow shortly.

Professor Grimes had been a member of the Management Committee of the Institute of Archaeology since 1943, and when Professor Gordon Childe retired in 1956 Professor Grimes was the obvious successor. The date was a turning point in the life of the Institute. It marked the transition from the easy, rural and attractive surroundings in Regents Park (providing as they did a detached, comfortable and perhaps somewhat amateurish outlook) to the more formal, prosaic and functional establishment in Gordon Square, in close proximity to and association with other branches of the University of London.

The change called for high qualities of administrative ability and tact and great praise is due to Professor Grimes for the way in which he supervised this operation and subsequently fostered that trans-formation into a fully professional body which has enabled the Institute, in its new Bloomsbury home, to take its due place among the institutions of the University. The last seventeen years have seen the Institute grow from strength to strength both in numbers and

A*

in the variety of disciplines for which it caters. The number of the staff has doubled since 1956, and the number of students has increased nearly threefold.

Professor Grimes soon recognized the anomalies caused by the limitation in the work of the Institute in catering only for post-graduate studies, and it was as a result of his enthusiasm and pressure that the Senate eventually agreed to the introduction in 1966 of a first degree in Archaeology. As a result the Institute has been able to extend its scope to provide for the teaching of both undergraduates and post-graduate students.

One of the most important duties of the Director of a Senate Institute is to cultivate close relationships with the authorities at the Senate House. In this respect Professor Grimes has been con-spicuously successful – to the great advantage of the Institute in its standing with the University.

The work of the Institute, its staff and students have naturally had the first call on the time and interest of Professor Grimes, although he has not neglected his own specialist contribution to research, to archaeological excavation and to field studies. In each of these spheres he has given leadership and inspiration to a wide group of followers, and perhaps his part in organizing each year a programme of field studies has been particularly appreciated by students. It was due to the initiative of Professor Grimes that the Institute decided in 1961 to publish an Annual Bulletin, which has become of substantial size and provides a convenient forum for publications by members of the staff and some of the students.

I have been impressed by the care taken by Professor Grimes to help and encourage individual students within their particular interest and research and, when necessary, with their personal problems.

Outside the Institute Professor Grimes has played a conspicuous and prominent part in nearly every National Society concerned with Archaeology, and has in time been President of the Council for British Archaeology, President of the London and Middlesex Archaeological Society, President of the Royal Archaeological Institute, Vice-President of the Society of Antiquaries, of the Society for Medieval Archaeology, and of the Prehistoric Society. This list is not exhaustive, and it has become almost trite to observe that no committee on an archaeological subject is complete unless graced with the presence of Professor Grimes, and none to which he does not from his wide experience make some notable contribution.

In addition to this special place among scholars Professor Grimes is known to a wider public as the discoverer of the Mithraic temple of the Walbrook, which was the culminating and most striking event in a long series of excavations undertaken, year by year, since 1946, for the Roman and Mediaeval London Excavation Council.

It is not for me to comment on the knowledge and scholarship in the many publications both in books and papers in the journals of learned societies which Professor Grimes has written. They all bear the stamp of painstaking workmanship and scrupulously careful statement, and are authentic records of scientific investigations that have made notable contributions to knowledge.

We express the gratitude of all associated with the Institute by offering him this testimonial volume of essays. We wish him many happy years of retirement and shall look forward to further publications from his pen of some still unrecorded excavations.

FLETCHER

May 1973

Contents

Abbreviations

C.A.H.	"Cambridge Ancient History"
C.I.L.	"Corpus Inscriptionum Latinarum"
I.L.S.	"Inscriptiones Latinae Selectae" (Ed. H. Dessay) 1892
P.I.R.	"Prosopographia Imperii Romani" Berlin from 1897
R.E.	"Pauly's realencyclopädie der Classischen Altertumswissenschaft"
R.I.B.	"The Roman Inscription of Britain", Oxford, 1965

Acknowledgements

This volume has been produced under the guidance of an Editorial Board consisting of Professors Dimbleby, Evans, Oates and Strong. Professor Strong and Mrs Marjory Hunt were responsible for the editorial work.

The Editors would like to thank the staff of the Siminar Press for the friendly way in which they have co-operated in the preparation of this book. Many of their colleagues have gladly assisted them in various ways; Miss Susan Johnson prepared the index and gave a great deal of secretarial assistance; Miss Christine Crickmore, Miss Roberta Crowder, Mrs Suzy Fellows, Mrs Frances McDonald and Mrs Penny Wyatt have also helped. Mrs Conlon's advice and expertize has, as always, been invaluable.

Landscape, with Figures

JOAN M. SHELDON

AT A RECENT SEMINAR instigated by the students at the Institute of
Archaeology, the question "Why Archaeology?" was put to members
of the academic staff. The Director expressed his belief that archaeology should be more than a study of Man and his artifacts in the past;
nor would it suffice merely to extend it to include the environmental
background; he felt that the only standpoint for an archaeologist was
to see man as yet another animal, though with a more profound
influence than most, in the world of nature. This ecological approach
is nowadays appearing more frequently in the archaeological literature but some workers, while accepting these ideas in theory, in
practice continue to treat all reports from scientists as discrete
appendices at the end of the archaeological section of their publications. No attempt is made to integrate the information obtained to
build up a picture of the landscape of the time and man's effect on it.
That Professor Grimes has never allowed the landscape to be left out
of his archaeological deductions is, however, clear from a study of
his published works (for example, 1936, 1951, 1963). The too facile
acceptance of the unsophisticated "clay-land-and-damp-oak-wood"
attitude, however, was always a source of danger (Grimes, 1945) and
Grimes (1935) saw the need "to-re-affirm the principle that we can
only obtain and use geological and botanical evidence by following
geological and botanical methods". Part of the teaching method of
the natural sciences has always been to include a period of practical
instruction in the field and it has equally been the Institute's practice
to combine practical work with theoretical instruction for undergraduates and graduates alike. This applies particularly to the courses
in the Human Environment Department and the outline course on
environmental subjects for First Year students culminates each year
in a period of study in the field. Through the years we have enjoyed
the Director's company on these field courses and generations of
students have benefited from his wide knowledge of archaeological
monuments and his great enthusiasm for field work.

Knowledge to be gained from the Landscape

To many archaeologists field work means either excavation or walking over the countryside looking for artifacts or archaeological features such as ploughed-out barrows, ancient field systems or some evidence of habitation sites. The recognition of such man-made features forms part of the instruction on our field courses and we try to cover the spectrum from Palaeolithic sites to mediaeval churches. In addition, however, we have always considered it necessary to include some natural phenomena and discuss the interaction between the two. Each site is thus viewed against its background of available resources and the effect the exploitation of these would have on the countryside at different technological levels. This paper is an attempt to outline some of the advantages in bringing students, even for only a short period, into actual contact with the geomorphological, pedological and biological aspects of the countryside. The knowledge they have of these subjects before starting the course varies widely, some school-leavers having taken geology, botany or zoology to A-level standard while others seem never to have learnt anything about the natural sciences or even to be aware of the backcloth against which we view man's activities through the ages. First

Fig. 1. Landscape near St David's Head, Pembrokeshire. (Photograph: M. Barton.)

and foremost, therefore, the field course is an opportunity to focus upon the *Landscape* and secondly to introduce *Figures* into the picture – not only the students (Fig. 1) but also their predecessors who have helped to make the canvas what it is today.

The term "environment" has become hackneyed; generally referring only to the artificial surroundings of urban life. In an archaeological context it often covers the botanical and zoological remains of domesticated plants and animals from a site, which are as much artifacts as any weapon or vessel manufactured from a natural resource. In trying to instil in students an ecological approach to the environment, we may feel that a walk across an open moorland or through a deciduous forest allows us to introduce them to a more natural background, but we need to keep in mind that a closer study has often revealed the anthropogenic nature of even these landscapes.

Perspective in Landscape Studies

We are well aware that it is misleading to discuss a region only in terms of present day conditions, so the selection of areas to be studied in the field has been partly governed by how much research into the past history of a region has already been carried out. In addition, personal knowledge and research by members of staff naturally played a part. For these reasons, areas visited have included Northeast Yorkshire; the Weald and Hampshire Basin; Salisbury Plain and the New Forest; and Pembrokeshire. Although this insular attitude has had its critics, we maintain, in the good company of Wooldridge (1960) that "Wisdom is before him that hath understanding, but the eyes of the fool are in the ends of the earth" (Proverbs xvii, 24).

Many ecological principles discussed in one country can be applied on a world-wide basis, such as the ecological status of areas of grassland and the results of intensive grazing by domestic animals. In other cases, there are positive advantages in working in a small country with a varied geological background. It is possible in one day's travel to traverse several different geological formations and to contrast man's exploitation of the ecological systems of each zone.

In all the areas selected basic rocks of chalk or limestone lie close to clay vales and acidic sandstones, making it possible to demonstrate the "optimal settlement sites" on the margins or ecotones, within easy reach of varying resources or where exchange of products becomes feasible. The importance of these situations for early man either with a hunting-gathering or an agricultural economy has been increasingly stressed in the archaeological literature (Harris, 1969).

Some of the plants which were important in the diet of early man are as indigenous to this country as to other parts of Europe or even Asia. In other cases, although the British plants may differ at species level, the ecological requirements of the genera may be homologous and it is, for example, possible to demonstrate the abundance of legumes and annual grasses growing in dry situations of Chalk hillsides, reflecting the importance of their counterparts in the diet of prehistoric man, as indicated by botanical remains in the Near East (Flannery, 1969). Other food supplies from Chalk areas include wild carrots, parsnips and other root crops as well as the fruit of many shrubs of the Rosaceae.

An even greater advantage of field work in the British Isles is that we are surrounded by sea so that it has been possible to include the littoral zone in our traverses each year. This has enabled us not only to look at geomorphological features such as ancient shorelines both above and below the present tidal range, but also discuss the possibilities of extended foraging territories for Upper Palaeolithic and Mesolithic people in the early Postglacial, for example, along the coasts of the Bristol Channel and Pembrokeshire. Whilst we have a certain amount of evidence that the coastal area probably was exploited on a seasonal basis by many prehistoric people, we perhaps underestimate the potentialities of this ecozone, particularly in the case of some food plants, the remains of which may not survive in the archaeological record. For example, many of our cultivated green and root crops, such as cabbages, beets, fennel, seakale and asparagus, were originally derived from plants of the coastal zone and can still be found growing wild in these habitats today.

Many of the plants which we regard as weeds were important sources of raw material to early man, not only in his diet but also for dyes, tannins and fibres. To young students with no practical experience of eradicating weeds from their gardens, many are but names in a textbook. Even more mature students, intimate with the pollen grains under a microscope, may be surprised at the sight of the whole plant in the field, particularly as so many weeds adapt their growth form to varying environmental conditions. Many useful weeds adapt themselves readily to disturbed ground conditions, whether naturally formed by earth movements or due to man's disturbance round habitation sites. The ideal situation to demonstrate the adaptability of plants has proved to be gravel and sand pits where the working face can first be used to explain geomorphological features such as cryoturbations, ice-wedging, glacial or river deposits and then the vegetation colonizing the abandoned floor and sand heaps examined. Salisbury (1964) has suggested that such disturbed conditions at the end of the Last Glaciation may have been the time when many of our common weeds speciated, producing, for example, the micro-species of *Taraxacum* (Dandelion), *Capsella* (Shepherd's Purse) and Whitlow Grass.

Gravel pits also present an opportunity to discuss some dynamic geomorphological processes on a minor scale – the erosion of bare slopes by water action and sheet erosion, the features of a stream bed, the formation and form of talus fans can all be encompassed within a small area. Geological text-books usually explain the mechanics of natural agencies as cause and effect, whereas environmental archaeologists usually have only the deposits before them from which to deduce the agencies which produced the sediments in the past.

Confusion in the Landscape

One of the major exercises, not only on field courses, but in environmental teaching as a whole, is to emphasize the possible confusion between natural and man-made features both on the ground and in excavation sections. Young archaeologists are becoming increasingly conscious of the obvious pitfalls but, in the past, members of staff have had difficulty in convincing excavators of the naturalness of iron-pans or humus horizons. The interpretation of changes in soil profiles is, therefore, an important part of field work combined with a discussion on biological and physical factors in soil genesis. The distinction between soil material as seen in the top few inches, possibly derived from elsewhere, and a soil profile formed *in situ* as a three-dimensional entity, is pertinent to many archaeological sections. It is unfortunate that the term "soil" is commonly used for both of them. The recognition of truncated soils buried under earthworks may be some indication of man's activities on the site.

Many phenomena continue to fall into a doubtfully natural category, particularly on Chalk sites, and we require more scientific information about solution weathering and the chemical effects of man's habitation on both basic and acidic bedrocks. Archaeological excavations are often one of the few occasions when large surfaces are uncovered so that features can be seen in plan as well as section. It is unfortunate, therefore, that once a feature is suspected of being natural it loses all interest in many cases. Periglacial features are, however, being recognized on archaeological sites in increasing number (Evans, 1971). In particular, ice-wedging with its regular pattern on the surface may be confused with man-made structures (Evans, 1972) and an example of this pitfall is always included on the field course to the North Yorkshire Moors.

The polygonal formations produced by this agency were first recognized in the area by Dimbleby (1952) from air-photographs. They seem to be confined to the Tabular Hills and, in particular, to the geological formation known as the Lower Calcareous Grit (Jurassic). This stratum has a non-calcareous constitution in this area (owing to the presence of siliceous sponge spicules) resulting in pod-solized soils, under today's conditions, carrying moorland or planted coniferous forests.

Once located, the polygons can be clearly seen on the ground by differences in vegetation over the cracks (cotton grass) from that in the centre of the polygons (heather). Indeed, in some cases the vegetational changes in the field distinguished "cracks" which were too poorly defined to register from the air. In addition, there is a detectable difference in level between the polygonal lines and their centres – anything from one inch to one foot on the surface configuration and even greater when the peat is stripped, as it lies thicker over the cracks. Thus the appearance in the field may well suggest hut circles or enclosures of some kind – raised centres, sub-quadrangular shape, diameters between 15 and 30 ft. Ice-wedges are known both under present day conditions in the permafrost zone (Leffingwell, 1915, 1919) and in their fossil state in present temperate zones (for example the British Isles: Shotton, 1960; Sparks and West, 1972). Péwé (1966) found that an average annual temperature of at least − 6°C. was required for their formation. A permanently frozen sub-soil is a requisite for the survival of the wedges from winter to winter as summer thaw disturbs the upper active layer.

It is usually only in vertical section that the true nature of the cracks is revealed and, in the case of the Yorkshire examples, sections dug across a number of them on Silpho and Suffield Moors (Figs. 2 and 3) exhibited a number of features in common. The width at the top was about 4½ ft, tapering to a few inches at about 7–10 ft below ground; there was marked disruption of the bedded gritstone at the edges of the wedge; the filling material contained non-local sands and, in one case (Fig. 3) erratics of Scottish origin in a purple-brown clay. It seems likely from this evidence, therefore, that these particular examples had been filled not by material from the peri-glacial zone but by ice-contact material. Other geomorphological evidence, also examined in the field, had suggested that during the

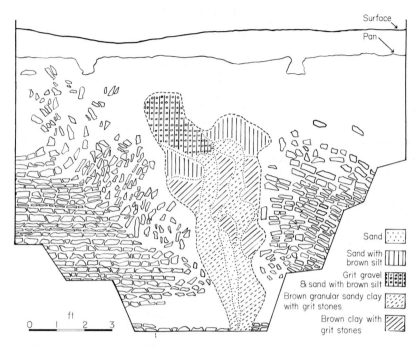

Fig. 2. Section of ice-wedge on Silpho Moor, Tabular Hills, N.E. Yorks.
(Courtesy British Soc. Soil Science.)

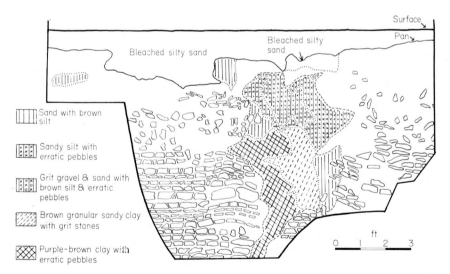

Fig. 3. Section across ice-wedge on Suffield Moor, Tabular Hills, N.E. Yorks,
showing infilling of crack with glacial material including erratic pebbles.
(Courtesy British Soc. Soil Science.)

Last Glaciation the ice-front had stood at less than 1000 ft (Kendall, 1902) leaving the Tabular and Cleveland Hills as nunataks (but see also Gregory, 1965). The polygons must belong to an earlier phase of the Pleistocene on this evidence, therefore.

One further horizon of the filling deserves mention; within the upper one to two feet there was a layer of burnt stones and other traces of fire, including charcoal of pine and oak. The identification of these trees in an area of open moorland leads to one of the most important discussions on any field course, namely the status of the vegetation cover which we see before us today. Although we have much to learn from ecologists' methods of study in an area under present day condition, it is of the time-factor that we are particularly conscious. While it is necessary to examine the interaction of climatological, physical and biological factors, it is the anthropological factor that particularly concerns us.

Anthropological Factor in the Landscape

Archaeologists are now becoming familiar with the impact of Neolithic Man on the landscape, but it remains necessary to emphasize the possibilities of change at the pre-agricultural stage also. Pollen analysis of buried soils has shown that the hold heather has gained in some landscapes, for example on the greensands in Surrey and Sussex (Keef et al., 1965) or Dartmoor (Simmons, 1969) was initiated by the activities of Mesolithic Man. The open, tree-less moorland of the Cleveland Hills is, however, a relatively late phenomenon. At the site of White Gill, at an altitude of 1250 ft on the main watershed between Farndale and Westerdale, microliths were found lying on the surface of a bleached mineral soil under a black humus layer. Pollen analysis of the soil in which the flints lay showed that Mesolithic Man would have been able to hunt under a closed forest canopy of oak, alder, birch and hazel (Dimbleby, 1961). The layer immediately above the cultural horizon showed that Mesolithic Man's activities had, locally at least, reduced the tree-cover. That this was likely to be the result of fire was suggested by the presence of charcoal with the microliths. Both in Yorkshire and in other areas visited we have always included an area of heathland where there are visible remains of the effects of fire under present land use. This can be seen not only in the blackened areas and blasted tree-stumps, but also in the distribution of the remaining trees and the fact that they all tend to be of the same age, unlike the situation in an area of natural regeneration. Hollows in the ground enable some clumps to survive the heat of the fire and, in general, the result of constant firing is floristic simplification to those species which are fire-resistant.

An examination of the soil and stones in a recently burnt zone also makes the point that it takes more than a moving fire of this kind, whether natural or started by man, to redden and crackle flints and other stones. The heat from a fire is very quickly blanketed by soil so that the objects just under the surface are protected and it is only with a constant bonfire in one place, implying a period of habitation, that such an effect is produced.

In the case of the Cleveland Hills, the forest cover was able to regenerate during the Neolithic, since man virtually avoided these acidic sandstones, and it was not until Bronze and Iron Age times that clearings began to coalesce. Even by the Iron Age, however, *Calluna* pollen had not reached today's proportions.

Over the same period, the status of the soils in the area can be shown to undergo degradation from brown forest soils under Bronze Age barrows to thin podsolic soils over their built-up surface and on the surfaces beyond the barrows. That this is due to changing vegetation and not changing climate is indicated by the fact that the process is reversible if certain trees are planted (Dimbleby, 1962). Podsols with mor humus and a thin hardpan can be converted to brown forest soils with mull humus within a period of 60 years when birch stands are planted instead of heather and conifers. If man had prevented his grazing animals from eating seedling trees, no doubt the area would be forested still.

The extent of burning of moorland under the present policy of land-use for new heather growth for sheep or grouse can be easily seen and we should be lacking in our role of educationalists if we did not bring young people into contact with modern problems of erosion and degradation resulting from thoughtless use of the countryside and a lack of understanding of ecological principles in the British Isles as a whole. Such areas as Bransdale Moor and others on the Cleveland Hills offer us splendid examples of the eroding effect of wind in a landscape when the balance of nature is disturbed. There is the added advantage that a surface of Mesolithic occupation has been uncovered in some places. Our teaching enthusiasm is tempered, however, by our dismay as conservationists at the sight of eroding peat hags and areas from where the top soil has been blown away, leaving bare sand.

The status of heathland in other areas where we hold field courses, such as the Presely Range in Pembrokeshire (Fig. 4), is less well known from pollen evidence. There are pollen analyses, however, that indicate that, at about the same altitude, oak/hazel forest covered most of Dartmoor during the Postglacial optimum (Simmons, 1964). It is always possible to discuss the difficulties of tree-growth at high altitudes when the students are experiencing for themselves the effects of wind and grazing domestic animals on the tree-less landscape.

Fig. 4. Tree-less landscape of eastern end of Presely Mountains with students walking up to Moel Trigarn (Foeldrygarn) hill-fort. (Photograph: M. Barton.)

We are on safer ground in the Chalk uplands of Southern England since, not only can it be seen that planted trees flourish on the highest points, but pollen (Dimbleby, 1965) and molluscan (Evans, 1971) analyses allow us to reconstruct past conditions. Pollen survives less well under the calcareous conditions of Chalk soils but, with the addition of charcoal remains, we can suggest a mixed oak forest, with abundant hawthorn, juniper and yew in local patches. To people used to seeing only maltreated yews in gardens, the gnarled giants of Kingley Vale Nature Reserve near Chichester (Fig. 5) are an impressive sight. Beech, we are reminded is only an Iron Age immigrant, in spite of the magnificent specimens now to be seen in hangers, such as that above Selbourne, where we pay homage to the early naturalist Gilbert White. Such specimens as those growing on Coombe Rock in Slindon Park lead us to the question of the shape of deciduous trees in a primeval forest. Pollarded and coppiced trees are worth examining to exemplify the use made of them by early man, but tall straight oaks, elms, alders and limes, if they can be found, are better examples of the growth form to be expected in the landscape of the Atlantic period. A walk through wooded areas also brings home to students the problems prehistoric men would encounter in surveying a distant horizon or sighting celestial phenomena.

Fig. 5. Professor Grimes and students examining the yew trees of Kingley Vale Nature Reserve, near Chichester. (Photograph: M. Barton.)

The practicalities of running a field course only allow a short empirical study of the difficulties of transporting men and materials on foot through a countryside devoid of roads, but established route-ways and the topographical reasons for their disposition are traced in the field. The search for ancient routes has long been one of Grimes' interests (i.e., 1951) and the Pembrokeshire field course enables him to demonstrate for the students the location of the Flemings' Way on his home territory. Walking along some of the more obvious examples, such as Chalk ridgeways, the Jurassic Way, or Roman roads leads to a search for introduced flora and a discussion of the possible spread of migrants in the past along such routes, much as occurs along railway embankments and motorways today. The problems of transporting stone for building at different periods in the past (particularly for religious monuments, from henges to medieval churches) can be appreciated in the field. Apart from land routes, we look at the possibilities of river transport, particularly the problems

of bringing the Presely rocks down the Eastern Cleddau on their way
to Stonehenge.

Many aspects of archaeology thus depend on environmental
factors and justify the importance we place on the landscape as a
focus on our field courses. In addition, we have tried to convey to
young students some of our own feelings of responsibility for the
world of nature. This attitude is so lacking in much of modern life
and we feel it should be part of the education of any graduate. Even
more should this be the case with archaeologists concerned as they
are about the increasing destruction of archaeological monuments.
In addition to responsibility, however, we need understanding if we
are to interpret the naturalistic information which is being produced
daily from archaeological sites. Unless we can appreciate the
interaction of climate, geology, flora, fauna and human beings
and cease to take one line of evidence to represent the whole, we shall
not be able to come to terms with those shadowy figures in past
landscapes.

References

Dimbleby, G. W. (1952). *J. Soil Sci.* **3**, 1–19.
Dimbleby, G. W. (1961). *Antiquity* **35**, 123–128.
Dimbleby, G. W. (1962). "The Development of British Heathlands and
    their Soils", Clarendon Press, Oxford.
Dimbleby, G. W. (1965). *In* "Windmill Hill and Avebury: Excavations by
    Alexander Keiller, 1925–1939" (I. F. Smith, ed.) pp. 34–42, Oxford
    University Press, Oxford.
Evans, J. G. (1971). *In* "Economy and Settlement in Neolithic and Early
    Bronze Age Britain and Europe" (D. D. A. Simpson, ed.) pp. 27–73,
    University Press, Leicester.
Evans, J. G. (1972). *P.P.S.* **38**, 77–86.
Flannery, K. V. (1969). *In* "The domestication and exploitation of Plants
    and Animals' (P. J. Ucko and G. W. Dimbleby, eds) pp. 73–100,
    Duckworth, London.
Grimes, W. F. (1935). *Antiquity* **9**, 424–434.
Grimes, W. F. (1936). *Arch. Camb.* 5–28.
Grimes, W. F. (1945). *Antiquity* **19**, 169–174.
Grimes, W. F. (1951). *In* "Aspects of archaeology in Britain and Beyond"
    (W. F. Grimes, ed.) pp. 144–171, Edwards, London.
Grimes, W. F. (1963). *In* "Culture and Environment" (I. L. Foster and
    L. Alcock, eds) pp. 93–152, Routledge and Kegan Paul, London.
Harris, D. R. (1969). *In* "The Domestication and Exploitation of Plants
    and Animals" (P. J. Ucko and G. W. Dimbleby, eds) pp. 3–16,
    Duckworth, London.

Keef, P. A. M., Wymer, J. J. and Dimbleby, G. W. (1965). *P.P.S.* **31**, 85–92.

Kendall, P. F. (1902). *Q.J. Geol. Soc.* **58**, 471–568.

Leffingwell, E. de K. (1915). *J. Geol.* **23**, 635–654.

Leffingwell, E. de K. (1919). *U.S. Geol. Sur. Proj. Paper* **109**, 205.

Péwé, T. L. (1966). *Biul. Peryglac* **15**, 65–73.

Salisbury, E. J. (1964). "Weeds and Aliens", Collins, London.

Shotton, F. W. (1960). *Geol. Mag.* **97**, 404–408.

Simmons, I. G. (1964). *New. Phytol.* **63**, 165–180

Simmons, I. G. (1969). *P.P.S.* **35**, 203–219.

Sparks, B. W. and West, R. (1972). "The Ice Age in Britain", Methuen, London.

Wooldridge, S. W. (1960). *Proc. Geol. Assoc.* **71**, 113–129.

Archaeological Science - Whose Responsibility?

G. W. DIMBLEBY

TODAY IN OUR LITERATURE we meet such terms as Archaeological Science, Scientific Archaeology, Systems Archaeology, or the New Archaeology (Clarke, 1972), though some would say that we are only talking about old concepts in a new guise (Hogarth, 1972). In choosing this title I am not implying any particular concept, but only referring to the general area of the application of so-called scientific methods to archaeology; it does not suggest that archaeology is a science or is not a science, or that it is "New" or "Traditional". Archaeological science can be applied to what are obviously scientific investigations, as for instance in the environmental field, or to projects such as art history which come clearly into the category of the humanities. It must be the responsibility of the archaeologist to control the applications of science to his problems. Jacquetta Hawkes' (1968) nightmare of a Frankenstein monster that threatens to take over archaeology is not a product of science *per se*. It is true that scientific literature contains many examples of methodology treated out of all proportion to the results it produces. To some extent this is inevitable in a developing field, but if balance is not restored in due course it becomes bad science. But science must not be judged by bad science any more than the humanities should be judged by their worst excesses; some of the research carried out in the humanities, and I do not exclude archaeology, is banal both in its subject matter and in the thought processes behind it. Let us not hold up science as the ogre; faults lie in the minds and capabilities of men, whatever their discipline.

Our concept of a fundamental distinction between science and the humanities arises largely from the history of the development of man's thought. In subjects such as archaeology, where man is the central figure, such a dichotomy breaks down and disciplines meet. While it is useful in practice to distinguish those areas of knowledge which do not involve man and his achievements – and which can usually (though not always) be tested by experiment – from those in which man, his mind and his culture are central, the distinction must not be pressed too far. Modern developments are tending to blur these boundaries; for example, doctors are increasingly linking medicine with the social sciences, psychology and with religion.

The Archaeologist's Philosophy

Turning to archaeology, we find that many archaeologists today are moving towards this unity in their thinking. I should like to pick out three expressions of their philosophy made recently by distinguished archaeologists, all of whom have done a great deal to foster the interdisciplinary approach to their subject. In doing so I admit at once that these are quoted out of context and could not justifiably be held to express the whole philosophy of these three people, and I ask them to forgive me for using their words somewhat narrowly in order to make a point. They all deal with this twilight zone between the humanities and science.

Professor W. F. Grimes (1969, p. xxiii), whom we are honouring in this volume, says: "It is the task of man-aligned disciplines to recover the material and to define its setting in terms both of date and culture. It is for the natural scientists to apply to that material the methods of analysis which will enable its status to be determined." Here, quite clearly, the archaeologist calls the tune; he poses the questions and provides the relevant material for the answering of those questions. The scientist has no say in the formulation of the problem – he merely provides the method of analysis, and ideally his findings should be expressed in terms of the archaeological problems. Professor Grahame Clark (1972, p. ix) is thinking in similar terms when he says: "archaeologists are not as such concerned with the environment, but rather with the use made of it by early man". In saying this he explicitly excludes certain areas from the archaeologist's sphere of interest, such as the environment for its own sake. or even the response of the environment to man's impact. Dr John Coles (1972, p. 10), another Cambridge archaeologist, sees the aim of prehistoric archaeology as "the writing of prehistory and the explanation of human behaviour". This is an interesting mixture of the historical approach and the social sciences, but it excludes the environment except so far as it is bound up with the behaviour of man. Each of these authorities is circumscribing the field of interest of the archaeologist, but none of them would deny the importance of scientific studies on archaeological material. Yet if these three statements are to be taken as creeds (which is quite unfair to those concerned, but which I do merely for the sake of argument), each one is slightly different. If it were possible for the same site to be excavated by three different people, it might happen that three reports were produced, differing in emphasis and perhaps even in detail. Such subjective variation will inevitably arise when basic philosophies differ, however slightly. But what should be noted is this : that each person will omit, or underdevelop, some aspects that the others have developed; and all will omit certain lines of investigation that fall outside the definition of archaeology as seen by all of them. In other words, no archaeological excavation will extract all the information about the past that a site contains (and may only extract a small fraction).

As long as our minds are polarized into the humanities or the sciences, whether by training, by tradition, or by sheer ignorance of the "other side", we shall fail to learn all that a site has to tell us. Indeed, we may make it impossible, by our methods of excavation, for the full story ever to be extracted. An archaeological site is a piece of the past which has survived to the present day. Of course it can tell us a good deal about early man, helped to an increasing extent by archaeological science; but it can also tell us about past conditions which are nothing to do with man himself, but which are important to the wider understanding of our world. For instance, excavations of long barrows on the English chalk have revealed periglacial soil phenomena. No doubt these originally covered the whole of the land-scape, but erosion, solution (itself of fundamental interest) and land use have obliterated them everywhere else except under these earth-works (Evans, 1968). My own association with archaeology grew from my interest in the evidence which earthworks held of soil and vegetation conditions in prehistoric times. This information is crucial to an understanding of some of the present-day landscapes. We can therefore see archaeological sites in the same category as peat bogs, lake deposits and similar situations where the past has persisted to the present. The determination of archaeomagnetism (Aitken, 1961), though having an archaeological feedback as a potential dating method, is another example of the contribution of archaeological sites to our knowledge of natural systems. Many other examples could be quoted from a wide range of scientific fields. When one looks at what a site may contain in absolute terms one wonders whether some key sites should be the prerogative of the archaeologist alone, since he will not and cannot attempt to extract information beyond what he can see to be relevant to his own reason for excavating. As Coles pertinently points out (*op. cit.*, p. 133), all excavation is destruction,

B

and non-archaeological material can be destroyed in the process without ever having been studied.

Why Excavate?

This leads us on to why and how excavations are carried out. The reasons for undertaking archaeological excavations fall into five main categories :
a. Research.
b. Rescue.
c. Training.
d. In the interests of sciences other than Archaeology.
e. Miscellaneous, mostly reprehensible.

The likelihood that scientific studies will be carried out in conjunction with the excavation varies widely from category to category. In e., for example, it is usually nil. In this category I include treasure hunting, which regrettably is still a force to be reckoned with. Not much higher comes the practice of some local societies to dig just to keep the members happy and interested. Such digging is seldom informed and co-ordinated; the possible technical aids of modern archaeology are not appreciated, and the result is that yet one more site is destroyed only half-assessed. At the other extreme comes category d., rare in this country, but well exemplified by MacNeish's work in Central and South America (Mangelsdorf *et. al.*, 1964) whose primary aim was to establish the history of maize as part of a wider scientific project into the origins of this cereal. It would, of course, have been indefensible if this work had failed to incorporate archaeological interests as well as the non-archaeological ones, but by proper planning both were achieved – the known history of man in the area being taken back several thousand years in the process – and indeed the interdependence of both the botanical and archaeological work was clearly demonstrated. In the same way directors of archaeological research excavations should show a similar degree of responsibility for the scientific investigation of materials relating to their own enquiries; but matters of non-archaeological scientific interest are unlikely to be given the attention they merit unless they have been taken into account at the planning stage. As for training excavations, where these are linked to a research programme the same responsibility to archaeological science may be expected and should be inculcated in the students, but where the dig exists only for training purposes little of scientific value seems to emerge. Inevitably rescue digs seldom do more than establish the salient archaeological facts and little emerges about the "fringe" material which the site may have contained. So again we find, as we did when considering the archaeologist's own outlook, that what the site contains in total is rarely considered. What is extracted is determined to a marked extent by the reason for excavation and it is seldom comprehensive.

It is not within my competence, being untrained in archaeological method, to evaluate the effect of excavation techniques on the extraction of material for scientific examination. I would, however, echo Coles' appeal to the archaeologist's conscience (*op. cit.*, p. 148), particularly in the matter of total excavation. This is rather like capital punishment; once it is done it is very difficult to reconsider the case in the light of new evidence. The contribution of new techniques for the extraction of relevant data from archaeological sites has in the last two or three decades greatly increased the scope of the interpretation which the archaeologist can make as the result of his excavation; and this trend is continuing. But once a site has been excavated to destruction no further developments can be applied to it. The archaeologist must be very sure – or very arrogant – before deciding that future generations cannot add to his own technical repertoire.

One other point arises out of my experience as a specialist visiting archaeological sites, and that is the value of the trench. This is shunned by many archaeologists, particularly if they are using open excavation. However, horizontal features are not only laid down by man. Percolating rainwater, for instance, can produce a horizontal zonation which can be recognized at once in a vertical section. I still meet excavators who assume that a humus-stained horizon must be a turf-line or an occupation level; they have not heard of illuvial horizons. Many archaeologists regard their excavation as complete when they have reached the "natural" (variously defined); a trench into this material may be of considerable interest to the natural scientist, and has even been known to change the archaeological picture.

Processing of Scientific Materials

So far we have been dealing with the problems and the variation of practice in providing materials for scientific examination from the site itself. Accepting that such material is going to add to the archaeological interpretation of the excavation, who deals with it? Another development since the Second World War has been a great increase in the number of sites excavated, and this is rocketing even more as the result of rescue operations rendered necessary by increasingly widespread and violent land disturbance. Whereas it was once possible to get material examined by experts, particularly at the universities, out of the goodness of their hearts, this is no longer possible with the volume of material now emerging. It is true that specialists may sometimes welcome material for their own interest, but this can no longer be the basis for a service covering hundreds of sites each year. It is not always realized that the examination of samples in the laboratory is not just a few minutes' work by an expert with a hand lens. It may take several months of a man's time to deal with just one aspect of a site. As a result we are in the position, as I have said elsewhere (1969), where the work on a small site can be squeezed in because it only involves a few samples, whilst the numerous samples from the large key sites lie untouched in the cupboard more or less indefinitely. The university specialist has his own duties to teach and to research into his own problems; with the best will in the world he cannot take on a heavy load of outside work.

For many years the small Ancient Monuments Laboratory, now under the Department of the Environment, tried to keep pace with the scientific investigations of materials from sites which had been excavated by the government archaeological service (Anon., 1969a). Recently this laboratory has been expanded in staff, equipment and premises, an enlightened development much to be welcomed (Anon., 1969b). Nevertheless, with rescue excavations alone now running at about 100 per year, this service can still make little impact on the total need in the country as a whole. Where else could expansion take place? I would suggest the museums. The time has surely come when the analysis of bone, wood, pollen, etc., is an essential complement to the artifacts; neither without the other can give a complete representation of what the site can tell us. Why, therefore, the distinction in treatment? Surely this is a matter of tradition rather than logic. Indeed, there are one or two museums in this country which have appointed specialists in the biological field specifically to meet this very need. In many of our museums the necessary expertise is already there, but it confines itself to the Natural History section (on your right as you go in) and never encounters the Local Archaeology section (on your left and up the stairs). Surely the local landscape should be the meeting point of these two disciplines; no naturalist can understand a landscape without putting man into it – even prehistoric man – and no archaeologist can understand human culture or human behaviour unless he puts man into an environmental setting. I would suggest that under one curator the artificial distinction between things cultural and things environmental could be removed with great advantage to the one theme – human ecology through the ages.

Even if the museums were to adopt this new rôle in the near future (I shall discuss the training of suitable staff below), there would still be a large residue of scientific analysis to be done, particularly on the longer research projects. Some of this work requires equipment which is only available at certain centres and which it would be unreasonable to expect less specialized establishments, such as the general run of museums, to acquire. In this category would come radiocarbon dating equipment, computer facilities, electronscan microscopes, etc. How such facilities should be distributed and how they should be related to the programme of field work needs to be worked out, but unless facilities of this calibre are made available the evidence which can now be extracted on an increasingly large scale will not be adequately processed. Equally serious, without such facilities new techniques will not be developed. Once it is realized that sites are irreplaceable and that they are disappearing at an ever increasing rate, the necessity to extract everything possible from those that are left becomes paramount.

Training of Personnel

Whatever expansion takes place will only be effective in so far as it can be staffed by suitably trained personnel. It may be putting the cart before the horse that certain training institutions have been offering appropriate courses even before the prospects of employment in these areas had become widely available, but it has been abundantly clear for some years that development must take place in this direction. Bachelor of Science degree courses combining science subjects with archaeology are offered at several universities, for instance, Belfast, Cardiff and Leicester, whilst in the last few years, under Professor Grimes' Directorship, degree courses have been introduced at the Institute of Archaeology in which selected archaeological courses can be combined with courses in environmental studies, agriculture and other field sciences. An increasing number of students are combining archaeology with the sciences at the higher degree level, coming with a science degree and adding archaeology afterwards, or building on an archaeology degree by taking science courses for the Master's degree. At present, regrettably, it is overseas students who are best able to take advantage of these options; though there is considerable interest from home students they are generally thwarted by the difficulties of obtaining grants for higher degrees (see below). It is sad that this enlightened and necessary development in training in archaeological science should benefit foreign archaeology more than archaeology in this country.

Financial Resources

In a minority of cases funds for research or development in archaeological science come from private sources, which generally are interested in the outcome of the work but do not attempt to advise on how it should be approached and carried out. Some of the most successful interdisciplinary projects have been financed in this way. Generally, however, appeal has to be made to sources of public funds. In Britain this immediately forces a decision as to whether a project comes within the humanities or whether it is a science, because different grant-giving bodies deal with the two areas.

If an application is being made for post-graduate research which involves training (e.g. the research worker is carrying out the research for a Ph.D.), it has gone to the Department of Education and Science if it is for a project in the arts, but if it is in the scientific field it goes to one of the Research Councils (NERC, SRC, SSRC) according to the topic. As one can imagine, the problems which arise with an interdisciplinary study in the area of archaeological science often need a research investigation to sort them out. If there is any taint of science in a project, DES pass it on to NERC (or SRC or SSRC). If it has a taint of archaeology, it is then rejected or passed on somewhere else. If one of these bodies eventually agrees to accept it, it is then put into the pool with the many other applications to this body, but it is given low priority "because you will realize that it is marginal to our main interest". The outcome of most of these applications can be predicted.

Where application is being made for funds to support projects which do not involve training the machinery is somewhat different but the result similar. On the arts side the British Academy administers public monies for this purpose, but on the science side the Research Councils, each circumscribed by its own terms of reference, deal with these projects as well. Again, projects involving both science and the humanities are in difficulty from the start, and even if they are eventually allocated to the science side the question then has to be settled as to which Research Council they come under.

It sometimes happens that the project as posed is unacceptable to any of the grant-giving bodies. In desperation, therefore, the applicant is forced to fragment his interdisciplinary work, submitting only those parts which are acceptable. Sometimes this is specifically suggested by the body concerned, which strikes me as quite unethical since they have declared that the subject as a whole is not within their competence to handle.

It is greatly to be regretted that domestic and administrative considerations of this sort should be allowed to interfere with the chosen direction of development of an academic subject, but without the resources which these bodies control no development at all would be possible. Unfortunately the Royal Society on the science side and the British Academy in the humanities themselves perpetuate these divisions. Though they have together run conferences on science and archaeology, they nevertheless retain their own separateness. The Royal Society has set its face against archaeology in any guise and however "scientific". The British Academy has shown some willingness to embrace work which is interdisciplinary, such as the Cambridge project on the History of Early Agriculture; but it is still bound, probably willingly, by its traditional terms of reference.

It is particularly, though not solely, in the environmental field that these divisions are the most serious, and it may be noted in parenthesis that even studies of the present-day environment are bedevilled by the same administrative divisions; this in a field which is vital to man's modern predicament. However, academic representations have been and will be made at every opportunity and it is to be hoped that before irreparable harm has been done to interdisciplinary research some adjustments will be made. One cannot help but note the contrast between our attitude in this country and that in, for instance, the USA or France, where government funding of research is unaffected by such obsolescent distinctions.

Society's Responsibility

We have seen that responsibility for the development of archaeological science falls upon the archaeologist, upon the scientist, upon the teacher and not least upon the financial administrator. But there is also a sense in which society itself bears a responsibility. If there is any virtue to man in understanding his past then society is at fault if it allows the irreplaceable evidence of that past to be destroyed, especially if that evidence has never been examined and assessed. We see this conflict in our towns whenever there is a proposal to pull down an old building in the name of progress. Even Victorian edifices are now fought over. How much more, then, should we be concerned about archaeological sites; they generally hold more information about the contemporary scene than does an old building, which depends for its value on its known historical associations (unless it has architectural virtues, which may be of overriding importance). Destruction of the old features of our towns is now matched by the destruction of archaeological monuments in our countryside. Intensive ploughing, urban sprawl and the development of airfields and motorways are revealing sites – and destroying them – in a hitherto unsuspected abundance. Archaeologists do what they can through local societies and organizations like "Rescue", but as we have seen, the likelihood of material for scientific study coming from such work is remote. One reason is, again, finance. Though much of this destruction has been carried out on behalf of society through the Department of the Environment, it is only recently that the same Department has set aside funds even to promote excavation. No funds have been earmarked for scientific investigation of samples, which, incidentally, could go on long after the site was destroyed. Nor have they been allocated towards the preparation of a report, without which no excavation is complete. The funds that have been allocated, welcome though they are, are little more than conscience money paid in recognition of the destruction of our heritage that we are not willing to halt. Society has indeed a responsibility, but it has scarcely acknowledged it.

There is one other, perhaps more concrete, reason why we should be worried about the destruction of our heritage from the distant past. I have argued elsewhere (in press) that our remote ancestors have left a mark on our landscape which we can see even today. They have also left us, in their monuments, the evidence which we can read about their environment and how they were modifying it, and often this evidence provides a yardstick by which we can judge our own environment. Taking the long term view, we can often see that over the generations we have degenerated our land, at first in ignorance but latterly often for gain. We are aware, then, that the processes of degradation are often still to be seen at work (e.g. moor burning) and in many ways our attitude to our environment today is little better than that of prehistoric man. No student of the past who looks at the environmental setting of man can fail to feel a unity and continuity with the people of those remote times. This feeling is not always obvious to those who only study man's material achievements, for technical progress may be so great as to give the impression of a gulf between the ages.

To end on a personal note, it is perhaps above all else this recognition of the unity of the past and the present which, for me, marks Professor Grimes as an archaeologist ahead of his time.

Though I took some words of his at the beginning of this paper to illustrate the persisting division between archaeology and science, Professor Grimes, in his work in the field, in his teaching and his capacity as director of a research institute, has always recognized that archaeology must be interdisciplinary and is not even confined to the past. He has sometimes been criticized for devoting time and energy to things which seemed to the critics to have nothing to do with archaeology – the Field Studies Council for instance. Professor Grimes sees no inconsistency between such involvement and his archaeology, and when one has heard him, on one of the "marginal" committees he sits on, advocating that archaeological monuments should be as important a reason for making a Nature Reserve or a Site of Special Scientific Interest as floristic or faunal rarity, one realizes that through this sense of unity he is doing more to save our archaeological heritage than those hundreds who are busy destroying it with the spade. I trust that his years of retirement will give him a greater scope to advance the cause of archaeological science. He has already honourably discharged his own responsibility.

References

Anon. (1969a). *Nature Lond.* **221**, 206–7.

Anon. (1969b). *Nature Lond.* **221**, 1099–1100.

Aitken, M. J. (1961). "Physics and Archaeology". Interscience Publishers, London and New York.

Clark, J. G. D. (1972). *In* "Papers in Economic Prehistory" (E. S. Higgs, ed.) pp. vii–x., Cambridge University Press.

Clarke, D. L. (1972). "Models in Archaeology". Methuen, London.

Coles, J. (1972). "Field Archaeology in Britain". Methuen, London.

Dimbleby, G. W. (1969). *Nature Lond.* **221**, 1176–7.

Dimbleby, G. W. (in press). *In* "Conservation in Practice" (A. S. Warren, ed.) Wiley, Chichester.

Evans, J. G. (1968). *Wilts. Archaeol. Nat. Hist. Mag.* **63**, 12–26.

Grimes, W. F. (1969). *In* "The Domestication and Exploitation of Plants and Animals" (P. J. Ucko and G. W. Dimbleby, eds) pp. xxiii–xxvi. Duckworth, London.

Hawkes, J. (1968). *Antiquity* **42**, 255–62.

Hogarth, A. C. (1972). *Antiquity* **46**, 301–4.

Mangelsdorf, P. C., MacNeish, R. S. and Gallinat, W. C. (1964). *Science N.Y.* **143**, 535–45.

B*

The Temple of Diana and the Devil's Quoits: Continuity, Persistence and Tradition

D. STURDY

LONG MEG AND HER DAUGHTERS, the Devil's Arrows, Waylands Smithy, and the other ancient sites which have their own idiosyncratic names, recall lost folk-traditions and hint perhaps at a local recognition of importance in ancient times, if indeed these names reflect more than the antiquarian suppositions of Renaissance scholars*

To pay tribute to W. F. Grimes and to honour his wide-ranging interests in fieldwork, it might be instructive to discuss two of these "named" monuments, to consider them in terms of their setting and to compare and contrast their local settlement patterns and land use in both prehistoric and mediaeval times.

Both regions are known to him: in Oxfordshire, Grimes (1943–4) conducted wartime rescue excavations on and around the Devil's Quoits at Stanton Harcourt; in Westmorland he participated in a training-course of the Institute around Diana's Temple at Levens (Sturdy, 1973). Even in the rushed conditions of war, he was at pains to attempt a whole prehistoric environment for the Stanton Harcourt area which Riley (1943–4) in the same wartime volume gave a regional context. Grimes' (1960) revised publication gives a refined and more detailed study of the Henge monument and its surrounding ring-ditches. But some of his other work reminds us that it is not enough to study the strictly "archaeological" evidence in isolation and against its physical setting alone: in his study of Charmy Down, Grimes (1960, pp. 232–41) hints at a technique of landscape study akin to peeling an onion and by stripping off layer after layer of human occupation working towards an understanding of man's

---

* Compare the disparate approaches of Weiss, R. (1969). "The Renaissance Discovery of Classical Antiquity". Oxford. Powell, A. (1948 rev. ed. 1963). "John Aubrey and his Friends". London; and Hunter, M. C. W. (1971). *Antiquity* **45**, 113–21 and 187–92.

impact on the countryside and of the effect of the environment on man. Grimes (1945) has taught us also to beware of accepting too simple an assessment of the effect of soils and rock on human settlement and in following his cautious acceptance of generalizations we could wonder just how much a "Lowland Zone" region in Fox's (1932) concept really differed from one in the "Highland Zone".

Both of the sites which we are to consider were recorded in the 17th century: Robert Plot (1677, pp. 350–51) said:

> But as for the *Stones* near the *Barrow* at *Stanton-Harcourt* called the *Devil's Coits*, I should take them to be *Appendices* to that *Sepulchral Monument*, but that they seem a little too far removed from it; perhaps therefore the *Barrow* might be cast up for some *Saxon*, and the *Stones* for some Britains slain hereabout (*aut vice versa*). . . . they are about eight foot high, and near the *Base* seven broad; they seem not *natural*, but made by *Art*, of a small kind of *stones* cemented together, where of there are great numbers in the Fields hereabout; which makes thus much for the Conjecture concerning those at *Stone-Heng*, that they may be *artificial*, it being plain from those, that they could, and did do such things in the ancienter times.

Plot's dating was hazardous (1677, p. 334):

> But for that at Stanton Harcourt, if a *Danish* monument, it was certainly a Memorial of some greater *Person*, because of the *Stones* set near it. . . . though it be possible too that these may be *Roman*, it being customary for them to set up such *trophies*, at the utmost Bounds of their *Victories*. . . .

but later he adopted a sounder position (Plot, 1686, pp. 397–8):

> And for other *British Antiquities* that are any way probably such, I met with none, unless the great *stone* in a field *South* of *Cannock* Church; and that other ... standing in a leasow near the two *Comptons* in the parish of *Kinfore* by some called *Baston*, by others *Bolt-stone*, there being a story that a *Gyant* threw it from *Aston* (a place under *Kinfare* edg) hither; may be accounted such. Which perhaps they may, and not without reason; whether we esteem them as *British Dieties*, as the *Devil's bolts* in *Yorkshire* and Devil's Coits in *Oxfordshire*, have been proved to be at large; or some memorials of *battles* fought *thereabout*.

And a few years later Edmund Gibson said (Camden, 1695, p. 810):

> And near it, *Levens*, where is a fair stone bridge over the river *Kent*, on the south-side of which river, are still to be seen the ruins of an ancient round building (now call'd *Kirkshead*) which is said to have been anciently a temple dedicated to *Diana*. And not far from it, appears the ruins of another building; which seems to have belong'd to the same place. In the Park (which is well stor'd with Fallow-deer,

and almost equally divided by the river Kent) is a spring call'd the *Dropping-Well*, that petrifies moss, wood, leaves, &c.

Later, less valuable comment adds (Camden, 1789, p, 294):

> In the fields of Stanton Harcourt stood three great stones called the *Devils Coits*, 65 paces asunder, but one of them was taken down several years ago to make a bridge. The third stone was smaller than the rest, and stood between the barrow and the church. Half a mile west by south from the church was a barrow, almost half of which to the north was cut down, and the earth carried away about 1777 by order of the Warden and Fellows of All Souls, perhaps to gratify curiosity, but report says to improve the field.

At the same time West (1778) said of Levens, "within the park is Kirkstead mentioned by Camden as a place frequented by the Romans, yet nothing of late belonging to that people has been discovered at that place".

Although discussions of both sites in the nineteenth and early twentieth centuries were, as Grimes said of Stanton Harcourt, "brief and add nothing to what is already known", one (Harcourt, 1876, p. 48) cannot be omitted:

> At a short distance from the village of Stanton Harcourt are some large upright stones, known by the name of the Devils Quoits. The tradition in the county is, that the Devil was playing at Quoits one Sunday on Wytham Hill, four miles distant, and that these stones were the result of his play. Mr Warton has suggested that these stones were erected to commemorate an engagement, fought near Bampton in the year 614.... Other accounts attribute the position of these stones to the Druids.

None of these spirited "literary" sources seems at first to be a rational archaeological description of an important site, but I have quoted them, more completely than is usual, to point out the kind of documentary material which we must use for a proper understanding of the landscape, whether we consider ourselves historical geographers, archaeologists, or local historians, or better, something of all three. Important early centres will probably be badly documented with strange tales, smacking of the strangest folklore and unlikely conjecture (Grinsell, 1939; Ravenhill, 1932).

We must try to appreciate all this and to see through the eyes of antiquaries whose work sometimes appears to be implausible conjecture piled on inadequate observation: after all, the next generation will soon look on us in just this light. The decline in the merit of conclusions reached, and the total absence of worthwhile observations between the late seventeenth century and the mid twentieth

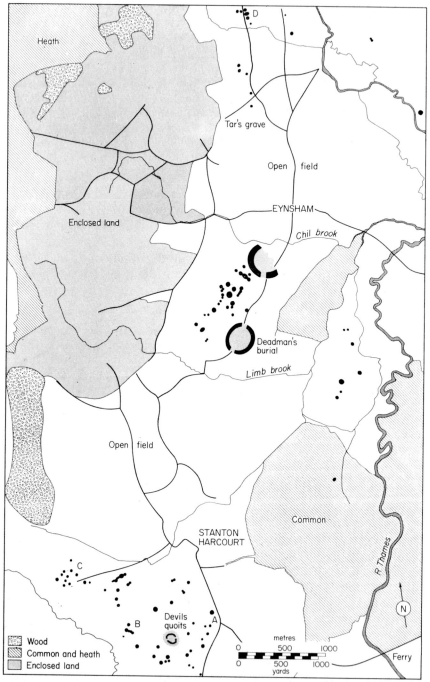

Fig. 1. Late Neolithic and Bronze Age sites at Stanton Harcourt plotted on the
Mediaeval landscape.

should distress those who believe in the steady improvement of scholarship or of human endeavour.

The Quoit circle itself, about 200 metres across was a "henge-monument", which are generally reckoned to date from the "Late Neolithic" period. One stone was in its proper place and two had later been moved for some mysterious reason several hundred metres out into the fields and the excavations now in progress may confirm Grimes' (1943–4, p. 33 and 1960, p. 154) suggestion that there were originally seven stones in a widely spaced circle.

The site is to be destroyed for gravel-digging and future genera-tions will view with disbelief the present pace of mutilation and destruction of these "henges", and the complete absence of any public pressure for their preservation intact except occasional murmurings such as Daniel (1967) or Ashbee (1972).

The many ancient sites which surround it are being completely destroyed: the evidence obtained in salvage-work has provided evidence for ancient settlement, and is discussed below. Of one class of site alone, ring-ditches of which there were once 60, more than 20 have been destroyed without record, less than 20 have been partially excavated (of which 8 have been published) and some 20 remain. (Fig. 1).

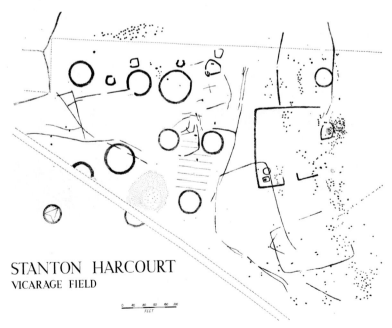

STANTON HARCOURT
VICARAGE FIELD

Fig. 2. A group of sites on the Thames gravel (detail of C. Fig. 1).

The "Temple" site is a subtriangular enclosure only about 50 metres across and dates from the Roman and sub-Roman periods, as far as limited excavation in 1970–1 seems to show.

The preservation of it and its setting seems to be properly assured for the future, following a vigorous legal battle and firm protest based largely on amenity grounds, since the site lies within the earliest surviving landscaped park in the country, although archaeological arguments played their part*.

The group of sites around Diana's Temple will, within a generation, be one of a small number, surviving for future enjoyment and scholarship. One small site a "ring-cairn" has been completely cleared and reconstructed, and a dozen or more sites of unknown date and character remain as low earthworks, with a substantial area of medieval plough-land.

So far there is no comparison between the sites: except that both lie among other sites and have unusual names: one is to be destroyed but the other preserved, one is Neolithic and the other Roman in date, one is of the class of great monuments which are usually reckoned to be "ritual" in function, the other is the sort of site usually considered to be a small farmstead, though a temple in name.

The "Dinnes Temple Well" recorded in 1581 at Doncaster is reckoned to be "literary" in origin by Smith (1961 and 1962). One would have assumed the same origin for the Levens site, but for the stray find of a jet statuette nearby (Fig. 3).

Fig. 3. Jet statuette found in Levens Park.

At first sight the environs have even less in common: one lies on flat gravel terrain a mile and a half (2 kilometres) from the banks of the upper waters of the placid Thames and the other among hills of

* Editorial in *The Times*, 15 Feb. 1969, and comment as widely dispersed as *The Estates Gazette*, 31 Oct. 1970, and *House and Garden*, March 1969, p. 33.

boulder-clay and limestone a few dozen yards (75 metres) from the fastest flowing river in England. (As locally reputed, without foundation so far as I can discover, to be in "The Guinness Book of Records".)

In terms of archaeological knowledge comparison seems equally ridiculous: around one the large square arable fields are known from air-photographs to cover thousands of ancient sites, and constant salvage-excavations on gravel-pits during the last century and a half have revealed plans and details of several hundred acres of archaeological sites, but around the other the small, elongated pasture fields have produced no crop-marks, no excavations have taken place and only a few casual finds are known.

Despite all these apparent differences, common sense suggests that the development of river-valleys that are reasonably well-drained and well-endowed will tend to follow a common course. I suspect that earlier settlement-patterns in the Kent Valley which are indicated only by scattered finds would be seen to bear a strong resemblance to those we know in the Thames Valley if the same conditions for air-photography and the same circumstances of excavation obtained.

Comment has often been made on the close similarity of the Stanton Harcourt "complex" with the dense group of sites around Dorchester-on-Thames, a dozen miles downstream and to the importance that both retained throughout prehistoric times with their henge-monuments and their river-forts. It has been suggested (most memorably by Professor C. F. C. Hawkes in private conversation) that the Stanton Harcourt area, since it lacks a Roman town, declined in importance at the Roman conquest, and that the Dorchester area too was overshadowed by the emergence of Oxford in late Saxon times. The siting of Oxford between the two "most favoured" areas symbolized their final amalgamation.

This may be too "dynamic" an interpretation since places and regions do not live a simple or a single "life". But it can be accepted as a broad generalization in our imperfect knowledge, or as a framework to hang our ideas on until we can work out something better. Perhaps more frequent comparison of region with region would point contrasts of history as well as the unevenness of evidence or study.

The most persistent feature of ancient settlement in the Thames valley is the small complex group, or one might almost call it "scrabble" of sites, which occur every few hundred or few thousand metres, clustering most densely around the Devil's Quoits. The groups are remarkably consistent in comprising sites of a variety of

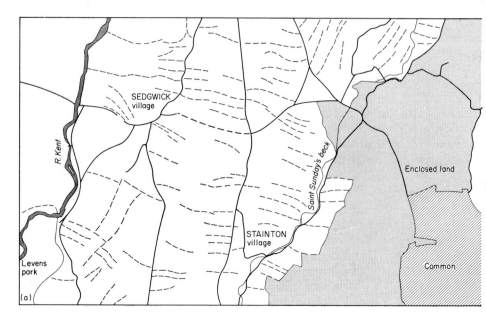

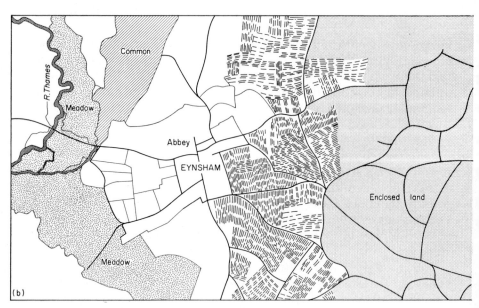

Fig. 4. Lansape patterns of Lowland and Highland can seem very similar.

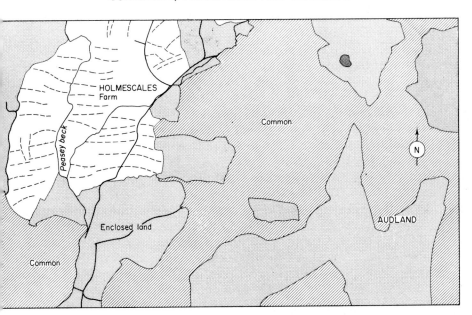

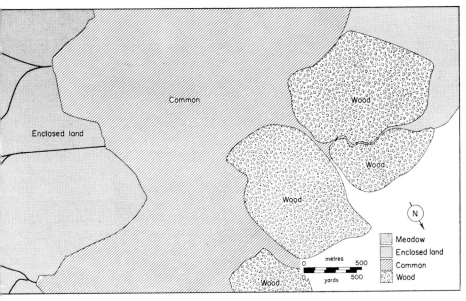

(a) Sedgwick, Westmorland (b) Eynsham, Oxon.

periods. Grimes himself (1943–4, pp. 47–60) tackled just such a group, 500 metres east of the Quoits and came across ring-ditches (Fig. 1,a) and a small Iron-age enclosure. There are normally storage or rubbish pits around this sort of enclosure and very often the list is concluded with a Roman farmstead or two and a few Anglo-Saxon burials.

Groups or complexes with most of these items were first competently excavated in the 1850s on Standlake Down, 2 kilometres west of the Quoits and in more recent salvage work 500 metres west of the Quoits (Fig. 1,B), 1500 metres to the north-west, as Mrs Grimes will remember (Fig. 1,C and Fig. 2) and 7 kilometres to the north at City Farm (Fig. 1,C) (Stone, 1857; Akerman and Stone, 1857; Hamlin, 1963; Williams, 1951; Case et al. 1964–5; Harding, 1972).

In all these groups the mixture of periods and within periods is the basic element. The six ring-ditches at City Farm, salvaged from haphazard loss by pell-mell excavation ranged, as Case lucidly demonstrated, from a small settlement and henge-monument of the Beaker period, through a "rather poor provincial barrow" of the Early Bronze Age and an elliptically laid-out enclosure with burials of a "prominent clan" of the period of the Wessex culture to "monuments of another generation or two of kinsman", perhaps "transhuming herdsmen" whose summer pastures were here and whose winter folds and corn-lands may have been in Wessex or the Cotswolds.

Such a wide range of date and function seems to be normal, and can be presumed to apply also to the great groups of barrows three times the number of the ring-ditches round the Quoits which surround Stonehenge. The ring-ditches of the Thames valley, however, were levelled and ploughed over in the Iron Age, while much of Salisbury Plain must have remained open downland until recent times, for some reason*.

Case's analysis of City Farm implies a strong element of continuity during part of the Bronze Age: to disentangle "continuity" of settlement from the persistent attraction of minor environmental factors demands more detailed evidence of this kind, and can seldom be conclusive, from the very nature of the material. But his analysis was the result of 9 years work and the clearance of 12 hectares (30 acres) by machine; without work on this scale discussion seems to be entirely a matter of whim or personal choice.

---

* The distribution-maps of round barrows on Salisbury Plain in Atkinson, R. J. C. (1959–70, 7th ed.). "Stonehenge and Avebury and neighbouring monuments", rear cover H.M.S.O., London; Cunliffe, B. (1972). "Cradle of England", p. 38, Fig. 8, B.B.C., London; and Pugh, R. B. (1957). "Victoria County History of Wiltshire", vol. 1, pt. 1, map V, Oxford University Press for Institute of Historical Research, London, display a good deal of variety.

But we can also gain another insight, which allows us to appreciate the tenacity of traditions and methods, but also to understand how the most radical changes of land-use and field-system can take place within an existing social order. We can use the deed-box and the estate map, the hedge-line and the "ridge-and-furrow" of pasture fields as source material and attempt to reconstruct the mediaeval field-systems, methods of farming, patterns of landowning and farms themselves, in the manner of Beresford (1957) or Hoskins (1970).

At Stanton Harcourt (Fig. 4,a), although the village itself remained, its farms declining into cottage status, the enclosure of the Open Fields in 1774 swept away the vestiges of medieval farming traditions and the interlocking tangle of land-holding in strips to produce the pattern of big squarish fields that lasted until 1940. Although these large arable fields seem unlikely material we can find beneath them traces of a mediaeval pattern of farming very like that which lies beneath the small largely pasture fields of the Kent valley. That there were Open Fields here (Fig. 3,b) is shown by their late survival, 8 kilometres to the North at Mints-feet in Kendal, enclosed by Act of Parliament in 1814, and in the upland hamlets of Selside where there were still "dales" in the "town-field" in 1809 and of Whinfell where there was still a regular arable "common field" held in strips in 1836*.

In both valleys the flatter central lands, whether on gravel or on boulder clay, were laid out in a strip-field system for arable rotation around the main villages. On the fringes of this in both cases, a zone of irregular enclosures separated central fields from the uncultivated heath or moor.

The settlement pattern for both areas was made up of large villages, small villages, hamlets and isolated farms: Stanton Harcourt was not exclusively nucleated, nor was the Levens area entirely dispersed as the conventional view has tended to imply.

Another aspect of mediaeval farming where we can draw evidence from both areas in the "demesne" lands. The holdings of the lord of the manor seems in both areas to have been in separate blocks from the villagers, although quite often in other areas they were inter-

*Kendal: Westmorland Record Office, WD/RG, Mints-feet Inclosure Act and Award.
Selside: Levens Hall MSS Map of 1809 inserted into early 18th century Estate Atlas; the strips appear to have gone by the time of the 1816 Atlas.
Whinfell: Westmorland Record Office: Kendal Corn-Rent map. For other open fields, see Rollinson, W. (1967). "A History of Man in the Lake District", p. 95, London, while a little known example at Drigg in Cumberland which was still partly in arable cultivation in 1933 is recorded by Fair, M. C. (1934). *Trans. of Cumb. and Westmorland Antiq. and Arch. Soc.* **34**, pp. 41–2.

mingled with the villagers' lands. At Eynsham (Fig. 5,a) the demesne lands (Chambers, 1936), which belonged to Eynsham Abbey through-out the Middle Ages, lay in a long belt between the river-meadows and the villagers' lands and are here plotted from the 1782 survey*.

At Helsington the demesne belonged to the mediaeval Barons of Kendal, and was bought in 1544 by the Bellinghams who later bought Levens. The farm called Helsington Laithes (Fig. 5,b) largely unchanged since the 1731 estate map†, occupied the northern quarter of the township, with a long frontage on the River Kent, and may have been separate from the village of Helsington (Farrer, 1923), if this is the "deserted Mediaeval Village" earthworks, in the centre of the township. Although there must have been many minor changes both these farms seem to be basically the same in the eighteenth century maps as in their first documentary reference in the thirteenth century (Chambers, 1936, pp. 100–102).

These examples may help us in our attempts to reconstruct ancient landscapes when we must always expect to find some sort of Roman landowner and some sort of Iron-age "chief", who would normally have had their own land and their own tenantry. In terms of continu-ity these big home-farms have a continuous existence as far back as records go. We may perhaps wonder whether they go further back and were set out as the lord's holding at the time of the Anglian colonization, at whatever date between the fifth and tenth centuries AD.

Robin Bagot, the Institute's host at Levens in 1971, is, however strange it may seem, the direct successor in the lordships and land of Heversham, Levens and Helsington for 800 years, and perhaps, though documents cannot help us, for 500 years before that. It might not be unreasonable to expect a similar sort of continuity in prehistoric times and on occasion to find a potential for survival matching his.

In soundly defeating an attempt to cut a motorway through Levens Park was he setting us an example of how a "member of a prominent clan" of the late Bronze Age might adopt the skills of the Iron Age? Or should we wonder how even Ministries "tend to be *absorbed*" in the Highland Zone (Fox, 1932, p. 77).

* The end plate in Chambers (1936), which may be compared with MSS Sur-veys of 1615 for Corpus Christi College and 1769 for Mrs Holloway which were experimentally reproduced by the Ordnance Survey for O. G. S. Crawford in c.1935 as a pilot-scheme for publishing early estate maps. The Inclosure Award map of c.1802 in Oxfordshire County Records Misc. Pal. IV/1.

†Levens Hall MSS in the early eighteenth century Estate Atlas studied by kind permission of Mr and Mrs O. R. Bagot.

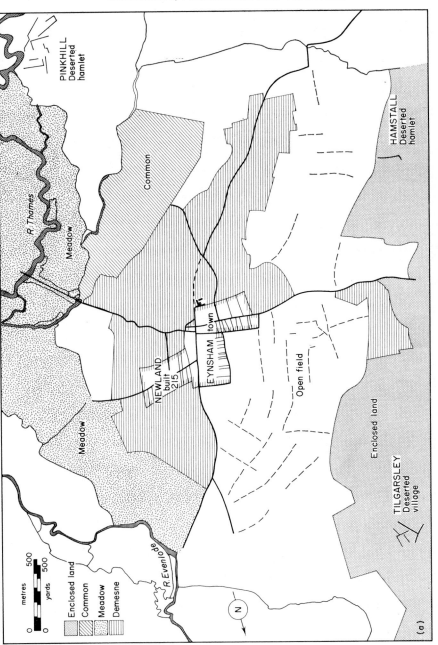

Fig. 5 (a). Demesne and open field at Eynsham, Oxon, in 1782.

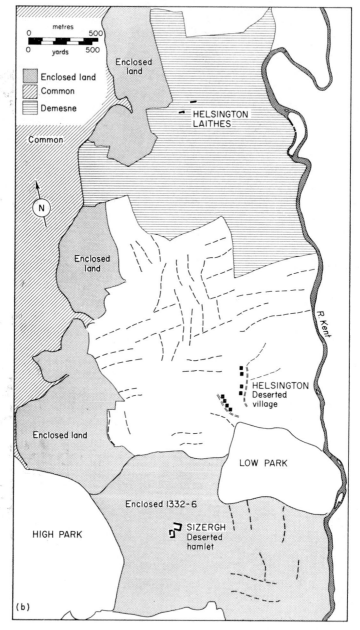

Fig. 5 (b). Demesne at Helsington, Westmorland, in 1731 with probable
mediaeval open field.

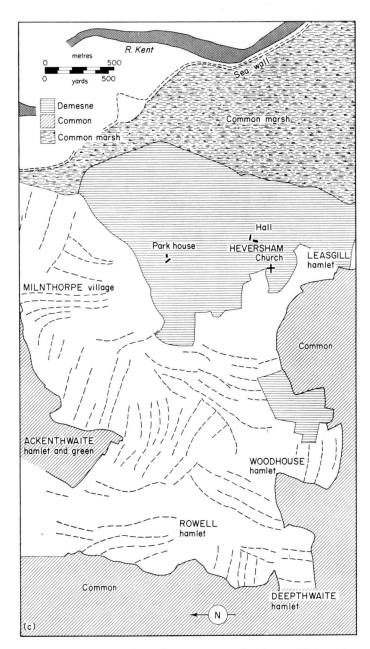

Fig. 5 (c). Demesne at Heversham, Westmorland in 1720 with probable
mediaeval open field.

We could ponder how the Devil's Quoits show the converse of Fox's precept: although the site lies, by an odd coincidence also, on the land of the direct successor of the mediaeval lords of Stanton Harcourt, its present setting in an industrial wasteland and its imminent destruction may symbolize the Lowland Zone, "easily overrun by invaders" where new cultures "tend to be *imposed*".

In all this we should view our evidence with Grimes' gentle scepticism and always remember uneasily how closely our distribution-map of finds represents the sources of road-metalling or the ditches which needed deep-clearances between about 1800 and 1950, how precisely our plotting of sites from air-photographs reflects a gravel subsoil, with regular barley-growing and an interested pilot passing overhead in late June and early July.

It would be foolish not to expect and to search for finds and sites on terrain where Victorian labourers refrained, because it was no good for road-making and did not need draining, from hacking away at pits and ditches. It would be quite sensible to look out for many new sites in areas which are well enough drained though not on gravel, where there are not always thousands of acres of barley with bright green marks on golden fields for a few weeks in the year and where flying conditions may not be conducive to pilots of light planes casting their eyes about the countryside.

In the interpretation of these finds and sites as a network of scattered farmsteads, or whatever we take them to represent we could perhaps question our own assumption that settlement takes the form of villages, hamlets or farms and recognize "straggles" or "clusters".

Always, when working on the archaeological problems we might bear in mind, and learn a good deal from all the minor puzzles of later settlement-geography, the odd place-names whose meaning must be searched for, the intricacies of township and parish boundaries, whose craziest meanderings must have once had a meaning and the network of roads, lanes and field-tracks, whose every kink and twist ought to be explained in terms of existing fields or structure that had to be threaded past, or of detours for what was once a very good reason. Dare we ask do any of the boundaries, lanes or fields go back to a period earlier than medieval times: or should we ask *which* of the boundaries, lanes or fields go back earlier?

References

Akerman, J. Y. and Stone, S. (1857), *Archaeologia* **37**, 363–70.
Ashbee, P. (1972). *Proc. Prehist. Soc.* **38**, 437.
Beresford, M. W. (1957). "History on the Ground". Methuen, London.

Camden, W. (1695). "Brittannia". (Gibson, E., ed.). Printed by F. Collins for A. Swale, A. and J. Churchill, London.

Camden, W. (1789). "Brittania". (Gough, R., ed.). Printed by J. Nichols for T. Payne and Son and G. G. J. Robinson, London.

Case, H. J., Bayne, Steel, Avery, and Suttermeister. (1964–5). *Oxoniensia* **29 30**, 1–98.

Chambers, Sir E. (1936). "Eynsham under the Monks", Oxfordshire Record Soc. **18**. Oxford.

Daniel, G. E. (1967). *Antiquity* **41**, 255.

Farrer, W. (1923). Records of Kendal. Cumberland and Westmorland. *Antiq. Archaeol. soc.* 4, V.1.pp 10, pp. 37.

Fox, C. W. (1932). "The Personality of Britain". National Museum of Wales, Cardiff.

Grimes, W. F. (1943–4). *Oxoniensia* **8 9**, 19–63.

Grimes, W. F. (1945). *Antiquity* **19**, 169–174.

Grimes, W. F. (1960). "Excavations on Defence Sites: 1". London.

Grinsell, L. V. (1939). "The White Horse Hill and surrounding country". London.

Hamlin, A. (1963). *Oxoniensia* **28**, 1–19.

Hamlin, A. (1966). *Oxoniensia* **31**, 1–27.

Harcourt, E. W. (1876). "The Harcourt Papers: 1" Privately.

Harding, D. W. (1972). "The Iron Age in the Upper Thames Basin". Oxford University Press, Oxford.

Hoskins, W. G. (1970). "History printed from the Farm". London.

Plot, R. (1677). "Natural History of Oxfordshire". Oxford University Press, Oxford.

Plot, R. (1686). "Natural History of Staffordshire". Oxford University Press, Oxford.

Ravenhill, T. H. (1932). "The Rollright Stones and the men who erected them". Birmingham.

Riley, D. N. (1943–4). *Oxoniensia* **8–9**, 64–101.

Smith, A. H. (1961). "The Place-Names of Yorkshire", vol. I, p. 34. Cambridge University Press, Cambridge.

Smith, A. H. (1962). "The Place-Names of Yorkshire", vol. VII. Cambridge. p. 73.

Stone, S. (1857). *Proc. Soc. Antiq.* (1st series) **4**, 92–100, 213–9.

Sturdy, D. (1973). *Scottish Archaeological Forum* (in press).

Thomas, N. (1955). *Oxoniensia* **20**, 1–28.

West, T. (1778). "Guide to the Lakes". London.

Williams, A. (1951). *Oxoniensia* **16**, 5–22.

A Page of "Punch"

W. M. BRAY

It is difficult for an Americanist to pay suitable tribute on the retirement of a colleague whose special interest is the archaeology of the British Isles. However even a serious occasion is improved by a good joke, and the lampoon which forms the subject of this paper is worth republishing in its own right (especially in these days when hominid fossils are once again front page news in the popular press)*. It is also interesting for what it reveals about the state of popular and scientific opinion at a critical moment in the emergence of Palaeolithic archaeology as a respectable, scientific discipline.

The official history of archaeology has been chronicled by Daniel (1950, 1964, 1967), but the unofficial history has still to be written. With the benefit of more than a century of hindsight it is not too difficult to pick out the men and the events which were to be significant for the long-term future of archaeology, but it is only through the ephemera – the cartoons and popular articles – that one can catch the mood of the moment, and can see how these goings-on appeared to the general public at the time when the controversies were still fresh.

"Monkeyana" (Fig. 1) appeared in *Punch, or the London Charivari* for 18 May 1861, only 17 months after the publication of the *Origin of Species,* and less than a year after the acrimonious Oxford meeting of the British Association where Thomas Henry Huxley, speaking on behalf of the absent Darwin, so conclusively routed Samuel Wilberforce, Bishop of Oxford and spokesman for the established Biblical view of creation. The dust raised by this encounter had not yet settled by 1861, and the leading scientific figures of the day were

* My attention was drawn to the *Punch* cartoon by Alan Moorehead, who reproduced it in his book on Charles Darwin (Moorehead, 1971, p. 267), and who made the connection with the Wedgwood medallion. He does not, however, discuss the archaeological implications. I am grateful to Mr William A. Billington, Curator of the Wedgwood Museum, Stoke-on-Trent, for providing further information about the medallion and for allowing me to include a photograph of it, and to the Library of the Zoological Society for finding several references to the Gorilla War.

206 PUNCH, OR THE LONDON CHARIVARI. [MAY 18, 1861.

MONKEYANA.

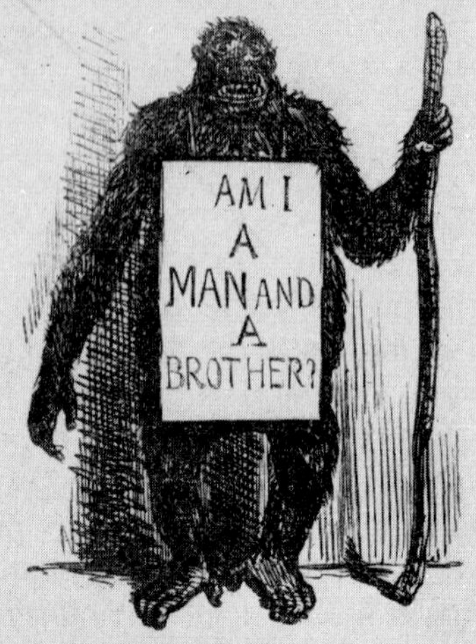

AM I satyr or man?
Pray tell me who can,
And settle my place in the scale.
A man in ape's shape,
An anthropoid ape,
Or monkey deprived of his tail?

The *Vestiges* taught,
That all came from naught
By "development," so called, "progressive;"
That insects and worms
Assume higher forms
By modification excessive.

Then DARWIN set forth.
In a book of much worth,
The importance of "Nature's selection;"
How the struggle for life
Is a laudable strife,
And results in "specific distinction."

Let pigeons and doves
Select their own loves,
And grant them a million of ages,
Then doubtless you'll find
They've altered their kind,
And changed into prophets and sages.

LEONARD HORNER relates,
That Biblical dates
The age of the world cannot trace;
That Bible tradition,
By Nile's deposition,
Is put to the right about face.

Then there's PENGELLY
Who next will tell ye
That he and his colleagues of late
Find celts and shaped stones
Mixed up with cave bones
Of contemporaneous date.

Then PRESTWICH, he pelts
With hammers and celts
All who do not believe his relation,
That the tools he exhumes
From gravelly tombs
Date before the Mosaic creation.

Then HUXLEY and OWEN,
With rivalry glowing,
With pen and ink rush to the scratch;
'Tis Brain *versus* Brain,
Till one of them 's slain;
By Jove! it will be a good match!

Says OWEN, you can see
The brain of Chimpanzee
Is always exceedingly small,
With the hindermost "horn"
Of extremity shorn,
And no "Hippocampus" at all.

The Professor then tells 'em,
That man's "cerebellum,"
From a vertical point you can't see;
That each "convolution"
Contains a solution,
Of "Archencephalic" degree

Then apes have no nose,
And thumbs for great toes,
And a pelvis both narrow and slight;
They can't stand upright,
Unless to show fight,
With "DU CHAILLU," that chivalrous knight!

Next HUXLEY replies,
That OWEN he lies,
And garbles his Latin quotation;
That his facts are not new,
His mistakes not a few,
Detrimental to his reputation.

"To twice slay the slain,"
By dint of the Brain,
(Thus HUXLEY concludes his review)
Is but labour in vain,
Unproductive of gain,
And so I shall bid you "Adieu!"

Zoological Gardens, May, 1861. GORILLA.

PUNCH'S ESSENCE OF PARLIAMENT.

MONDAY, *May* 6. The Lords had a discussion about the Canal of the Future, that is to say, the impossible trench which M. LESSEPS pretends to think he can cut through the Isthmus of Suez. The Government opinion upon the subject is, that if the Canal could be made, we ought not, for political reasons, to allow it, but that inasmuch as the Canal cannot be cut, the subject may, and the wise course is to let the speculators ruin themselves and diddle the Pacha. This seems straightforward and benevolent enough.

MR. SPEAKER DENISON, who had had a relapse into indisposition, re-appeared, and made his apologies for having been ill. The House cheered him so loudly that he began to think he had done a clever thing, rather than not, in catching the rheumatism. *Mr. Punch* hopes to behold the brave Speaker "astir in his saddle" (as MR. DISRAELI's song goes) in due season, and to see him, like a true Whig, following Fox and avoiding pit.

LORD JOHN RUSSELL made an important reply to an important question from MR. GREGORY. The American Difficulty is beginning to create English difficulties. The North is calling on PRESIDENT LINCOLN to blockade the ports of the South, and the South is sending out Privateers to intercept the commerce of the North. LORD JOHN announced that England can recognise no blockade except a real one, and that she is prepared to regard the South as sufficiently consolidated to entitle her to be treated as a Belligerent, not as a mere rebel, and therefore her right to issue letters of marque must be acknowledged. This is a very prosaic paragraph, but *Mr. Punch* "reserves to himself" the right to be grave, gay, lively, and severe exactly when it pleases him.

Our Daughter ALICE is to have £30,000 down, and £6,000 a year, LORD PALMERSTON remarking, very properly, that she is not our Eldest Daughter, and may not require the same allowance as the future QUEEN OF PRUSSIA, but that it is not for the honour of England that her Princesses should go out as paupers. Quite the reverse, and what is more, *Mr. Punch* insists that all the money be settled on his amiable young friend ALICE, so that she may draw her own cheques, and not have to ask her husband for money every time she wants to buy pins or postage stamps, or a little present to send over to her dear *Mr. Punch*.

Then was the Paper Resolution moved by MR. GLADSTONE. LORD ROBERT CECIL opposed it, and hoped the Lords would reject the Bill to be based on it: MR. LEVESON GOWER approved it, and paraded the

Fig. 1. 'Monkeyana'. Punch 18th May 1861. (Mansell Collection).

still divided in their attitudes towards the inter-related problems of the antiquity of man and of his place in the natural order. Mr Punch's doggerel verses give some indication of the bitterness of the controversy, but are even more remarkable as a piece of scientific journalism. The anonymous author shows a detailed knowledge of the scientific literature and of the lectures given to learned societies, and he clearly takes for granted a similar degree of familiarity on the part of his readers. I doubt whether many editors could rely on that today.

Even the picture is full of topical allusions. With the publication of Du Chaillu's book (see below), the gorilla was the subject of enormous public interest, and the wording on the placard around its neck is a reflection of the troubled international politics of the time. The legend on the card parodies the inscription on an anti-slavery medallion (Fig. 2) designed in 1786 by William Hackwood for Josiah Wedgwood, who was himself a strong supporter of the anti-slavery cause*. By May of 1861 the American Civil War had begun, Parliament was debating whether or not to recognize the blockade of the southern ports, and the pages of *Punch* were filled with comments and drawings attacking slavery and plantation life. At a time when the negro's place in nature was so much under discussion (and Biblical authority could still be quoted in defence of slavery) the relevance of Darwin's theories would have been obvious to any intelligent reader.

Daniel has already paid tribute to the work of the geologists, notably Darwin's mentor Charles Lyell, in pushing back the date of the creation beyond the traditional Biblical figure of 4004 BC, but in 1861 the *nature* of creation and of the observed change in the fossil record were still matters for speculation. The second verse of the lampoon refers to the anonymously published, but enormously popular, work by Robert Chambers entitled "Vestiges of Creation" which in 1844 introduced the general public to Lamarck's theory of evolution, with its emphasis on the inheritance of acquired characteristics, the spontaneous generation of the simplest forms of plants and animals, and the belief that change came about through an innate, but divinely ordained, tendency towards improvement. Darwin provided an alternative explanation for evolutionary change, and the third verse of the lampoon incorporates a direct quotation

---

* He was also a Fellow of the Society of Antiquaries and, through his daughter, was the grandfather of Charles Darwin. The connection was further strengthened when Darwin married his cousin Emma Wedgwood in 1837. Darwin's personal antipathy towards slavery is evident from the pages of his journal (Darwin, 1905, p. 490).

Fig. 2. Wedgwood anti-slavery medallion of 1786 (Photograph: Josiah Wedgwood & Sons Ltd.).

from the book's full title: "On the Origin of Species by means of Natural Selection, or the preservation of favoured races in the struggle for life".

For the historian of archaeology, one of the most interesting figures in this all-star cast is Leonard Horner (verse 5), better known as an educational and industrial reformer than as an archaeologist. He was, however, a fellow of the Royal Society, and in 1861 was president of the Geological Society of London (T. H. Huxley was its Secretary at the time, and the fellowship included 93 clergymen). The author of the verses had obviously heard or read Horner's presidential address, delivered in February of that year, in which he gave an account of the state of geology and of what he regarded as the most significant developments within the subject (Horner, 1861).

After praising the geological aspects of Darwin's research, Horner included a section which he entitled "Evidence of the early Existence of the Human Race". The tone is set by the opening sentence:

> Numerous newly discovered facts, and a more attentive and un-prejudiced estimate of many of a similar kind, long since recorded, seems to prove indisputably that Man must have been an inhabitant of this earth at a far earlier period than we have been accustomed to believe him to have existed (Horner, 1861, p. 36).

To prove his point, he quotes an impressive body of evidence which demonstrates the close liaison existing between British scholars and their continental colleagues. Besides the work of Pengelly and Prestwich (discussed below), he was able to cite the work of Gaudry and Collomb at St Acheul, Beaudoin in the Seine Valley, Verneuil in the department of Oise, Lartet's paper on man-made incisions on the bones of extinct animals from the Seine gravels (Lartet, 1860), the Marquis de Vibraye's discovery of a human jaw with extinct fauna in a cave at Arcy-sur-Yonne, and the recognition by Falconer and Baron Anca of artifacts and fossil bones in several caves of north-west Sicily (Lyell, 1863, p. 174).

The discussion also ranged over chronology as established by landscape changes, with reference to "the soil surrounding Cyclopean and Druidical monuments which have existed for more than 2000 years", and to dugout canoes buried under more than 20 ft of sediment in the valley of the Yorkshire Aire. Even the technique of glottochronology is foreshadowed in his appreciation that it might be possible to determine the time taken to develop one language from another within what is now called the Indo-European group.

Horner's most scathing and amusing comments were reserved

C

for the traditional Biblical chronology, which placed the creation in
the year 4004 BC:

> My own conviction is that this wide-spread belief in the recent exis-
> tence of man is to be ascribed, so far at least as this country is con-
> cerned, to the impression made by the lesson taught in early youth,
> the soundness of which is not questioned in after-life, by that marginal
> note in our Bibles over and against the first chapter of the book of
> Genesis. . . . It is more probable that of the many millions of persons
> who read the English Bible, a very large proportion look with the
> same reverence upon that marginal note as they do upon the verse
> with which it is connected (Horner, 1861, p. 44).

Writing as a palaeontologist, Lyell (in the seventh edition of
"Principles of Geology", 1847, p. 637) had already shown that the
supporters of the 4004 BC chronology were caught in a trap of
their own making:

> If all the leading varieties of the human family sprang originally from
> a single pair, a much greater amount of time was required for the
> slow and gradual formation of such races as the Caucasian, Mongoloid
> and Negro, than was embraced in any of the popular systems of
> chronology.

Horner attacked from a different quarter, employing textual
criticism to prove that, far from representing the word of God, the
figure of 4004 derived from a relatively recent calculation and was
therefore not an essential item of belief.

This argument was prefaced by a stirring declaration of faith in
the value of science, with the demarcation line between religion and
geology very clearly defined:

> I make no allusion to any part of the learned prelate's [Archbishop
> Ussher] system except the date he assigns for the creation of the
> world: that date comes properly within the province of the geologist;
> for, as the almost religious belief in its accuracy is an obstacle to the
> acceptance of the conclusions to which he is led by a careful study
> of the facts which the structure of the earth exhibits, he is fairly
> entitled to deal with it (Horner, 1861, p. 44).

Horner, in his own way, had already made a practical attempt to
deal with it, and it is to this research that the lampoon specifically
refers. Inspired by Lyell's calculations of rates of deposition in the
Mississippi Valley, Horner had since 1847 been considering the
possibility of making a similar attempt in Egypt:

> If, as in Egypt, there were in the valley of the Mississippi monuments
> of human art of remote antiquity, the age of which was pretty

accurately known, round which the alluvial soil was accumulated, the monuments resting on a soil of the same nature, we should have a better measure, a standard scale of some accuracy to begin with: and if we had sections or borings at various points in the valley . . . we should be able to form a tolerably correct estimate (Horner, 1847, p. 26).

In the 1850's, with the aid of grants from the Royal Society and the Egyptian government, Horner was able to put his ideas into practice (Horner, 1855, 1858).

At Heliopolis he sank shafts close to the twelfth Dynasty obelisk of Sesostris I (then thought to date from 2300 BC), in order to record the nature and depth of the strata, their shell content, and "any fragments of human art" in a stratified context. At Memphis he excavated a huge pit beside the colossal statue of Ramesses II, and 95 further test pits were dug in various parts of these two valleys. Several of the excavations went down for 50–60 ft, and artifacts were found throughout. Horner calculated the average rate of sedimentation as 3·18 ins per century in the Heliopolis region and about 3·5 ins near Memphis, giving him a date of 11517 BC for an unglazed red sherd found at a depth of more than 41 ft in one of the Memphis pits. This date, wrong though it is in the light of present knowledge, seemed at the time to dispose of the Mosaic chronology, and in addition came out 7625 years older than Lepsius's then accepted date for King Menes and the foundation of Memphis. Lyell (1863, p. 38) later noted that Horner's calculations were "not considered by experienced Egyptologists to have been satisfactory" and pointed out certain flaws in the method. Horner's date, however, is reasonably close to Lyell's own figure of circa 8000 BC for pottery found in a shell bed 98 m above sea level near Cagliari, Sardinia (Lyell, 1863, p. 177). It was indeed, as Mr Punch wrote, "a right about face".

Unlike Horner's research, the work of the geologists Pengelly and Joseph Prestwich (verses 6 and 7) is already well known, and its significance for archaeology has been fully discussed (Daniel, 1950, pp. 57–67; 1964, pp. 38–46; 1967, pp. 67–78). In the late 1840s Pengelly had followed up MacEnery's original excavations of 1824–9 by further digging at Kent's Cavern, and in 1858–9 was engaged in the excavation of Windmill Cave, Brixham, on behalf of the Geological Society and the British Association. The geologists Prestwich, Lyell and Hugh Falconer were among the members of the excavation committee. The new excavations confirmed the results of Falconer's preliminary work at the site, producing flint tools in association with the bones of extinct animals in a deposit of cave earth sealed by a stalagmitic layer containing mammoth, reindeer, rhinoceros, hyaena, bear and lion.

By 1859, Lyell and Prestwich were publicly advocating the great antiquity of man on the basis of evidence from cave sites and from excavations in river gravels (Daniel, 1950, pp. 58). Falconer (who had examined the Abbeville pits in November 1858) persuaded Prestwich and John Evans to make a special journey in 1859 with the purpose of examining the Somme gravels where Boucher de Perthes had discovered handaxes in association with extinct fauna, and the two scholars came back convinced by what they had seen (Daniel, 1972). On 26 May of that year Prestwich gave a paper to the Royal Society entitled "On the Occurrence of Flint-implements, associated with the Remains of extinct Mammalia, in Undisturbed Beds of a late Geological Period" (Prestwich, 1860), and this was followed by a communication from John Evans on the typology of the flint tools.

In 1859, scientific opinion was becoming receptive to the idea of man's great age, and we must keep these discoveries in mind when considering the sections of the lampoon which deal with evolution and anatomy. As Glyn Daniel has already pointed out (1950, p. 66), "The doctrine of evolution not only made people more ready to believe in the antiquity of man; it made the roughly chipped artefacts from Devon and the Somme not only credible, but essential." This is true enough – provided, of course, that you first believe in evolution – but there were still, in 1861, some influential scholars who believed in evolutionary change but not in Darwinism, and others who accepted neither natural selection nor the antiquity of man.

The second half of the lampoon deals more with anatomical controversies than with archaeology, but certain figures spanned the frontiers of the different disciplines and concerned themselves with both fossil man and his living relatives. One such biologist was T. H. Huxley. Huxley was one of Darwin's most vehement supporters, and his popular book "Evidence as to Man's Place in Nature" (1863) spelled out, for anyone who had not yet grasped the point, the full implications of the theory of natural selection. The book discussed the comparative anatomy, brain structure and behaviour of man and the anthropoid apes, leading to the conclusion that

> whatever systems of organs be studied, the comparison of their modifications in the ape leads to one and the same result—that the structural differences which separate Man from the Gorilla and the Chimpanzee are not so great as those which separate the Gorilla from the lower apes (Huxley, 1863, p. 103).

The link with archaeology is provided by the human fossils from continental caves. Schmerling in 1833 ("Recherches sur les ossements fossiles découverts dans les cavernes de la Province de Liège") had made the Engis skulls available to scholars, and in 1857 the Neanderthal skeleton had been discovered in a cave near Düsseldorf. The Neanderthal skull, in particular, was still attracting considerable interest in 1860–1, and Lyell has left a description of a visit he made to the site in the company of Dr Fuhlrott, who had helped with the recovery of the bones. The account concludes with a reference to Huxley: "When on my return to England [in 1860] I showed the cast of the cranium to Professor Huxley, he remarked that it was the most ape-like skull he had ever beheld" (Lyell, 1863, 79). Huxley's own published assessment appears on p. 157 of "Man's Place in Nature":

> In no sense, then, can the Neanderthal bones be regarded as the remains of a human being intermediate between Men and Apes. At most they demonstrate the existence of a Man whose skull may be said to revert somewhat towards the pithecoid type. . . . And indeed, though truly the most pithecoid of known human skulls, the Neanderthal cranium is by no means so isolated as it appears to be at first, but forms, in reality, the extreme term of a series leading gradually from it to the highest and best developed of human crania.

At the time when the *Punch* lampoon was being composed, the Neanderthal skull was once more in the public eye, for George Busk (in the *Natural History Review* for April 1861) had just produced an English translation of Schaaffhausen's original German memoir, adding some comments of his own on the relationship between the Neanderthal skull and those of the chimpanzee and gorilla (Busk, 1861).

These remarks reintroduce the theme of the gorilla, and with it the holy alliance of Bishop Wilberforce and Sir Richard Owen. Owen, at this time superintendant of the natural history departments of the British Museum, was one of the most eminent anatomists and palaeontologists of his day. He had studied with Cuvier, was a friend of Dean Buckland (of "Red Lady of Paviland" fame), had written up the zoological specimens collected by Darwin during the voyage of the Beagle, and examined materials from cave excavations in France. He was also one of the first specialists to handle a gorilla skeleton (Owen, 1859, p. 68), and had written several papers on the subject.

When "The Origin of Species" was published, Owen was one of the scholars who found themselves unable to accept the theory of natural selection, though his writings show that he was well aware of the process of continuous evolution (Owen, 1859, pp. 55–63; 1868, Chap. XL). He himself had argued that each organism was adapted to a particular set of conditions, and had recognized "one cause of extinction as being due to defeat in the 'contest which, as a living organized whole, the individual of each species had to maintain against the surrounding agencies which might militate against its existence'" (Owen, 1868, p. 789). He refused, however, to draw the Darwinian conclusion that the same forces were responsible for the origin and differentiation of species. It was not the *fact* of evolution which upset him, but Darwin's explanation of its *cause*. Owen could not bring himself to accept the non-purposive character of evolutionary change. In his Fullerian Course of Lectures in Physiology for 1859 he wrote:

> . . . surely we must be more strikingly impressed with the wisdom and power of that Cause which could produce so much variety, and at the same time such perfect adaptations and endowments, out of means so simple. . . . Everywhere in organic nature we see the means not only subservient to an end, but that end accomplished by the simplest means. Hence we are compelled to regard the Great Cause of all as . . . an active and anticipating intelligence (Owen, 1859, p. 62).

What was missing from Darwin's scheme was the presence of what Owen elsewhere called "a predetermining intelligent Will' (Owen, 1868, p. 789) which, for the religious-minded, was synonymous with the Will of God.

These sentiments were expressed in an unsigned, but sarcastic and cantankerous, article which Owen wrote for the *Edinburgh Review* (1860, pp. 487–532), quoting extensively from his own earlier works to rebut Darwin on both physiological and philosophical grounds. It was widely believed, by Darwin among others, that Owen also provided such scientific data as there were in another, unsigned, article by Bishop Wilberforce in the *Quarterly Review* (July 1860, pp. 225–64), written in the superior, pulpit style which earned him the sobriquet "Soapy Sam" Wilberforce. His review has a number of memorable lines ("Is it credible that all favourable varieties of turnips are tending to become men?"), several weak arguments, and a peroration which admirably sums up the traditionalist view of the proper relationship between science and the Bible:

> Now we must say at once, and openly, that such a notion (natural selection) is absolutely incompatible not only with single expressions in the word of God on that subject of natural science with which it is not immediately concerned, but, which in our judgment is of far more importance, with the whole representation of that moral and spiritual condition of man which is its proper subject matter (*op. cit.*, p. 258).

Comparison of this statement with the one by Horner (quoted on p. 50) illustrates very clearly the conflict of authority between two different kinds of "truth", the revealed truth of the Bible, and the empirical truth of the new science.

Huxley's involvement in the controversy was at an anatomical rather than a spiritual level, and the history of his running battle with Owen is contained in a section of "Man's Place in Nature" which he titled "A succinct History of the Controversy respecting the Cerebral Structure of Man and the Apes" (Huxley, 1863, pp. 113–18). By 1861 the quarrel had all the ingredients of good journalism, with each professor calling the other's factual knowledge and scientific competence in question. As the *Punch* lampoon demonstrates, the dispute was not confined to the scientific journals.

Verses 9 to 11 are a remarkably accurate paraphrase of Owen's views on the relationship between the brains of man and the great apes, as put forward in his Reade Lecture at Cambridge (May 1859) and in a number of earlier papers. In 1859 he had written:

> The posterior development of the cerebral hemispheres in man . . . is so marked that anthropometrists have assigned that part of the character the name of a "third lobe": it is peculiar and common to the genus *Homo*: equally peculiar is the "posterior horn of the lateral ventricle", and the "hippocampus minor" which characterize the hind lobe of each hemisphere. The superficial grey matter of the cerebrum, through the number and depth of its convolutions, attains its maximum extent in man.
>
> Peculiar mental powers are associated with this highest form of brain, and their consequences wonderfully illustrated in the value of the cerebral character; according to my estimate of which, I am led to regard the genus *Homo* as not merely a representative of a distinct order, but of a distinct subclass, of the Mammalia, for which I propose the name of ARCHENCEPHALA (Owen, 1859, p. 26).

Huxley maintained that all these characteristics were in fact present in apes as well as man. His opinion of those who felt that the relationship endangered man's special status can be gauged from a comment he made a few years later: "it is not I who seek to base Man's dignity upon his great toe, or to insinuate that we are lost if an Ape has a hippocampus minor" (Huxley, 1863, p. 109).

During the months before the publication of the *Punch* verses, each side had publicly defended its position, Owen in a lecture to the Royal Institution on 19 March 1861 and subsequently in the *Athenaeum* of 23 and 30 March, Huxley in the *Natural History Review* for January 1861 and the *Athenaeum* for 13 April. There can be no doubt that Mr Punch was either present at these meetings or had been closely following the literature.

The joker in the pack is Paul Belloni Du Chaillu, an American who had lived for some time on the west coast of Africa. He was neither an anatomist nor an archaeologist, though his story is inextricably tangled with the anatomical squabbles of 1861, and he was later to write a detailed and surprisingly useful book* on Scandinavian archaeology (Du Chaillu, 1889). At the time of the *Punch* verses, his claims to fame derived from his explorations in the interior of Equatorial Africa, which were written up and published early in 1861. In Du Chaillu's own words,

> It has been my good fortune to be the first white man who can speak of the gorilla from personal knowledge; and . . . I can also vouch that no description can exceed the horror of its appearance, the ferocity of its attack, or the impish malignity of its nature (Du Chaillu, 1861, p. 347)

This is dramatic stuff, and the book reached the British market at just the right moment. Although a stuffed gorilla had been exhibited in the Mammal Gallery of the British Museum since 1858, it was not until October 1887 that the London Zoo received its first live specimen. With its splendid gorilla pictures (Fig. 3), and exciting eyewitness accounts of gorilla shooting, Du Chaillu's book at once became a best seller, running to a second edition in the same year, and becoming a major topic of drawing room conversation†. Public interest was insatiable. The author was invited to lecture and exhibit his specimens at the Royal Geographical Society on 18 March, and on the following day Owen spoke at the Royal Institution, basing his

---

* The purpose of this work was to answer the question "Why is it that, wherever the English-speaking peoples have settled, or are at this day found, even in small numbers, they are far more energetic, daring, adventurous, and prosperous, and understand the art of self-government and of ruling alien peoples far better than other colonizing nations?". His answer was: Norse vigour, introduced by the "numerous warlike and ocean-loving tribes of the North" at the time of the Viking conquest (Du Chaillu, 1889, pp. vii, viii). The book is, however, lavishly illustrated with engravings of objects and monuments from Bronze Age to Viking date, and is based on first-hand study of museum collections.

† See for example the cartoon in *Punch* for 1 June 1861. The scene is a fashionable ball: a weedy bespectacled youth is trying to make conversation with a stern-looking girl about the current long-running success at the Adelphi theatre. Beneath the picture is the following exchange:

MILD YOUTH. "Have you seen 'The Colleen Bawn'?"

HORRID GIRL (with extreme velocity). "Seen 'The Colleen Bawn'! Dear, dear! Yes of course. Saw it last October! And I've been to the Crystal Palace, and I've read the Gorilla Book!"

MY FIRST GORILLA.

Fig. 3. Paul du Chaillu hunting the gorilla (from *Explorations and Adventures in Equatorial Africa*).

C*

talk on material provided by Du Chaillu, and giving "an explanation of the distinctive characters between the Negro (or the lowest variety of Human Race) and the Gorilla" (*Athenaeum* 23 March 1861, pp. 395–6).

Besides describing his adventures, Du Chaillu made serious, scientific claims for his book, maintaining that it was the first study of gorilla behaviour in the wild, and incorporating a chapter on the comparative anatomy of man and the great apes. The anatomical data derive mainly from papers written by Owen between 1848 and 1861. Du Chaillu also claimed to have discovered 48 new birds and 18 animal species, including two new anthropoid apes of roughly chimpanzee size: a bald-headed one which he named *Troglodytes calvo*, and the *kooloo-kamba*, a big-eared one with a singular cry (kooloo) and "an expression curiously like to an Eskimaux or Chinaman" (Du Chaillu, 1861, p. 361). This new species, of which Du Chaillu obtained only one specimen, was said to bear "a closer resemblance to man that any other ape yet known" (*op. cit.*, p. 360).

It was these scientific claims which roused the academics to battle and sparked off the ludicrous "Gorilla War" of 1861, giving birth in the process to a number of other fine parodies (see *Temple Bar*, 1861; Entellus, 1861; *Punch*, 15 June 1861, p. 245). The most convenient summary of the case against Du Chaillu is contained in a two-part review by J. E. Gray (1861), published in June and July of that year, but to really enjoy the comedy it is best to follow the story through successive issues of *The Times* and the *Athenaeum*.

Public and scientific opinion was divided on the merits of Du Chaillu's research, and the battle raged through editorials and correspondence columns for the rest of the year. Trivial issues (did Gray ever call Livingstone a "great humbug" in Du Chaillu's presence?) were jumbled together with important scientific controversies, as the charges against Du Chaillu mounted up. Much of this is subsequent to the *Punch* lampoon, but the first doubts were raised by Gray ("The New Traveller's Tales") in the *Athenaeum* of 18 May, the very day on which the *Punch* verses appeared.

Over the year it gradually became evident that Du Chaillu's narrative was full of inconsistencies, that he had lifted his most striking incidents and most of his gorilla data from the works of earlier travellers (Huxley, 1863, p. 53), and that none of his species was new to science. His *T. calvo* and the *kooloo-kamba* were plain chimpanzees, and most of the engravings of apes turned out to be borrowed without acknowledgement from other more learned books. Even the illustrations of Du Chaillu's new anthropoids were copied, and had been originally published as pictures of chimpanzees!

Things went from bad to worse for Du Chaillu when information from his native companion seemed to prove that he had not visited many of the areas he described, and had in fact purchased most of the specimens which he claimed to have shot himself (*Athenaeum*, 14 December 1861, pp. 806–7).

The division between the scientists followed the already familiar lines. Huxley and most of the anatomists were against Du Chaillu; Owen (who had been Du Chaillu's patron in England) was isolated in his rather embarrassed support of the man who, it must be admitted, had provided him with useful raw material for his study of anthropoid anatomy.

The final word must be allowed to J. E. Gray:

> I believe, and have thought from the commencement, that M. Du Chaillu is more sinned against than sinning; for I presume that when he lent his name and, perhaps, furnished a few notes to the American publisher, neither he nor the author of the work (for it is generally allowed that M. Du Chaillu did not write it) intended it as more than a cheap, popular book of travels, written to meet the taste of the American public . . . a community who are always seeking excitement and telling wonderful tales, and whose newspapers are so full of "sensation paragraphs" (Gray, 1861, p. 60).

Gray's words have a familiar ring today, when the cheap popular book and the mass media are, for good or ill, the main purveyors of science to the public. From this it follows that no historian of archaeology can afford to ignore the journalistic literature which provides the most sensitive barometer of public interest in the subject, and – more importantly – that professional archaeologists must not leave the work of popularization to the writers of "wonderful tales" and "sensation paragraphs". Public concern – and public money – are still, as they always have been, an essential component of archaeological research. It is exactly one hundred years since George Smith's discovery, at the *Daily Telegraph*'s expense, of the second half of the Assyrian flood tablet at Nineveh (Daniel, 1950, p. 133), and (with Olduvai, Masada, Abu Simbel, the Nubian sites, Silbury Hill and South Cadbury in mind) there is good reason to look back at the long and often honourable history of "newspaper archaeology".

References

Busk, G. (1861). *Natural History Magazine* **2**.
Daniel, G. E. (1950). "A Hundred Years of Archaeology". Duckworth, London.

Daniel, G. E. (1964). "The Idea of Prehistory". Penguin Books, Harmondsworth.

Daniel, G. E. (1967). "The Origins and Growth of Archaeology". Penguin Books, Harmondsworth.

Daniel, G. E. (1972). *Antiquity* **184**, 317–320.

Darwin, C. (1905). "The Voyage of the Beagle: Journal of Researches into the Natural History and Geology of the Countries Visited during the Voyage Round the World of H.M.S. Beagle". Amalgamated Press, London.

Du Chaillu, P. B. (1861). "Explorations and Adventures in Equatorial Africa: with accounts of the manners and customs of the people, and of the chase of the *gorilla*, crocodile, leopard, elephant, hippopotamus and other animals". John Murray, London.

Du Chaillu, P. B. (1889). "The Viking Age; the early history, manners, and customs of the English-speaking nations, illustrated from the antiquities discovered in mounds, cairns, and bogs, as well as from the ancient Sagas and Eddas". John Murray, London.

Entellus (1861). "Account of the Milling-match between Entellus and Dares, translated from the fifth book of the Aeneid, by one of the Fancy: being an account in doggerel verse of the Gorilla Contest between Dr J. E. Gray and P. B. Du Chaillu". London.

Gray, J. E. (1861). *Ann. Mag. nat. Hist.* **7**, 463– 470; and **8**, 60–65

Horner, L. (1847). "Address delivered at the Anniversary Meeting of the Geological Society of London on the 19th of February 1847". Richard and John Taylor, London.

Horner, L. (1855). *Phil. Trans. R. Soc.* **145**, 105–138.

Horner, L. (1858). *Phil. Trans. R. Soc.* **148**, 53–92.

Horner, L. (1861). "Address delivered at the Anniversary Meeting of the Geological Society of London on the 15th of February 1861". Taylor and Francis, London.

Huxley, T. H. (1863). "Evidence as to Man's Place in Nature". Williams and Norgate, London.

Lartet, E. (1860). *Q. Jl. geol. Soc. Lond.* **16**, 471–479

Lyell, C. (1863). "The Geological Evidence of the Antiquity of Man, with remarks on the origin of species by variation". John Murray, London.

Moorehead, A. (1971). "Darwin and the Beagle". Penguin Books, Harmondsworth.

Owen, R. (1859). "On the Classification and Geographical Distribution of the Mammalia, to which is added an Appendix 'On the Gorilla' and 'On the Extinction and Transmutation of Species'". Parker and Son, London.

Owen, R. (1868). "On the Anatomy of Vertebrates: Vol. III, Mammals". Longmans Green, London.

Prestwich, J. (1860). *Proc. R. Soc.* **10**, 50–59.

Temple Bar (1861). "With Mr Gorilla's Compliments", *Temple Bar; a London Magazine for Town & Country Readers*, **3**, 482–91.

Old and New Views on Primate Fossils

I. W. CORNWALL

THE MIDDLE NINETEEN-SIXTIES saw the Theory of Continental Drift gain respectability and general acceptance in a way that its main proponent, Alfred Wegener (1915) could never have foreseen. It has solved many problems of apparently trans-oceanic migration of plant and animal species, which have long bedevilled geology with impossible demands from palaeontologists for former land-bridges everywhere.

It now seems probable that Wegener's postulated supercontinent of Pangaea persisted almost up to the end of the Mesozoic. The successive separation of Laurasia (the northern part) from Gondwanaland (the southern) by the Tethys Sea (of which the Mediterranean is a remnant) and that of North America from Europe and South America from Africa, by the "conveyor-belt" of the widening Atlantic, have all taken place within the last 100 million years.

Before that, more or less the same kinds of dinosaurs (for instance) had coexisted in all the continents. After the rifting, populations of early Tertiary mammals became progressively isolated. Among Primates, for instance, while members of Lemuroid and Omomyid stocks were common to all save Australia in the Palaeocene and early Eocene, by the later Eocene and early Oligocene there were no Lemuroids left in South America while, in Europe, a specialized Tarsiid had developed, probably from the Omomyids. By the later Oligocene, Platyrrhine (New-World) monkeys had evolved in South America, while only Omomyids persisted in the North; Tarsiids had migrated to south-eastern Asia (where their sole-surviving representative still lives); Catarrhine (Old-World) monkeys and Lorisids had developed in Africa, while the true Lemurids remained only (as they still do) in Madagascar. From the mid-Miocene up to the present North America has had no sub-human Primates at all; South America only the Platyrrhines. Catarrhines and Lorisids are common to Africa and Eurasia.

The re-closure of much of the western part of the east-west Tethys rift during the Miocene, by the northward drift of Africa, enabled Cercopithecid (monkey-like) and Pongid (ape-like) Primates, already differentiated there, to migrate into Europe and Asia, along forested routes which no longer exist in the Near East. In the late Miocene, these were followed by Hominids, which, in the present state of our knowledge, were almost certainly also African in origin.

By the end of the Mesozoic, mammals must have became numerous and active, if mostly small in size and perhaps nocturnal in habit – all features favourable to inconspicuous survival in the presence of reptilian predators. Their characteristic coats of hair, high and constant body-temperature and four-chambered hearts (among other important changes) led to greater physiological efficiency than that of the reptiles. The habit of suckling and caring for their young reduced wastage by infant mortality and rendered unnecessary the prodigal egg-production characteristic of reptiles.

The opening of the Tertiary found the mammals, thus equipped, all ready for explosive development, in size, variety of species and numbers of individuals, expanding to fill the varied ecological niches made vacant by the extinction of most of the reptiles. Among them, some still-unspecialized small insectivores took to the trees for greater safety and founded the Order Primates. They are found as an already-distinct group as early as the Lower Eocene.

Primate fossils are scarce, because the chances are slender of their remains being quickly buried and preserved. On the tropical forest floor, biological and chemical dissolution are rapid.

If we first look to the Eocene of Burma, there is a long-known, but generally disregarded or misinterpreted fossil, *Pondaungia cotteri* (Pilgrim 1927), from the Upper Eocene Pondaung Sandstone. Pilgrim thought it to be a Primate at the very root of the Anthropomorph stem – i.e. not even a catarrhine monkey, but an ape. Abel (1931) regarded this conclusion as too far-reaching (though he did not rule out its possibility), in the case of a fossil "which is not even certainly a Primate". Von Koenigswald denied it this status, regarding it as a generalized ancestor of the carnivores. Other authorities, however, notably E. L. Simons, judge it to be a "bridge between the higher and lower Primates". It might have crossed from Burma to India, to north Africa roughly 40 million years ago. Thus Pilgrim's original determination is supported.

Another "poor relation" among presumably Primate fossils is *Apidium phiomense* (Osborn 1908). It consists of the fragment of a mandible with a premolar and three molars *in situ*, from the Lower Oligocene beds of the Fayum. Abel (1931) says that it is superficially pig-like, but Schlosser (1911) regarded it as a possible ancestor of

Oreopithecus (vide inf.). Piveteau (1957) was of the opinion that it was a distinct primitive Catarrhine, and so, perhaps, a common ancestor of Old-World monkeys, apes and man. A number of new specimens of *Apidium* has recently been found by a Yale University expedition to the Fayum and its Catarrhine status is now more widely admitted.

The star of the show, among these remote cousins of man, is a small monkey-sized creature known as *Propliopithecus haeckeli* (Schlosser, 1911). It is not found in the Lower or Upper Oligocene forest-beds which have yielded the greater number of mammalian fossils, but from the intervening Middle level, dated to about 30 million years BP. As the generic name given to it by its discoverer suggests, it was, by him, regarded as ancestral to *Pliopithecus*, an Upper Miocene small European ape of gibbon affinities, which still retains that status in most palaeontologists' opinions.

A recent American expedition to the Fayum (Simons, 1962) found, in the Lower Oligocene beds, a small early catarrhine monkey, called *Oligopithecus*, and in the Upper a probable ancestor of the Ponginae (great apes) which is named *Aegyptopithecus*, both new to Science. Whatever the contemporary environment of the deposition of the Middle beds, it was certainly not forest, and the implication, therefore, is that it was open country. *Propliopithecus*, complemented by several new finds, is unlike either of those others. It has a short and deep jaw, a tooth row without a diastema, a short, stumpy canine, almost vertically-set incisors, a low, bicuspid lower third premolar and a reduced third molar. All these features relate it rather to the Hominids than to the Pongids, while the other two species are clearly Cercopithecid and Pongid respectively, by their high canines, procumbent incisors, sectorial lower third premolars and enlarged third molars. It is a possible conclusion, therefore, that the Pongid and Hominid stems were already clearly separate by the Middle Oligocene.

In a recently-published popular book, entitled "Not from the Apes", (1972), Björn Kurtén, of Helsinki, proposes the theory that the apes branched from the Hominids, instead of the reverse, which has hitherto been the orthodox view. It is notable that Abel (1931), though regarding *Propliopithecus*, as did his predecessors, as an ancestral gibbon, nevertheless notes all the *un*-gibbon-like features on which Simons and Kurtén now rely in concluding that it is, perhaps, a Hominid!

African Oligocene Pongidae gave rise to apes which, in the Miocene, spread thence, not only to other parts of Africa but to Eurasia. The larger species, originally given a multiplicity of generic names, are now usually assigned to two main genera: *Dryopithecus* and *Sivapithecus*. The smaller, *Limnopithecus* and *Pliopithecus*, are clearly specialized in the direction of the modern gibbons. About most of the former, there is little doubt that they are apes, the forerunners of gorilla, chimpanzee and orang-utan. They have the characteristic ape dentition.

In one case, however, *Ramapithecus*, from the Nagri Zone (Upper Miocene) of the Siváliks, northern India (Lewis, 1934), the Hominid features are numerous: no "simian shelf" at the symphysis of the jaw, small canines, a bicuspid lower third pre-molar and so on. Further material was described by Gregory, *et al.* (1937), who concluded their article by saying that, though they regarded *Ramapithecus* as a "simian by definition", it was "almost at the human threshold, at least in respect of (its) known anatomical characters".

In 1963, E. L. Simons, after re-studying the *Ramapithecus* material, decided that it represented a true early Hominid, not a Pongid. In the interval the early Pleistocene Australopithecines had also been accorded Hominid status by a general consensus of opinion, so that this announcement was not as startling as it might otherwise have been.

A Hominid, then. But in Asia? Did this mean that Asia, not Africa, was the scene of Hominid differentiation? L. S. B. Leakey's (1962, 1967) *Kenyapithecus wickeri* from Fort Ternan, dated at about 14 million years BP, was assimilated to *Ramapithecus* by Simons (1969), though Leakey strenuously opposed such generic identification. This view now seems to be accepted by most authorities. Since the East African species should be the earlier by some tens of thousands of years at least, the African origin of the genus and its later diffusion into Asia by the same route as the other African Hominoids is likely.

Thereafter, in Africa, between about 14 and 5 million years BP, the Primate fossil record is represented by only a single tooth, from near Lake Baringo, northern Kenya (Bishop and Chapman, 1970), which might, morphologically, as in time (9 million years BP) lie between *Ramapithecus* and *Australopithecus* in the Pliocene.

In Europe, we have a solitary Pliocene Hominoid, *Oreopithecus bambolii* (Gervais, 1876), from Lower Pliocene lignites in Tuscany, rescued from obscurity by Johannes Hürzeler of Basel in the 1950's. A number of fragments of jaws and loose teeth had been poorly illustrated and the originals in their museum drawers were practically unknown to specialists. On searching the trucks of brown-coal from the Baccinello mine, Hürzeler found several more pieces. He later had the opportunity to go underground himself and was lucky enough to find an entire skeleton *in situ*. The remains were severely crushed and an exhaustive study has, even now, not appeared.

The jaw and tooth-material showed some man-like characters, such as the upright incisors and small canines. Hürzeler concluded (1958) that this was an ape with unusually advanced features, which might be a link between the ordinary great apes and primitive Hominids like the Australopithecines. *Oreopithecus*, however, has a molar pattern peculiar to itself and the limb-proportions and environmental evidence betray a still-arboreal creature living in a forest-swamp, rather like the cedar-swamps of Florida today. Most authorities, therefore, regard it as a terminal side-branch of the Hominoidea, instead of a progressive, transitional form, and so in no sense a Hominid. Simons regards it as possibly derived from *Apidium*. Furthermore, we have, by the later Pliocene, already-recognizable Australopithecines in east Africa, which are, according to present-day opinion, undoubted Hominids, even if of a genus, or even a sub-Family, distinct from the genus *Homo*.

These have been discovered only within the last few years at a number of sites near Lakes Baringo and Rudolf, and in the Omo Valley in Ethiopia (1967–71), not to mention the now well-known later specimens from South Africa and Olduvai in Tanzania. The earliest of the new finds dates from more than 5 million years BP and so is clearly late Pliocene. No *Elephas* is older than some 4 million years BP, and this is one criterion for drawing a Plio-Pleistocene boundary.

Early Hominids, then, we have, but what of *Homo*? There are those (not all) human palaeontologists who saluted L. S. B. Leakey's "pre-*Zinjanthropus* child", of 1·75 million years ago, from Bed I, Olduvai, as *Homo habilis*, a likely transition-form between *Australopithecus* and *Homo erectus* (Leakey *et al.*, 1964). The grounds for this were the larger brain-capacity indicated by the parietal bone and the advanced detailed morphology of foot and hand, suggesting an almost fully-developed striding gait and a manipulative potential quite capable of working the associated pebble-tools.

If that were all, we might have been well satisfied. But behold! another Leakey (Richard), his father's own son, confounds the pundits by presenting to the world "Hominid 1470", from the Lake Rudolf region, only a few months ago (Leakey, R. E. F., 1972)! It is a skull-cap even in newspaper photographs unmistakably larger and more advanced in the direction of *Homo*, even than *Homo habilis*. Its potassium/argon date, 2·5 million years BP, is three quarters of a million years older yet than *H. habilis* and must give us something to think about in rearranging our ideas about the origins of our genus.

This will take some time to digest, and yet, so fast, nowadays, does new evidence overtake theory, that no one can say whether we may not have to reconsider even this remote representative of man before very long.

There is plenty of time (11·5 million years) and unexplored space in Africa (to say nothing of Asia!) for many more "missing links" to lie hidden between *Ramapithecus* and 'Hominid 1470" – perhaps even enough for the mermaid-like lady conjured up by Elaine Morgan (1972) to explain so much that is still obscure about the evolution of specifically human physical and psychological equipment!

References

Abel, O. (1931). "Die Stellung des Menschen in Rahmen der Wirbeltiere". Jena.

Bishop, W. W. and Chapman, G. R. (1970). *Nature* **226**, 914–918.

Gervais, P. (1876). "Zoologie et Paléontologie générales", 2e série.

Hürzeler, J. (1958). *Verhandlungen naturforschender Ges., Basel* **69**, 1–48.

Kurtén, B. (1972). "Not from the Apes", 183 pp. Gollancz, London.

Leakey, L. S. B., Tobias, P. V. and Napier, J. R. (1964). *Nature, Lond.* **201**, 967; **202**, 3–9.

Leakey, L. S. B. (1967). *Nature* **213**, 155–163.

Leakey, L. S. B. (1962). *New Scientist* **447**.

Leakey, R. E. F. (1972). *New Scientist* **56**, 385–387.

Lewis, G. E. (1934). *Am. J. Sc.* **27**, 161.

Morgan, E. (1972). The descent of woman, 288 pp. Souvenir Press, London.

Osborn, L. (1908). *Bull. Am. Mus. Nat. Hist.* **24**, 265–272.

Pilgrim, G. E. (1915). *Rec. Geol. Surv. India* **45**, 1–74.

Pilgrim, G. E. (1927). A Sivapithecus Palate and other Primate fossils from India, *Pal. Ind.* **14**, 1–26.

Piveteau, J. (1957). "Traité de Paléontologie V. 7: Primates". Masson, Paris.

Schlosser, M. (1911) *Paläont. u. Geol Österrich-Ungarns u. des Orients* **24**, 51–167.

Simons, E. L. (1962). *Peabody Mus. Postilla, No. 57*.

Simons, E. L. (1969). *Nature, Lond.* **221**, 448–451.

Wegener, A. (1915). (4th ed. 1928) "Die Entstehung der Kontinente und Ozeane"

The Late Middle Acheulian Industries in the Swanscombe Area

J. d'A. WAECHTER

BARNFIELD PIT, SWANSCOMBE, for many years considered the type site of the 100 ft Terrace of the lower Thames has, since the original investigations of Spurrell in the 1880's, provided a rich haul of artifacts to both excavators and collectors, as well as three human fragments – so far the oldest human remains in Britain. The richness of the site, both archaeologically and faunal, as well as its geological significance has led, over the last sixty years, to a number of excavations and a considerable amount of literature.

The recent excavations, particularly those of 1971 and 1972, (Waechter, 1971, 1972), although primarily concerned with the lower part of the sequence, investigated the upper deposits by re-cutting sections over a wide area. This re-examination of the upper levels raises the question of the date of some of the Acheulian, not only from Barnfield Pit but from other deposits between Northfleet and Dartford.

The generally accepted sequence at Barnfield, established by Smith and Dewey in 1912 (Smith and Dewey, 1913), is as follows:

Chalk.
Thanet Sand. Surface 75 ft OD.
Lower Gravel.
Lower Loam. Surface 88 ft OD.
Lower Middle Gravels.
Upper Middle Gravels.
Upper Loam. Surface 110 ft OD.
Upper Gravel. 115 ft OD.

The Lower Gravel and Lower Loam have produced a Clactonian industry (in mint condition in the Loam) and a rich temperate fauna attributed to the Great or Hoxnian Interglacial (Elster/Saale). The surface of the Lower Loam is weathered, suggesting a period as a land surface.

Resting on the surface of the Lower Loam, which forms its bench, is a second series of river gravels, coarse at the base and passing into current bedded sands. From both parts of these Middle Gravels came a rich industry of pointed Acheulian hand-axes, generally unpatinated, and a temperate fauna similar to that from the Lower Loam and Lower Gravel. The Middle Gravel has been equated with the 100 ft Terrace of the Thames dated to the same inter-glacial (Oakley, 1938). It was from this horizon that the human remains came.

Smith and Dewey's section shows the Middle Gravel passing from its rather coarse base directly into the current bedded sands, now generally called the Upper Middle Gravels, and thence into the Upper Loam which was considered as part of the aggradation. The Upper Gravel is a solifluction representing one of the stages of the Riss or Saale glaciation.

Chandler's section (Chandler, 1930), drawn from nearly the whole of the south side of the pit, about 280 yards, modifies the original section by showing that the Lower Loam pinches out at the eastern and western ends and where it is missing the Middle Gravels rest directly on the Lower Gravels. The Upper Loam also pinches out and the whole deposit dips slightly in the middle of the section.

Marston in his report on the finding of the first two skull fragments (Marston, 1937) modifies the earlier sections very significantly, publishing a composite section made up of three separate faces, one running northeast to southwest containing the Middle Gravels and the deposits above, a second immediately opposite the first with the Lower Gravel and Lower Loam only and the third around the corner outside the pit, running east to west, showing only the Lower Gravel and Lower Loam.

Marston's section shows a major channel feature cutting through the lower part of the Lower Middle Gravels and down through the Lower Loam and Lower Gravels to the surface of the Thanet Sand, a channel over 25 ft deep. (Fig. 1) This channel is filled with the

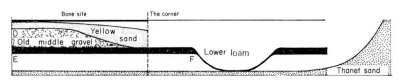

Fig. 1. Barnfield Pit (Marston, 1937).

current-bedded sand of the Upper Middle Gravels, which overlaps the Lower Middle Gravel and passes upwards to the Upper Loam, and is thus the upper part of Smith and Dewey's Middle Gravel.

If this downcutting does exist then there is a considerable time interval between the deposition of the Lower Middle Gravel and the cutting and filling of the channel.

Marston considered that there were two stages of Acheulian represented in the Middle Gravels, the first, from the lower part, being more primitive than those from the channel filling which were associated with the skull. (Marston, 1937, pp. 344, 353). This view was not supported by the Swanscombe Committee (Swanscombe Committee, 1938, p. 41), who considered both the industries as being the same : a view which requires further consideration.

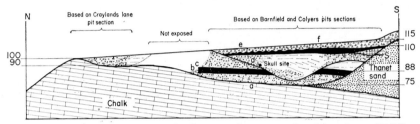

Fig. 2. Barnfield Pit and Craylands Lane (Swanscombe Committee, 1938).

Marston's published section (Marston, 1937) was accepted by the Committee (Committee report, 1938, Fig. 3) (Fig. 2) but they make no comment on Marston's section F outside the pit which purports to show the Lower Loam and Lower Gravel cut out by the channel at the eastern end and re-appearing at the western, (Fig. 3). Smith and Dewey, and apparently Marston, include the Upper Loam as part of the Middle Gravel aggradation, suggesting that it has the same significance to the Middle Gravel as the Lower Loam has to the Lower Gravel, thus raising the surface of the terrace to 110 ft OD.

Dines in the Committee report (Committee Report, 1938, p. 27) mentions "a wedge-shaped mass of contemporary solifluction resting on the surface of the Middle Gravel and against its sloping upper surface the horizontal laminae of the Upper Loam abut". This solifluction wedge is very localized and was not seen by Smith and Dewey, nor apparently by Chandler, though it is odd that Marston makes no mention of it although it occurs at the western end of his section F. Paterson publishes a section (Paterson, 1940, Fig. 2) showing Marston's channel, the solifluction wedge and the deposits abutting on to the rising Thanet Sand. Paterson also maintains that the upper part of the Middle Gravel suggest colder conditions for their deposition. The presence of this solifluction wedge, confirmed by the recent excavations, clearly separates the Upper Loam from the underlying Upper Middle Gravel and a cold phase intervenes between the two.

The archaeological material associated with the upper part of the Upper Middle Gravels and the Upper Loam is often inadequately marked as such, and that from the former is frequently attributed to the Middle Gravels as a whole. What seems to separate these two series from the bulk of the hand-axes, apart from typology, is the white patina, which is virtually absent in the material from the lower levels.

Smith and Dewey, (1913, pp. 191–2) though not themselves finding any hand-axes in the Upper Loam quote the workmen as saying that white patinated ovate hand-axes were found at the base of the Upper Loam, though it is not clear whether these came from the surface of the gravel or were actually in the Loam. Smith and Dewey mention these hand-axes again in their following paper (Smith and Dewey, 1914, p. 189) and Dewey refers to these implements in a later paper (Dewey, 1932, p. 42). His remarks are worth quoting in full: "The higher parts of the Middle Gravel, although containing fewer implements, are richer in better fashioned pieces and there is a gradual incoming of cordate and oval forms (the limande of French authors)". These presumably refer to the implements mentioned in his earlier publications with Smith. Burchell (1931, p. 256) also mentions ovate hand-axes exhibiting a porcelain white-patina apparently coming from the Upper Loam, though he follows this remark by referring to Smith's Stone Age Guide to the British Museum where Smith repeats his original remarks of 1913 and 1914, but illustrates a typical twisted ovate with white patina as coming from the uppermost beds at the base of the Upper Loam (Smith, 1926, p. 30 and Fig. 18).

Hawkes in the Committee report (Swanscombe Committee report, 1938, p. 45) is more specific regarding implements from the Upper Loam, and illustrates two with a porcelain-white patina (Fig. 10 nos. 9, 10). It is, however, not clear where these hand-axes were found, as the Upper Loam had already been removed when the Committee started their excavation (Committee report, 1938, p. 49). Two further hand-axes from Marston's collection are illustrated, both sub-cordate or sub-ovate. (Committee report, 1938, Fig. 12, nos. 1, 2).

Paterson also refers specifically to implements from the Upper Loam and describes them as

> thin tongued pointed bifaces (Micoquian) oval, pyriform and linguate bifaces, S-twists, developed controlled secondary working which may be so good that retouch is unnecessary to produce regular outlines, feather flaking retouch, some controlled step retouch, edges and outlines regular, symmetrical biconvex and plano-convex sections, and a fair number made on flakes (Paterson, 1940 p. 169).

He also refers to their porcelain-white patination.

Roe in his analysis of the British Acheulian industries (Roe, 1968, p. 21 and Fig. 36) accepts eighteen hand-axes as coming from the Upper Loam, considering only those clearly marked as coming from this level. These hand-axes are strikingly ovoid and 22% show twisted profiles and 39% tranchet finish.

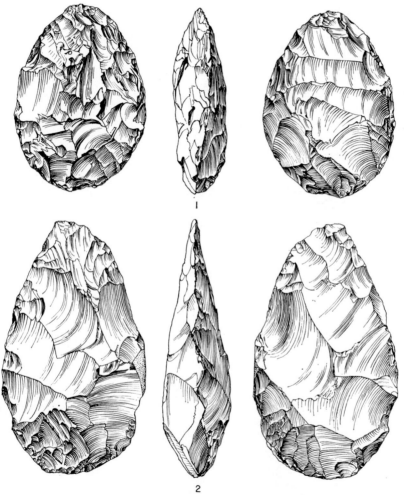

Fig. 3. Upper Loam, Barnfield Pit. (scale $\frac{1}{2}$)

Wymer, arguing that white patination is virtually absent on the Upper Middle Gravel hand-axes selected those with white patina from the Stopes collection (Wymer, 1964, p. 47, Figs. 25, 26) and (Wymer, 1968, p. 343, Fig. 106). A large proportion of these patinated hand-axes are not typologically distinct from those from the Middle Gravel, but there are two ovates illustrated by Wymer with markedly twisted profiles (Wymer, 1964, Fig. 26 nos. 3, 4).

A number of patinated hand-axes have come from the Upper Gravel solifluction, including two from the present excavations (Waechter, 1971, Fig. 3, and 1972, Fig. 3), the latter, though not twisted is typical of the small Upper Loam ovates.

Further evidence for the presence of ovate hand-axes comes from Colyer's Pit, an extension on the south side of Barnfield Pit. Oakley, in a footnote (1939 p. 357) mentions Marston finding ovate

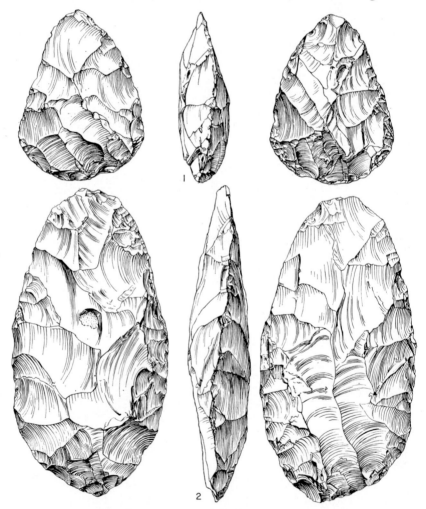

Fig. 4. Upper Loam, Barnfield Pit (scale ½).

hand-axes immediately below the Upper Loam. The three specimens illustrated here (Figs. 3, 4), come from the Institute's own collection.

It seems clear from the above that there are at least two series of hand-axes above the Upper Middle Gravels, the first apparently resting on the Gravel surface, occurring at both Barnfield and Colyers. They are predominantly ovoid and characteristically patinated white. Dewey implies that there is a gradual development from the pointed hand-axes below. As these hand-axes appear to belong to the surface of the gravel, and not in it, there may well be a time interval. The second series is from either the Upper Loam or in the Upper Gravel, presumably derived from the Loam. This group, also white patinated ovates, are markedly twisted.

The Committee report, due no doubt to its composite authorship, contains some curious anomalies. In Hawkes' report, in collaboration with Oakley and Hazzledine Warren, the yellow sands overlying the skull horizon were uniformly sterile and the Upper Loam also, but in the following paragraph he discusses the industry from the Upper Loam, remarking that the material came from the surface of the Loam and not in it. This is at variance with the evidence of ovate hand-axes occurring at the top of the Upper Middle Gravel and immediately beneath the Upper Loam and also the evidence for an industry in the Loam itself.

The recent cutting of long sections in the western end of the pit, covering Marston's section F, has confirmed some of the older ideas but has made it necessary to re-consider others. The presence of the solifluction wedge between the Upper Middle Gravel and the Upper Loam is confirmed, but there is now more detailed climatic evidence. Immediately above the solifluction wedge are current bedded sands with clay layers; in this horizon are ice wedges, cryoturbation and micro-faulting. This is followed by clayey fine sand with thin clay layers in the upper part. Above this is the solifluction gravels, the Upper Gravel. At the junction of the Loam and the Upper Gravel are ice wedges and drag structures.

These new sections also exposed both parts of the Middle Gravels and there is no evidence for the channel as conceived by Marston. Chandler always maintained that this channel never existed and has also said that Marston admitted that he had never in fact seen it. (Chandler, 1942, p. 21). If this is so, then it is necessary to put a rather different time profile on the sequence from the base of the Lower Middle Gravels to the Upper Gravels.

If the major erosion of the channel and the time interval this implies does not exist, then the Lower Middle Gravel and Upper Middle Gravel would appear to be a continuous aggradation without interruption, and the contained Acheulian industries almost con-temporary, as the Committee maintained. In the upper part of this aggradation the climate, previously temperate, becomes progress-ively colder, with lemming and a cool molluscan fauna (Kerney, 1971, p. 79). Following the final deposition of the Gravel and sand of the Middle Gravels is the onset of marked cold conditions, in the middle of which occurs the undisturbed Upper Loam.

These cold conditions place not only the ovate implements from the Upper Gravels at the very end of the Interglacial and immediately preceding the onset of the Gipping or Saale glaciation but also suggest that the whole of the Middle Gravel aggradation occurs towards the end of the Interglacial, and it seems probable that these ovate hand-axes are a development of the typical pointed hand-axes of the lower part of the Middle Gravels, as Dewey suggested.

The industry associated with the Upper Loam, either in it or on its surface, represents a different phase, demonstrably later in time, typologically different, and occurring in an interstadial of Gipping or Saale.

The twisted ovate industry from Swanscombe is by no means an isolated phenomenon, and there are a number of sites in the Swans-combe area as well as elsewhere, not only with the same industry but apparently associated with similar geological conditions. There are six sites between Dartford and Northfleet with archaeological material and geological conditions similar to Barnfield, and although some were investigated many years ago, it is possible to extract a considerable amount of information from them.

Craylands Lane

This pit, on the east of Craylands Lane, is now dug out and the sections obscured. During Smith and Dewey's time at Swanscombe a section was available, although its exact position is not now known (Smith and Dewey, 1914, p. 169, Figs. 1, 2,). Their section is as follows:

  a. Contorted clayed gravel, 3 ft.
  b. Even bedded gravel and sand, 7 ft.
  c. False bedded gravel and sand, 4 ft.
     Chalk surface, c.90 ft OD.

Although the distance between Craylands Lane pit and Barnfield is short and the Craylands Lane bench at about 90 ft is comparable to the surface of the Lower Loam at Barnfield, the bench of the Lower Middle Gravels, it is impossible to relate Craylands Lane directly with the Barnfield sequence. The Committee's suggestion that is represents a separate channel (Dines Committee report p. 24 and Fig. 2) is probably correct.

Recently further sections have been cut in the sides of the pit (Harrison, 1972) which show a different set of deposits from Smith and Dewey. The main difference in Harrison's sections is that in all of them the gravels lie not directly on the Chalk, but on a "Combe Rock", suggesting solifluction due to cold conditions.

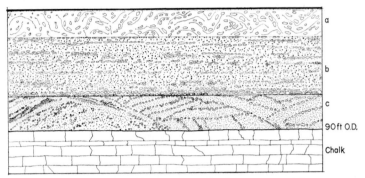

Fig. 5. Craylands Lane (Smith and Dewey, 1914).

The implements illustrated by Dewey (1914, plates 15, 16) came from the surface of the false bedded gravel and sands, Layer C. They are all ovoid and a number have S-twists, in fact the same industry as that associated with the Upper Loam and Upper Gravel at Barnfield: and apparently occurring between two cold phases, the second being represented by the Contorted Clayey Gravel of Dewey's Layer A.

Rickson's or Barracks Pit

This pit lies on the opposite side of Swanscombe village to Barnfield Pit and overlooks the Ebbsfleet valley of which it forms the northern edge. The site lies near Rickson's farm and also the local barracks, hence the two names, the latter used by Burchell. There are two descriptions of the section, one by Dewey (1932, Fig. 2) and one by Burchell (1934, p. 163 and plate XX). As the two sections do not agree in detail it is necessary to give both.

DEWEY'S SECTION
    a. Current-bedded sand and gravel.
    b. Even-bedded ochreous sand.
    c. Shell bed.

d. Bed of coarse gravel with cores and large flakes.
e. Chalk.

BURCHELL'S SECTION
  g. Surface soil.
  f. Upper Gravel.
  e. Upper Loam.
  d. Middle Gravel and Sand.
  c. Lower Loam.
  b. Lower Gravel and Sand.
  a. Chalk.

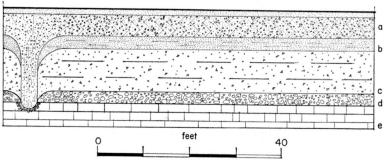

Fig. 6. Rickson's Pit (Dewey, 1932).

The major differences between the two sections is Burchell's inclusion of two loams missing in Dewey's section. Burchell however, does mention that the Upper Loam is rarely present in the sections.

The Lower Gravel has produced a rich Clactonian, some in mint condition and some slightly abraded. The sands and gravels above contained hand-axes, which, according to Dewey, are ovoid and some are the most beautiful small twisted ovates ever found in Britain. (Figs. 7, 8, 9)

Burchell found Levallois material in the overlying Upper Loam. (Burchell, 1931, Fig. 3). He also mentions Levallois material from his Middle Gravel. No Levallois technique has been proved with certainty from either Barnfield or Craylands Lane (Waechter, 1968, p. 494).

The dating of Rickson's Pit presents several difficulties. Harrison's recent work in this area (Harrison, 1972) shows that east of Barnfield Pit there is extensive channelling of which Craylands Lane is only one example. The condition of some of the Clactonian suggests that the Lower Gravel may well be a remnant of the Barnfield Pit, but there is no evidence for the Barnfield Middle Gravels, which appear to have been eroded away. The archaeological content of the Rickson's Middle Gravels suggest that they are contemporary with the Upper Loam cycle at Barnfield, since the Upper Gravel of Rickson's strongly suggest similar cold conditions to those of the Barnfield Upper Gravel.

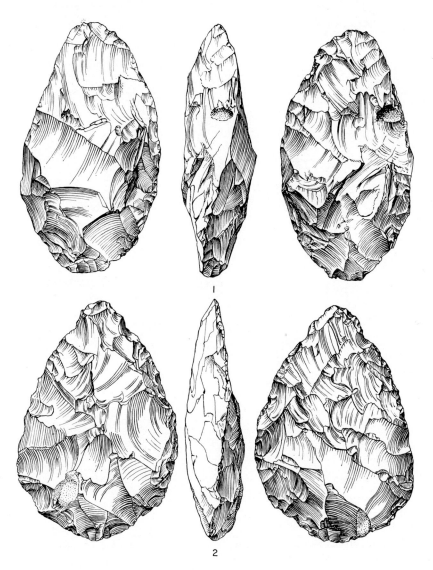

Fig. 7. Rickson's Pit (scale $\frac{1}{2}$).

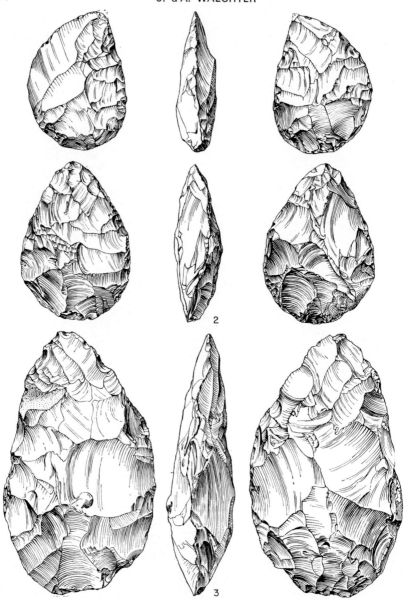

Fig. 8. Rickson's Pit (scale ½).

The Globe Pit, Greenhythe

This pit, abandoned for many years, lies west of Barnfield Pit on the south side of the Dartford-Gravesend Road, a quarter of a mile south-east of Greenhythe station.

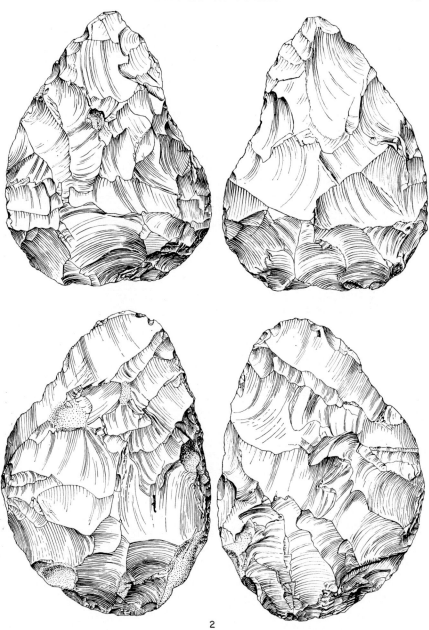

2

Fig. 9. Rickson's Pit (scale ½).

Smith and Dewey (1913, p. 192) investigated the pit but found only a few worked flakes, and we are dependent on material collected during the commercial digging for any ideas of the industry. The deposits rest on Thanet Sand at between 90 ft and 100 ft OD, and consists of gravel filling irregular channels cut in the Thanet Sand. Filling what appears to be a further channel cut into the gravel is a "Brickearth" overlaid by what seems to be disturbed gravel. This sequence is based on the section published by Dewey, (1932, Fig. 6.) (Fig. 10).

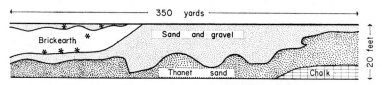

Fig. 10. Globe Pit Greenhythe (Dewey, 1932).

Smith and Dewey's description is of a deposit without visible stratigraphy. It is therefore difficult to place the implements in any geological context, and we must depend on the typology of the hand-axes themselves. Most of them came from either the brickearth, or on its eroded surface. They are markedly ovoid (Fig. 6, no. 2) and were compared by Smith and Dewey to the material from Wansunt Channel (see below), although there is no certainty that twisted ovates have been found in the Globe Pit.

Pearson's Pit, Dartford

This is one of the three pits on the Dartford Heath Gravels, the others being Wansunt Channel and Bowman's Lodge. These pits have been dug in the large sheet of gravel which forms Dartford Heath. The age of these gravels has been variously interpreted. The generally accepted altitude is 136 OD, some 20 ft higher than the surface of the aggradation at Barnfield.

Hinton and Kennard regarded the Dartford gravel as being earlier than the 100 ft or Boyne Hill Terrace of Barnfield (Hinton and Kennard 1905, p. 80). Chandler and Leach (1912), estimating the base of the Dartford Gravels as between 90 ft – 100 ft OD, equate them with the Gravels at Swanscombe. Taking the base level of the Barnfield Middle Gravels as about 90 ft, the surface of the Lower Loam, this correlation is reasonable, but the height of the Dartford Gravels,

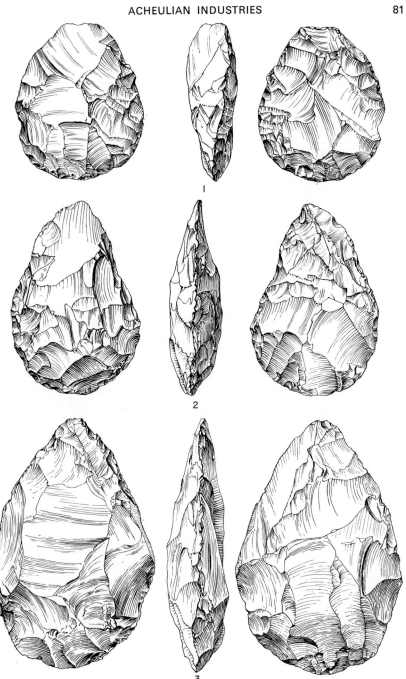

Fig. 11. Pearson's Pit (scale $\frac{1}{2}$).

D

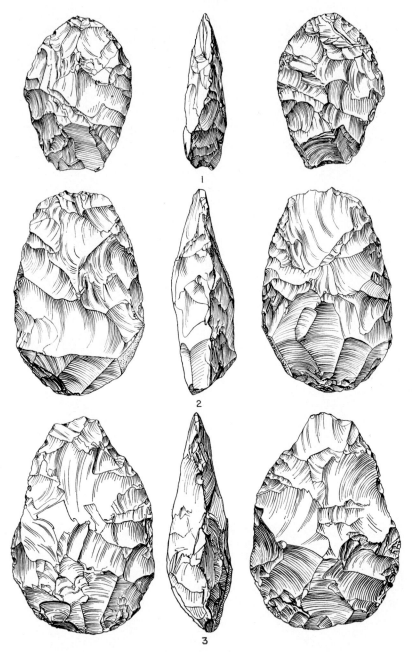

Fig. 12. Pearson's Pit (scale $\frac{1}{2}$).

136 ft, seems too high compared with the surface of the Upper Middle Gravels at Barnfield, just over 100 ft OD.

Zeuner (1959 p. 155, footnote) has made the suggestion, followed by Cornwall (1950, Fig. 1, p.36), that the gravel on the heath is composite, the older part belonging to the Kingston Leaf series, and banked against these are younger gravels belonging to the Boyne Hill Terrace at approximately 100 ft OD. The age of these younger gravels is important as the deposits of the three pits under consideration are fillings of channels cut into, and therefore post dating them.

There is no published section of Pearson's Pit, but the hand-axes appear to have come in, or immediately under, a loam filling a channel cut into gravels. The position of the pit suggests that the underlying gravels belong to the later phase of the Dartford gravels, e.g. the Swanscombe Middle Gravel series.

The implements (Figs. 11 and 12) are in mint condition: predominantly ovoid or cordiform, with twisted ovates present. No fauna has been recorded.

Wansunt Channel

This pit, which lies to the west of Pearson's Pit, has received more attention and the implements and sections have been published. (Smith and Dewey, 1914) and (Chandler and Leach, 1912). Chandler

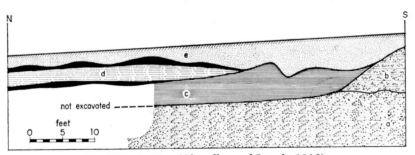

Fig. 13. Wansunt (Chandler and Leach, 1912).

and Leach's section is more detailed (Fig. 13). Resting on a Thanet sand bench of 90 – 100 ft are two deposits of gravel, the lower described as false-bedded gravel, the upper red gravel. Chandler and Leach ascribe both these gravels to the 100 ft or Boyne Hill Terrace, the Middle Gravels at Barnfield. Cut into these gravels is a channel filled with three deposits described by Chandler and Leach as (c) dark clay, (d) stratified loams and clay, and (e) unstratified loamy gravel (Fig. 12). Flakes have come from the clay of layer (c), but the hand-axes come from layer (d). These are unrolled and little patinated; characteristically they are small ovates, many in Smith and Dewey's series twisted.

Bowman's Lodge.

This site is to the east of Wansunt Pit but it is not clear whether the two deposits are continuous. The pit as it is now is extremely confusing, the basal gravel is much channelled and filled with a variety of deposits, and Tester's original deposit does not appear to be extant. The deposits at Tester's site are as follows: Thanet Sand; Gravel 19 ft with base at 96 ft OD; Loam 1 ft; Surface soil, 1 ft (Tester, 1951). From the surface of the gravel, Tester obtained a total of 279 artifacts, of which 28 were hand-axes. The industry is completely fresh and a number patinated white. The hand-axes are predominantly ovoid, some with twisted profiles. Tester claims evidence for Levallois techniques on some of the cores, but the material is not very characteristic (Waechter, 1968, p. 494).

The industries from the six sites described above have a strong typological unity; the hand-axes are characteristically ovate or cordiform, they have in common the strong tendency towards twisted profiles, and appear to occupy the same chronological position.

In Barnfield Pit the twisted ovate industry clearly post-dates the last of the Boyne Hill aggradation represented by the Upper Middle Gravels, and is associated with cold conditions. In some of the other pits the climatic evidence is not so precise, though the upper levels of Craylands Lane and Rickson's suggest cold conditions and the channelling indicates lateral erosion due to fall in base level in response to the oncoming of cold conditions.

If the temperate deposits of the Barnfield Middle Gravel are of Elster/Saale age, which the existing evidence suggests, then the ovoid hand-axe industries with twisted profiles are to be correlated with one of the interstadials in the succeeding glaciation, Saale or Gipping. In all the other sites the evidence of erosion and down cutting suggest that they too belong to the same glaciation.

The twisted ovate industries are by no means confined to the Swanscombe area, and occur over south and east England; Gaddesden Row, Herts: (Smith, W. G., 1916); Santon Downham, Suffolk: (Smith, R. A., 1931); Caddington, Beds.: (Smith, W. G., 1894) and Elveden, Suffolk: (Paterson, 1940). The industry from Elveden is particularly relevant as it is almost identical to that from the Swanscombe area (Paterson, 1940, Fig. 5). Unfortunately, no fauna is available but the artifacts occur between two distinctly cold deposits which Paterson refers to as Saale or Gipping and Wiechsel or Würm respectively. In view of the Swanscombe evidence an inter Saale date would seem more acceptable.

At Gaddesden Row the implements were on the surface of a brickearth channelled and filled with re-deposited brickearth which is in turn covered by a contorted drift, and at Caddington the material came from a brickearth filled depression formed in a boulder clay. (Smith, W. G., 1894, Figs. 4, 5 and 6).

It is not possible in a short paper to re-examine the deposits with twisted ovates outside our original area but the existing evidence suggests that they are probably all inter-Saale in date. Some confirmation of this chronological position comes from France, where similar industries are associated with the Older Loess, (Breuil and Koslowski, 1931, Figs. 11, 12 and 13), but also see Bordes (1954, p. 438 and footnote 2). Bordes re-publication of Commont's Atelier (Bordes and Fitte, 1953) shows twisted ovates similar to those in Britain, though the twisting seems to be less developed; similar material from the same workshop are illustrated by Vayson (1920, No. 39).

Bordes puts the Atelier Commont at the base of the Older Loess, which would make it slightly earlier than the material from the Upper Loam at Barnfield, but a chronological position closer to that attributed to Hoxne, (West and McBurney, 1954) which has an industry very similar to that from the Atelier Commont.

The French evidence and that from Hoxne suggest that there may be not one, but two industries with twisted ovates; one, slightly earlier than the other and less developed, is represented by Hoxne in the Elster/Saale interglacial and possibly the ovoid hand-axes claimed as coming from the surface of the Upper Middle Gravels, and dating, like the Atelier Commont, from the very end of the same interglacial, to be followed by the more extreme twisted ovates in an interstadial of Saale.

References

Bordes, F. and Fitte, P. (1953). *L'Anthropologie* **57**, 1–2, 1–45.
Bordes, F. (1954). *Archives de l'Institut Paléontologie Humaine, Paris, Mem* **26**, 1–472.
Breuil, H. and Koslowski, L. (1931). *L'Anthropologie* **41**, 449–488.
Burchell, J. P. T. (1931). *P.P.S.* **6**, 253–303.
Burchell, J. P. T. (1934). *A.J.* **XIV**, no. 2, 163–166.

Chandler, R. H. and Leach, A. L. (1912). *Proc. Geol. Ass.* **23**, 102–111.

Chandler, R. H. (1930). *P.P.S.* **6**, 76–116.

Chandler, R. H. (1942). *Proc. Geol. Ass.* **53**, 21.

Cornwall, I. W. (1950). Univ. of London, Inst. of Archaeology, *6th Annual Report*, 34–43.

Dewey, H. and Smith, R. A. (1914). *Proc. Geol. Ass.* **25**, 90–97.

Dewey, H. (1932). *Quart. J. Geol. Soc. Lond.* **88**, 35–54.

Hinton, M. A. C. and Kennard, A. S. (1905). *Proc. Geol. Ass.* **XIX**, part 2, 76–100.

Harrison, R. W. (1972). B.A. Dissertation, Institute of Archaeology, University of London.

Kerney, M. P. (1971). *Quart. J. Geol. Soc. Lond.* **127**, part 1, 69–86.

Marston, A. T. (1937). *J. Roy. Anthrop. Inst.* **67**, 339–406.

Oakley, K. P. (1938). *J. Roy. Anthrop. Inst.* **68**.

Oakley, K. P. (1964). "The Swanscombe Skull" (Cameron D. Ovey ed.) Roy. Anthrop. Inst.

Paterson, T. T. and Fagg, B. E. B. (1940). *P.P.S.* **6**, 1–29.

Paterson, T. T. (1940). *P.P.S.* **6**, 166–169.

Roe, D. A. (1968). *P.P.S.* **XXXIV**, 1–82.

Smith, R. A. and Dewey, H. (1913). *Archaeologia* **64**, 117–204.

Smith, R. A. and Dewey, H. (1914). *Archaeologia* **65**, 187–212.

Smith, R. A. (1926). "Guide to the Antiquities of the Stone Age", 3rd edition. British Museum.

Smith, R. A. (1931). "The Sturge Collection", Vol. 1. British Museum.

Smith, W. G. (1894). "Man the Primeval Savage". Edward Stanford, London.

Smith, W. G. (1916). *Archaeologia* **67**, 49–74.

Swanscombe Committee (1938). *J. Roy. Anthrop. Inst.* **68**, 17–98.

Tester, P. J. (1951). *Arch. Cant.* **63**, 122–34.

Vayson, A. (1920). *L'Anth.* **30**, 441–496.

Waechter, J. (1968). "La Préhistoire, Problèmes et tendances", 491–497. Éditions du Centre National de la Recherche Scientifique, Paris.

Waechter, J. (1971). *Proc. Roy. Anthrop. Inst.* 1971, 43–49.

Waechter, J. (1972). *Proc. Roy. Anthrop. Inst.* 1972, 73–7.

West, R. G. and McBurney, C. M. B. (1954). *P.P.S.* **20**, 131–154.

Wymer, J. J. (1964). "The Swanscombe Skull" (Cameron D. Ovey ed.) Roy. Anthrop. Inst. 1960.

Wymer, J. J. (1968). "Lower Palaeolithic Archaeology in Britain". John Baker, London.

Zeuner, F. E. (1959). "The Pleistocene Period". Hutchinson, London.

Constellation Analysis of Burins from Ksar Akil

M. H. NEWCOMER AND F. R. HODSON

Introduction

As a result of trial and a good deal of error, archaeologists have over the last decade managed to adapt some general computerized techniques to their own specific problems of classification. A great deal more experimentation and adaptation remain to be done; however, some of the techniques have passed beyond the initial stages of testing and are now accepted and available for a wide range of archaeological situations. The most successful of these fall under the general heading of *multidimensional scaling*: they allow archaeological material described by many variables (hence multidimensional) to be summarized, so that the archaeologist is helped in one of the more difficult and neglected aspects of his craft: seeing the wood for the trees. Multidimensional scaling harnesses the computer to sift through masses of data, to pick out general agreements and trends, and, effectively, to reduce the dimensionality of the whole problem. The results are presented as a simple scatter diagram in as few dimensions as seem reasonable when judged by an associated measure of distortion.

The initiation and development of multidimensional scaling in archaeology has largely centred on the London University Institute of Archaeology, and this volume provides a fitting context for recording the active encouragement which Professor Grimes has always given to this research.

A recent development in this approach is "Constellation Analysis"*, where different aspects of a problem are considered

* The computer programme for Constellation Analysis was developed with the help of a grant from the Leverhulme Foundation. We would like to thank the Computer Centre at University College, London and Mrs Rosaly Evnine for help in running this programme. For access to the Ksar Akil material we are indebted to Emir Maurice Chehab and Dr. J. d'A. Waechter.

separately and then in relation to each other. In fact, a series of multi-dimensional scaling analyses are carried out, one for each aspect or *constellation* of the evidence, and the results are compared by fitting one to another and measuring the residuals (Gower, 1971a; Azoury and Hodson, 1973).

Constellation Analysis provides a very general technique, but in this paper it is applied to a specific problem: how to decide on a satisfactory level for classifying items of study. Palaeolithic archaeologists accept one such level in their classification of stone tools under headings like "hand-axe", "end-scraper" or "burin", but they also agree that for useful cultural interpretations something more than these general classes is required. However, at a more detailed level there is no longer agreement about the definitions of sub-types or even about whether sub-types should be defined. Perhaps, rather, individual attributes of the tools within the several categories should be isolated and studied, even if it is not quite clear how (Movius *et al.*, 1968).

Although it is not difficult to suggest any number of possible subdivisions of, or descriptive attributes for, such general archaeological classes as "hand-axe" or "burin" (or "beaker" or "La Tène fibula" for that matter, since the problem is the same), it is far more difficult to assess the merits of these alternative approaches. A related study (Azoury and Hodson, 1973) demonstrated how Constellation Analysis could be used to make such comparisons. A suitable group of assemblages is chosen as the basis for comparison. Any proposed descriptive list, whether by sub-types or morphological attributes, or by a mixture of both, forms a descriptive constellation for the assemblages, which are then interrelated according to this information. These interrelationships are discovered and presented by means of a multidimensional scaling analysis. Thus for each constellation of information about the assemblages, a different analysis is performed, and a different configuration or "map" results (like Figs. 1–3). Constellation Analysis quantifies the relationship between each pair of configurations and so between the descriptive systems that lie behind them. In the study of Azoury and Hodson (1973), a number of general descriptive constellations were compared using a series of stratified assemblages from Ksar Akil. The constellations referred to entire assemblages of tools and debitage, and included type-lists at two levels of detail (one with 54 and the other with 17 types), technological information on butts, blanks and cores, and alternative forms of weighting this evidence. One of the more surprising results of this general investigation was that the long type-list (54 types) gave little if any additional information about the overall interrelationships between assemblages, than a reduced type-list (17 types) made up by amalgamating some of the more detailed types. Since both the time needed to study assemblages and the insight derived from the study are directly dependent on the type- and/or attribute-list followed, this result calls for further investigation.

This present study focuses this problem narrowly down to one of the major accepted classes of Palaeolithic tools – burins. A similar but more extended set of stratified assemblages from Ksar Akil are taken as the basis for assessment. These assemblages are described by different categories of information about their burins, each category forming a constellation. Most interest will concentrate on four such constellations defined by alternative type-lists with 23, 15, 8 and 4 types of burin respectively. However, other burin attributes are also studied and their significance investigated.

The Data Analysed

The data used in this study were prepared as part of a doctoral study, where, alongside more general interpretations, interest was centred on the detailed study of burins from all of the Upper Palaeolithic levels at Ksar Akil (Newcomer, 1972). This site and its burins provide an obvious basis for investigating the general taxonomic problem posed above: how best to study and if necessary to sub-divide general tool classes.

Few really detailed investigations of single Upper Palaeolithic tool classes have been carried out. Sackett (1966) attempted such a study for end-scrapers, and the results of his preliminary morphological study were used to seriate a number of assemblages in south-western France. This was an interesting methodological study, but in our opinion unrealistic: the attributes or descriptors for end-scrapers were few in number and debased beyond the point where an accurate or even an approximate impression of the object would be given by its symbolic description. This is especially true for the fully quantified attributes which were split into only three measurement divisions. The next stage of the analysis involved estimating the statistical association between these measurement intervals, judged via the end-scrapers in the sample. It was thought that "significant" association between these intervals could be taken to define attribute clusters (or, rather attribute *state* clusters) and so a kind of "type", but in fact, this would simply reveal that the attributes concerned were statistically correlated. This is irrelevant for the definition of types, which depends on finding discontinuities rather than correla-

D*

tions (see Doran and Hodson, 1973). The subsequent unidimensional seriation of assemblages on this basis is again perhaps a little unrealistic since a single, linear relationship between such assemblages cannot and need not be assumed *a priori*. No comparison was made between this approach to end-scraper classification and any of the other more obvious approaches. Numerical studies in archaeology have advanced considerably since 1966, and a more comprehensive and realistic attempt to investigate this basic problem should be made. Ksar Akil, with its series of rich assemblages in known stratigraphic order provides a suitable starting point for such an investigation. Burins offer the widest range of technological and typological variation of any group of Upper Palaeolithic tools and provide a natural choice for this specialized study.

Of course, it would be unwise to limit any site-study to the burin tool group alone : no reliable characterization of assemblages poor in burins is possible, and no firm conclusions about the cultural similarities or differences between any two assemblages can be made without reference to the total assemblages. The complementary work of Azoury on the total tool assemblages from some of the levels at Ksar Akil (Azoury and Hodson, 1973), including some burin-poor levels, provides a basis for judging any comparison of assemblages based on a detailed study of burins alone.

The site of Ksar Akil is a deeply-stratified rock-shelter about 6 kilometres to the north-east of Beirut, Lebanon. Although there have been several excavations at Ksar Akil, our material comes from the 1937–8 campaigns of the Boston College Expedition to Lebanon (for references to preliminary reports on the stratigraphy and archaeology, see Newcomer, 1970).

Full reports on the stone tool assemblages found in the 23 m of archaeological deposits at Ksar Akil have never been published, but in the broadest terms the sequence includes Mousterian assemblages at the bottom (levels 37–26), followed by a long series of Upper Palaeolithic levels (25–1), containing 5,112 burins.

Of the 25 Upper Palaeolithic levels, only 16 have more than 50 burins; the remainder were considered too poor in burins to study statistically and were omitted from our analysis. Although the site was dug in 2 m square excavation units, and some levels were divided into arbitrary units of depth or "spits", these squares and spits are ignored and the assemblage of burins from each level is taken as the basic unit of study.

The burins from Ksar Akil were studied by two main approaches. The first set up a series of 23 morphological types. A type is taken to represent a discrete group of related tools where each tool is more similar to all the other tools of its type than to any tool of another type. A 24th category, miscellaneous, was needed for broken and unclassifiable burins, although this is not regarded as a type. This typology provided a basis for the general description and comparison of assemblages. By defining conditional attributes specific to certain of these types, it was further possible to study variation within them during the occupation of the site. This type-specific information is not used for this present study.

The second approach studied features that cut across this type-list: information about the blanks on which tools were made, details of the actual burin edge, and so forth.

From these various categories of information the following constellations have been defined for this present study:

Constellation 1: General

This provides a reference constellation with all of the available cross-cutting information on burins. It in fact combines the information of constellations 2 and 6–10 below.

Constellations 2–5: Typology

Four alternative type-lists of varying complexity were defined. It is possible to divide burins, first, into four major groups:

  a. Dihedral burins (comprising 1–7 of the detailed types below),
     where the spall removal surface or "SRS" (Movius *et al.*, 1968) is an unretouched surface.
  b. Truncation burins (types 9–16),
     where the SRS is a line of retouch.
  c. Multiple burins (types 8, 17–18),
     combining two or more burin edges on the same blank, and
  d. Composite burins (types 19–23),
     combining a burin with a tool from another tool group, e.g. an end-scraper.

This fourfold division constitutes one constellation (C5).

At the opposite extreme, it is possible to define another constellation made up of 23 types (C2). There is no need to discuss them in detail here, but brief descriptions follow. It will be seen that they correspond to a large extent with the well-known types given by de Sonneville-Bordes and Perrot in their list for the European Upper Palaeolithic (1956). Types are mainly distinguished by their technology as shown by the SRS, although in some cases a set of attributes is used, similar to those employed to define French Noailles burins (Tixier, 1958; Newcomer, 1971). Percentages in brackets give the largest recorded occurrence for each type and so indicate their relative importance.

1. *Single-blow burin*: The spall removal surface (SRS) is a flat natural surface, a cutting edge, or cortex (17·8%).

2. *Burin on a break*: The SRS is a break (9·0%).

3. *Axial dihedral burin*: The SRS is a burin facet (or set of facets) and the burin edge is on or near the axis of the blank (8·8%).

4. *Offset dihedral burin*: As type 3, but the burin edge is clearly off the axis of the blank (30·4%).

5. *Angle dihedral burin*: As type 3, but the burin edge is on a corner of the blank, and the two facets or sets of facets meet in a near right angle (11·7%).

6. *Flat-faced carinated burin*: The SRS is a burin facet or flat natural surface, against which three or more facets are made on the ventral surface of the blank (23·3%).

7. *Carinated burin*: The SRS is a burin facet or flat natural surface, against which three or more facets are made, but these are not confined to the ventral surface of the blank and are often curved in profile (30·0%).

8. *Multiple dihedral burin*: Tool combining two or more burins of types 1–7 on the same blank (12·3%).

9. *Burin on straight normal truncation*: The SRS is a straight line of retouch (truncation) which is perpendicular or nearly perpendicular to the axis of the blank (5·6%).

10. *Burin on concave normal truncation*: The truncation is concave and perpendicular or nearly perpendicular to the axis of the blank (7·8%).

11. *Burin on a notch*: The SRS is a Clactonian or retouched notch, and the burin is usually small and thick, frequently sharpened, etc. (see Newcomer, 1971) (13·8%).

12. *Burin on straight oblique truncation*: The truncation is straight and oblique to the axis of the blank (23·6%).

13. *Burin on concave oblique truncation*: The truncation is concave and oblique to the axis of the blank (17·0%).

14. *Burin on an end-scraper*: The SRS is a line of retouch which previously defined an end-scraper, usually a narrowed front (nosed or shouldered) variety (5·4%).

15. *Burin on convex oblique truncation:* The truncation is convex and oblique to the axis of the blank (18·8%).

16. *Burin on lateral preparation*: The SRS is a line of retouch up the edge of the blank; both this SRS and the burin facet(s) are oblique to the axis of the blank (12·8%).

17. *Multiple truncation burin*: Tool combining two or more burins of types 9–16 on the same blank (5·1%).

18. *Multiple mixed burin*: Tool combining one or more dihedral burins (types 1–7) with one or more truncation burins (types 9–16) on the same blank (8·3%).

19. *Dihedral burin/end-scraper*: Tool combining one or more dihedral burins (types 1–7) with an end-scraper (12·9%).

20. *Truncation burin/end-scraper*: Tool combining one or more truncation burins (types 9–16) with an end-scraper (7·5%).

21. *Burin/chamfered piece*: Tool combining one or more burins with a chamfered piece (see Newcomer, 1970) (6·4%).

22. *Burin/beak*: Tool combining one or more burins with a beak or spur (*bec* or *épine*) (3·2%).

23. *Burin/truncation*: Tool combining one or more burins with a retouched truncation (3·2%).

Between these basic constellations with 4 and 23 types, two intermediate constellations were defined with 15 (C3) and 8 types (C4) respectively. These result from progressive amalgamations of single, detailed types. Thus C3 is made up of 1–2, 3–5, 6–7, 8, 9–10, 11, 12–13, 14, 15–16, 17, 18, 19–20, 21, 22, 23. C4 is made up of 1–2, 3–5, 6–7, 9–11, 12–14, 15–16, 8 and 17–18, 19–23.

Constellation 6: Burin edges

For the study of the contours of burin edges, a feature which cross-cuts the burin type-list, a shortened form of the list devised by Ronen (1965) was used:

E1 ("E" standing for "edge shape"): *Squared*. The burin edge is a straight line, more or less perpendicular to both surfaces of the blank.

E2: *Bevelled*. The burin edge is formed by the intersection of a curved line and a straight line.

E3: *Rounded*. The burin edge is more or less smoothly curved.

E4: *Pointed*. The burin edge is formed by the intersection of two more or less straight lines which meet in an acute angle.

Constellation 7: Blanks

Three widely used categories expressing the length/width ratios of blanks were used to characterize the blanks on which burins were made at Ksar Akil:

Flake: any product of debitage whose length is less than twice its width.

Blade: any product of debitage whose length is twice or more than twice its width, and whose maximum width is greater than 12 mm. (Bordes, 1961; Tixier, 1963.)

Bladelet: any product of debitage whose length is twice or more than twice its width, and which is narrower than 12 mm.

Since the process of converting a flake, blade, or bladelet into a burin involves some shortening of the blank, the length/width ratios given above were used cautiously, and for the classification of blades and bladelets other features of the blank were taken into account, such as the nature of the lateral edges and ridges, which should be parallel or sub-parallel (Tixier, 1963).

In practice, bladelets were only rarely used as blanks for burins at Ksar Akil (20 of 4,383 classifiable blanks or 0·5%), and for all statistical analyses these bladelets were counted as blades.

Constellation 8: Butts

Although the butts of blanks are not normally studied in Upper Palaeolithic assemblages, they seemed important at Ksar Akil, where a general shift in the dominant butt type from faceted to punctiform to plain could be observed. Three categories for butts were used:

Faceted: The butt is composed of two or more flake scars, the result of faceting the striking platform of the core. Three varieties of faceted butts are included under this heading: faceted straight, faceted convex, and faceted dihedral (Bordes, 1961).

Punctiform: The butt of the blank is narrower and thinner than the full width and thickness of the blank. These butts usually result from the special preparation of the striking platform of blade cores as described by Bordes and Crabtree (1969), and both punctiform and linear varieties are included under this heading.

Plain: The butt is formed by one flat wide surface, usually part of a striking platform formed by one large flake scar (Bordes, 1961). Both plain and cortex butts are counted as "plain".

Constellation 9: Other technological features

The attributes noted under this heading refer to the blanks on which burins are made, cross-cutting the "flake, blade, bladelet" divisions discussed above. These features include: the use of a core tablet as a blank; the presence of a large area of cortex on the blank's dorsal surface; the phenomenon named "offset debitage" in which the axis of percussion of the blank (usually a blade) does not coincide with the main axis of symmetry of the blank (*cf.* Bordes, 1961); and the presence of two patinas on the burin, the burin facets having the more recent patina.

Constellation 10: Retouch and stop notch

Two further technological features were appended: the presence of continuous retouch on one or both edges of the blank, and the use of a stop-notch to interrupt the run of burin facets.

Constellation 11: Chronology

This rather different constellation was included to aid interpretation of the others. It records the mean depth of each level and so gives a very approximate idea of the date of burins relative to each other.

The Analysis and its Results

As discussed in the introduction, Constellation Analysis starts out from two or more preliminary analyses of the same set of archaeological units. Here each unit is an Upper Palaeolithic level at Ksar Akil. Each preliminary analysis provides a configuration for these levels, when described by a given constellation. For example, Fig. 2, C2 shows the interrelationships between these levels described by C2, the 23-type list (i.e. by the percentage representation of each type in each level). Fig. 2, C3 shows a similar representation for the 15-type list (C3). In each case the numbers in the diagram represent the relevant levels at Ksar Akil. Clearly, these two configurations are very similar indeed. Constellation analysis operates by quantifying the difference between one such representation and another. This may be taken to reflect the difference between the descriptive systems that underly them. Quantification allows these relationships to be described and subsequently analysed more or less objectively.

It has been mentioned above that these preliminary configurations are given by multidimensional scaling, a general form of data analysis which may follow two distinct approaches, metric and non-metric. The former, in the guise of Principal Co-ordinates Analysis, is followed in this study, but the relative merits of the two approaches need not be discussed here (see Kruskal, 1971 and Doran and Hodson, 1973). Each diagram, then, represents the first two major dimensions, in fact a summary of a configuration set up algebraically in a space of many dimensions. An associated percentage value records how

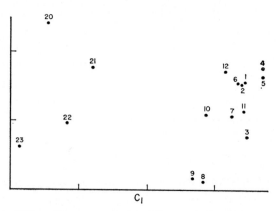

Fig. 1. Principal Coordinates analysis of Upper Palaeolithic burins from Ksar Akil, based on Constellation 1: overall burin information. Levels are numbered downwards. 75% (i.e. 75% of the total variance for this Constellation is preserved in the two-dimensional diagram).

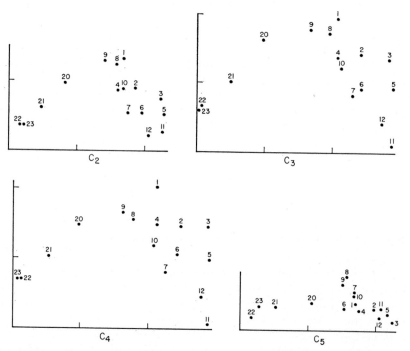

Fig. 2. Constellation 2–5: "Typology". Conventions as for Fig. 1. C2: 23 types (66%); C3: 15 types (80%); C4: 8 types (81%); C5: 4 types (98%).

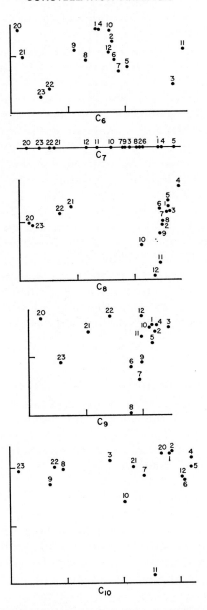

Fig. 3. Constellations: 6–10: Conventions as for Fig. 1. C6: Burin edges (89%); C7: Blanks (100%); C8: Butts (100%); C9: Other information on blanks (95%); C10: Retouch and stop-notch (100%).

much of the total spread of the original values is preserved by this summary representation.

When these preliminary analyses have been carried out, a measure of difference M^2 is calculated between each pair and the values recorded in a matrix like a mileage chart: Table 1 (the M^2 differences between constellations corresponding to the miles between cities). Each M^2 value is calculated by fitting one configuration to another as exactly as possible and summarizing the distances remaining between corresponding points. This fitting is carried out algebraically in as many dimensions as seem suitable (in this analysis, in six dimensions). This whole fitting procedure is described in detail by Gower (1971a and 1971b).

The overall structure within this set of M^2 values may then itself be portrayed visually by a multidimensional scaling analysis, Fig. 4. (This results from a metric, Principal Co-ordinates Analysis, see Gower, 1966 and 1971a). On this diagram, distances between the points reflect differences between the constellations.

The results of this analysis, then, are essentially given by the diagrams: Figs. 1–3, showing the detailed performance of each separate constellation, Fig. 4 showing the overall relationship between constellations.

Discussion of the Results

Since the results of the analysis are summarized by diagrams, Figs. 1–4 will form the basis for the following discussion. To recapitulate, Figs. 1–3 portray relationships between levels at Ksar Akil when judged by different aspects of the burin evidence. The levels are numbered downwards (i.e. later levels have smaller numbers). These diagrams will be discussed first. Although the levels at Ksar Akil are mainly considered here as a basis for assessing different descriptive systems, the constellations, it will also be possible to extract from these diagrams useful information about the mutual relationships between these levels. The final diagram, Fig. 4, then represents a more general summary of relationships between the constellations.

Figure 1 results from an amalgamation of all of the burin information considered (i.e. from amalgamating constellations 2 and 5–10). It suggests a dichotomy between the earlier levels (23–20) and the later (12–1); but also within these later levels, an interrelationship and discreteness for levels 9 and 8. There is clearly a general chronological progression from the left of the diagram to the right, but this is distorted by other effects. The discontinuity between the first four and all the later levels corresponds with a gap in the information: levels between 20 and 12 were too poor in burins to be analysed here. Whether this discontinuity corresponds with a major cultural break as well as an interlude of impoverishment could hardly be decided from the information included in this analysis alone; but a more general analysis, which was able to include some of these intermediate levels, did imply a cultural as well as a depositional break (Azoury and Hodson, 1973). The point is of considerable interest since in general terms, the upper levels would be considered as clearly Upper Palaeolithic in character, whereas the lower levels might not. If anything, the burin evidence summarized in Fig. 1 would imply a rather marked contrast between the two groups. This represents a summary of the more detailed evidence seen in Figs. 2–3 which will be discussed next.

The typological constellations C2–C5 may be taken together. C2 and C3, with 23 and 15 types respectively, have clearly given a very similar result. The quantified estimate of this relationship by M^2, $0·12$ (see Table I) emphasises this overall similarity. This value is calculated from more comprehensive information than may be displayed in a two-dimensional diagram. C4 with 8 types, is still remarkably close to 2 and 3 with M^2 values of $0·15$ and $0·03$ (see Table I). However, the constellation with 4 types only, C5, does differ widely from C2–C4, with M^2 values of $0·38$, $0·30$ and $0·29$ respectively. These four results together provide perhaps the most striking result of the whole analysis: progressive reduction, by amalgamation of the type-list from 23 down to 8 types had relatively little effect. However, the reduction from 8 to 4 types seems to have broken a barrier: this last, very general amalgamation has lost the patterning recovered by the other three. In general, these typological constellations show, first, less emphasis on the discontinuity between earlier and later levels than seen in the overall summary of C1; and second, relatively little correlation between the detailed ordering of levels and the known chronological order.

The burin edge constellation C6 preserves a division on the major horizontal axis between the four earlier and the later levels, but it separates perhaps more emphatically 11 and 3 from the rest. This separation is not seen in any of the other diagrams and here presumably results from the exceptional importance of rounded edges (E3) in level 11, and pointed edges (E4) in level 3, and the corresponding under-representation in both these levels of the more usual squared edges (E1).

Constellation 7 (flake/blade ratio of burin blanks) again demonstrates the usual separation between the four earlier and the later levels, but also, although perhaps not so obvious at first sight, a more detailed relationship with stratigraphy than the other constellations. Level 11, for example, is located unambiguously between 12 and 10, rather than as one of a mixed bag (*cf.* C1) or as an extreme (*cf.* C6). This chronological significance is emphasised by the M^2 value of 0·13 between this constellation and depth (C11), reflecting chronology. No other constellation shows this close relationship. It may be taken to reflect the very general and relatively regular increase of flake to blade production for blanks during the whole period of occupation: in fact a remarkable, long term trend, independent of more detailed, possibly cyclic or simply irregular effects seen via constellations like C6.

Constellation 8, butts of burin blanks, quite simply emphasizes the separation between the four early and the later levels. This clearly

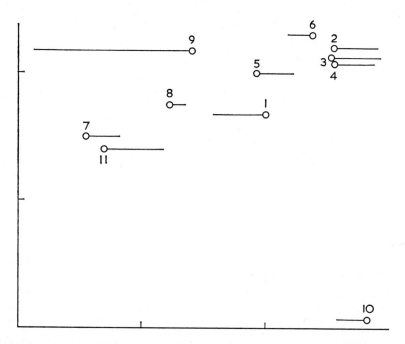

Fig. 4. Overall relationship between the constellations as shown by a Principal Co-ordinates analysis of the M^2 matrix (see Table 1 and text). 70% of the relevant variance is accommodated. (The first two dimensions account for only 56% of the variance, and so a third dimension is indicated by horizontal lines proportional to coordinate values on this third dimension.)

TABLE I

CONSTELLATION	1	2	3	4	M² VALUES 5	6	7	8	9	10	11
1) All information	—	0·36	0·31	0·26	0·42	0·46	0·55	0·31	0·42	0·68	0·59
2) 23 types	0·36	—	0·12	0·15	0·38	0·45	0·81	0·56	0·69	0·87	0·79
3) 15 types	0·31	0·12	—	0·03	0·30	0·40	0·74	0·48	0·66	0·80	0·71
4) 8 types	0·26	0·15	0·03	—	0·29	0·38	0·75	0·48	0·65	0·75	0·70
5) 4 types	0·42	0·38	0·30	0·29	—	0·42	0·56	0·45	0·58	0·89	0·50
6) Burin edges	0·46	0·45	0·40	0·38	0·42	—	0·89	0·63	0·68	1·01	0·83
7) Blanks (flake/blade)	0·55	0·81	0·74	0·75	0·56	0·89	—	0·31	0·63	1·22	0·13
8) Butts	0·31	0·56	0·48	0·48	0·45	0·63	0·31	—	0·57	1·03	0·39
9) Blanks (other info.)	0·42	0·69	0·66	0·65	0·58	0·68	0·63	0·57	—	1·23	0·70
10) Retouch and stop-notch	0·68	0·87	0·80	0·75	0·89	1·01	1·22	1·03	1·23	—	1·12
11) Depth	0·59	0·79	0·71	0·70	0·50	0·83	0·13	0·39	0·70	1·12	—

reflects the contrast between the earlier emphasis on faceted, and the later emphasis on plain and punctiform butts.

Constellation 9, miscellaneous blank, information does not bring out so strongly this separation of the 4 earlier levels, but rather groups 21 and 22 and isolates 8 on the second, vertical axis (clearly a reflection of the large count there of double-patinated burins and the relatively small count of burins with large areas of cortex on the dorsal surface).

Constellation 10, continuous retouch and use of a stop-notch disturbs the consistent pattern of distinction between early and late seen more or less clearly in all of the other constellations. Here, levels 8 and 9 are clustered with the two earliest levels 23 and 22, and these four are separated from all the others. These are the four levels with most burins with continuous retouch. Level 11 is further isolated on the vertical dimension, a separation dictated by the unique frequency of burins with stop-notches from that level.

All of these detailed results for individual constellations are generalized on Fig. 4 which, as stated earlier, results from a Principal Co-ordinates analysis of the M^2 distances of Table I. Values on a third dimension are shown by directed lines. The most striking general effects already previewed in considering the individual constellations are

1. The marked clustering of the type-lists with 23, 15 and 8 types respectively (C2–C4), and the relative alienation of C5, with only 4 types.
2. The relative proximity of C6, burin edges, to the detailed typology constellations.
3. The close relationship between flake/blade ratio (C7) and time, reflected by depth (C11). C8, butts, as would be expected, falls in this same general part of the diagram.
4. C10, continuous retouch and stop-notch on burins, presents a clear contrast with all the other categories of information.

More speculatively, these dispositions seem to imply three contrasting effects. Blank production (C7 and C8 and to a lesser extent C9) represents one relatively straightforward technological aspect of the assemblages that follows a progression through time. The top left part of the diagram at the bottom right. It is perhaps not too fanciful Continuous retouch and stop-notch, C10, occupies its own distinct part of the diagram at the bottom right. It is perhaps not too fanciful to regard these features as basically "stylistic", unnecessary for the production or presumptive function of the tools, but more the expression of arbitrary traditions. Any general significance for the constellations in the upper right hand part of Fig. 4 (basically detailed typology and burin edge type) must be even more uncertain, but it could well reflect fairly subtle functional differences within any general function that burins as a whole may be thought to have served. In the absence of detailed faunal, climatic and comprehensive locational evidence for these levels at Ksar Akil, such interpretations are bound to remain rather remote speculations. In more felicitous circumstances, it would certainly have been instructive to locate "faunal" and "climatic" constellations on Fig. 4 as well as the time constellation C11.

Summary and Conclusions

Constellation Analysis provides a new analytical technique that seems especially suited to archaeological data. Basically, it allows different aspects of a problem, or the same aspect described by different systems, or both, to be considered together. After the few archaeological applications so far attempted, it is still difficult to assess the ultimate scope for Constellation Analysis in archaeology. However, it already seems to be producing valuable and rather unexpected results. In the present case-study, alternative descriptive systems for a major class of Palaeolithic tool, burins, have been compared by testing them out on a group of stratified assemblages from Ksar Akil. Without a suitable computer programme, it would have been difficult, first, to assess the interrelationships between these assemblages for each of the different descriptive constellations in turn, since no *direct* diagrammatic (or other) representation is possible for this kind of multivariate information. The results of these preliminary Principal Co-ordinates Analyses are presented in Figs. 1–3. Without this specific approach and computer programme, it would then have been virtually impossible to compare these preliminary configurations objectively. The result of this second stage of the analysis (by rotational fitting) is presented in Table I and Fig. 4. Taken as a whole, these results suggest that no one of the current descriptive systems for tool classes will be sufficient by itself to capture their full significance. It may prove possible to reduce the complexity of descriptors within these systems (to reduce the number of types in a given type-list, for example), but at present, more insight seems likely to come from the successful integration, by suitable computer programmes, of more rather than fewer cross-cutting categories of information.

References

Azoury, I. and Hodson, F. R. (1973). *World Archaeology* **4**, 3, 292–306.
Bordes, F. (1961). "Typologie du Paléolithique Ancien et Moyen". Delmas, Bordeaux.
Bordes, F. and Crabtree, D. (1969). *Tebiwa* **12**, **2**, 1–21.
Doran, J. E. and Hodson, F. R. (1973). "Mathematics and Computers in archaeology: an introduction". Edinburgh University Press, Edinburgh.
Gower, J. C. (1966). *Biometrika* **53**, 325–338.
Gower, J. C. (1971a). *In* "Mathematics in the archaeological and historical sciences" (F. R. Hodson, D. G. Kendall and P. Tautu, eds) pp. 138–149. Edinburgh University Press, Edinburgh.
Gower, J. C. (1971b). *J. Roy. statist. Soc.*, A, **134**, 360–365.
Kruskal, J. B. (1971). *In* "Mathematics in the archaeological and historical sciences" (F. R. Hodson, D. G. Kendall and P. Tautu, eds) pp. 119–132. Edinburgh University Press, Edinburgh.
Movius, H. L. Jr., David, N. C., Bricker, H. M. and Clay, R. B. (1968). "The analysis of certain major classes of Upper Palaeolithic tools". *American School of Prehistoric Research, Peabody Museum Bull.* **26**, Harvard.
Newcomer, M. H. (1970). *Bull. Inst. Arch.* **8–9**, 117–191.
Newcomer, M. H. (1971). *Bull. Soc. Préhist. Franç.* **68**, 267–72.
Newcomer, M. H. (1972). "An analysis of a series of burins from Ksar Akil (Lebanon)". Doctoral thesis, London University.
Ronen, A. (1965). *L'Anth.* **69**, 465–86.
Sackett, J. R. (1966). *Am. Anth.* **68**, 356–94.
Sonneville-Bordes, D. de and Perrot, J. (1956). *Bull. Soc. Préhist. Franç.* **52**, 408–12.
Tixier, J. (1958). *Bull. Soc. Préhist. Franç.* **55**, 628–44.
Tixier, J. (1963). "Typologie de l'Epipaléolithique du Maghreb". Arts et Métiers Graphiques, Paris.

Island Southeast Asia and the Settlement of Australia

I. C. GLOVER

HISTORIANS OF SOUTHEAST ASIA concerned themselves, for many years, almost exclusively with the activities of outside peoples in Southeast Asia, and their influence on events there; Indians, Chinese and the various European nations who exercised political power in the region from the sixteenth century AD onwards*. Archaeologists, too, shared many of the prejudices of their colleagues and were content to interpret the prehistoric record in terms of a series of migrations into Southeast Asia from areas of more advanced cultural traditions. Bierling (1969) has shown how much of the archaeology in the period of colonial rule was undertaken within the hyper-diffusionist framework associated with the Vienna school of anthropology, and how field workers were particularly influenced by the writings of Robert Heine Geldern. Archaeologists such as Colani and Mansuy in Indochina, van Stein Callenfels and van Heekeren in the Netherland East Indies, and later in Indonesia, and Collings, Evans and Tweedie in Malaya, and Beyer in the Philippines were inclined to see culture only in terms of stone artefact technology, and they too readily assigned known, or supposed ethnic groups, to particular stone tool traditions. And since, together with most archaeologists of their day, they accepted that stone age cultures were essentially static, only population movements could be invoked to account for the observed developments in artefact technology.

Thus, Southeast Asia was usually seen as no more than a stage,

* I would like to thank Professor J. E. van Lohuizen-de Leeuw of the Instituut voor Zuid-Aziatische Archaeologie, Amsterdam, for permission to examine the Houbolt Collection which is housed there; Win Mumford (Australian National University) for preparing the maps; and Peter White (Sydney University) for the drawings of the material from Kosipe, Papua.

The paper has been revised and extended since it was presented at a symposium of the 8th Congress of the Far Eastern Prehistory Association, 28th International Congress of Orientalists, Canberra, January 1971. My attendance was partly supported by the Organizing Committee of the Orientalists' Congress, and by the Institute of Archaeology, London.

where transitory cultures of diverse origins could be recognized, briefly, before they passed on, or merged with others to give rise to new configurations. Such an approach to the prehistory of the region enabled Clark (1962, p. 201) to write, "one of the main reasons why the mainland of Southeast Asia merits study is that it forms a kind of funnel through which peoples have spread over Indonesia, Melanesia, and farther afield. Another is its intermediate position between the two main foci of culture in India and China, respectively".

In recent years research interests have been turning towards an investigation of the indigenous cultural traditions of the region itself, which has long had its own distinctive life style, and whose people contributed more to man's stock of technological achievements than has often been admitted in the past (e.g. Christie, 1961, p. 291). Perhaps it was in the field of plant domestication that the prehistoric people of the monsoon lands of southeastern Asia gave most to the modern world, for an impressive number of the world's important food crops appear to be native to this area (Harris, 1967, p. 96; Sauer, 1952, p. 24; Vavilov, 1951, pp. 21–9).

Nevertheless, it would be absurd to deny that there have been many movements of people, and diffusion of techniques, ideas and material through Southeast Asia, and that this contributes an interesting and valid field of study.

The Australian Evidence

Australian archaeologists, for instance, look at Southeast Asia as a "donor" area from which, at various times, people, techniques, and cultural equipment have been obtained. And in this paper I want to examine some of the evidence for the earliest period in the prehistoric settlement of Australia, and the relevance to this of recent archaeological work in the islands immediately to the north of Australia (Fig. 1), whence, it is presumed, the ancestors of the Australian Aborigines came.

Although knowledge of the prehistory of Australia is still at a rudimentary level, recent excavations seem to indicate that the continent was first colonized during the Late Pleistocene by a physically modern man who, adapting to a new and largely unfamiliar continent, quickly evolved a distinctively Australian way of life. The archaeological evidence for the settlement period in Australia has recently been discussed in detail (Jones, 1968, 1971; Mulvaney, 1969; Golson, 1971a), and in this paper I will mention only some of the evidence,

Fig. 1. Southeast Asia, New Guinea and Australia, with the islands of *Wallacea*.

and particularly the flaked stone tools, which may be valuable in relating the prehistory of Australia to that of island Southeast Asia. In any case, with the exception of the important "Mungo Man" site in western New South Wales (Bowler *et al.*, 1970, pp. 52–6; Thorne, 1971, pp. 85–9), the evidence for the earliest phase of settlement depends largely on the distribution and associations of stone tools.

In older typologies these artefacts were mostly lumped under the labels "generalized" or "miscellaneous" flake scrapers, "horsehoof" cores, and pebble choppers (Mulvaney, 1969, pp. 143–50). Some of the elements in these collections, particularly the unifacial and bifacial flaked pebbles, have long been compared with the Middle Pleistocene flake and core tools now roughly grouped under the term, "Patjitanian" (McCarthy, 1940, pp. 30–2; Van Heekeren, 1957, pp. 27–35). Although, as McCarthy well realized, neither the relative chronologies, nor descriptions of the assemblages were sufficiently precise for any reasonable inferences to be drawn from these general similarities. Today, over thirty years later, the picture has not changed much. Movius's (1944 pp. 91–3) and Van Heekeren's (*ibid.*) analyses of the Patjitanian were based on fairly small and selectively collected assemblages of unstratified finds (Mulvaney, 1970), while in Australia detailed work on the older industries is only now under way (Jones, 1971).

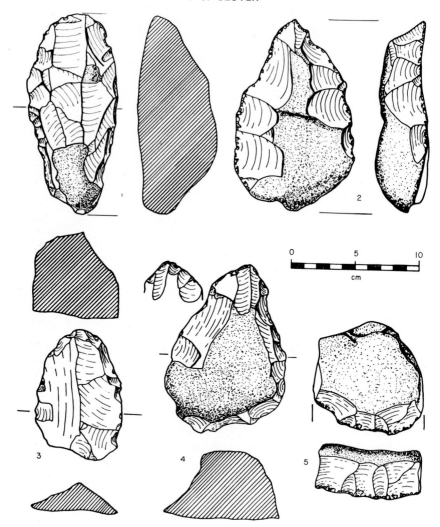

Fig. 2. Stone tools of the Patjitanian industry from Central Java of presumed
Middle Pleistocene Age.

1. Chopper on a large flake with unifacial working around the margin; H 43 in
   the Houbolt Collection, Amsterdam.
2. Proto-handaxe, redrawn from Movius 1948: Fig. 7.
3. Flake scraper of silicified limestone: Houbolt H 29.
4. Chopping-tool of silicified limestone from Punung, with bifacial working at
   the pointed end, parallel with the long axis: Houbolt H 7.
5. Hand adze with steep unifacial working at one end: more common in the
   Anyathian industry of Burma, than in the Patjitanian. Redrawn from Movius
   1948: Fig. 7.

The essential characteristics of the Patjitanian as defined by Movius (*ibid.*) were summarized by the label "chopper, chopping-tool complex" under which he grouped the Lower Palaeolithic assemblages of East and Southeast Asia. Although recognizing the large number of worked flakes, and the occasional crude biface in the Javanese collections of von Koenigswald, Movius stressed the importance of the large pebble tools which were unifacially or bifacially worked, parallel to the long axis of the tool. The principal categories of tools in Movius' classification (Fig. 2) were:

Chopper: pebbles unifacially worked, often on one margin only.
Hand adze: choppers which are more rectangular than oval in outline.
Chopping-tool: pebbles bifacially worked, often on one margin only.
Proto-hand axes: implements, mostly on flakes, and worked on the upper surface only, into crude or roughly pointed types of hand-axes of plano-convex section.
Scrapers: flakes, unifically worked on one or more margins. Scrapers are smaller than choppers.

From later work in Java, van Heekeren (1957, p. 30) subdivided the choppers into four sub-types, flat-iron choppers, side choppers, tortoise choppers, and cleavers, but continued to stress the unifacial pebble tool as the essential Patjitanian type.

In Australia, on the other hand, flake and core scrapers are the

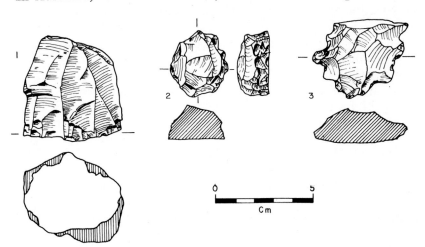

Fig. 3. Scrapers of the early Australian core-tool and scraper tradition.
1. Core-scraper, or "horsehoof" core.
2. Steep-edge scraper.
3. Flat scraper.

dominant type (Fig. 3), and in a preliminary classification of early Australian assemblages, Jones (Bowler *et al.*, 1970, pp. 48–52) has defined their characteristics as follows:

Core-scrapers with a single platform from which flakes have been removed around the entire perimeter, leaving a circular, dome-shaped implement. Secondary retouching around the platform leaves a step-flaked, overhanging edge. Edge angles range from 90° to 120°. These are the tools commonly called "horsehoof" cores in Australian terminologies. They are heavy tools, weighing from 100–1000 g.

Steep-edge scrapers manufactured on thick flakes with steeply re-touch edges ranging from 70° to 90° and an edge height of 1·0–2·4 cm. Edges are usually straight or convex and slightly step-flaked.

Flat scrapers form another class of flake tools with a lower profile and finer, oblique secondary working on edges ranging from 45° to 70°. Worked notches are common on some of these scrapers.

Jones (1971, p. 52) has suggested the term "Australian core tool and scraper tradition" as a convenient label for the older stone assemblages, which, though yet little known from well excavated, dated deposits, do seem to have common features throughout the continent.

Although these ancient core and scraper industries are difficult to characterize, especially in words, distinct differences can be seen between the Patjitanian and the old Australian tradition. This is, of course, not too surprising, since no Australian material can yet be dated to more than 30 000 BP with certainty, and the Patjitanian may be anything up to 500 000 years old, on present estimates.

McCarthy (1940, p. 33) was more specific in claiming a direct link between the flaked pebble tools of the Hoabinhian cultures of Indo-China, Malaya and northwest Sumatra, and the pebble tools from the sandstone rockshelters and shell middens of the Australian south-east coasts (Fig. 4). More recent fieldwork in Australia has shown that these tools have little regularity in form, and yet are remarkably long-lived, persisting through several changes in stone-working traditions. Mathews (1966) analysed the pebble tools from several Australian sites, and from Sai Yok in Thailand, and found little to relate them. Not surprisingly, the Australian tools were generally closer to each other in terms of size, shape, edge-angles and position-ing of retouch, than to the Thai material.

Much later than the period of initial settlement, there are Australian stone industries which undoubtedly can be derived from Indonesian, or even Indian origins (Mulvaney, 1969, pp. 123–7)

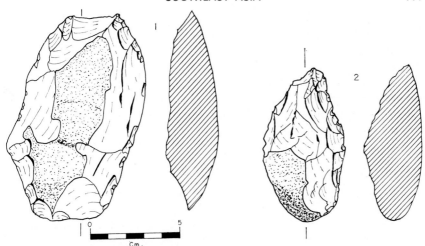

Fig. 4. Unifacially flaked pebble choppers.
1. Green Gully, Keilor terraces, Victoria; redrawn from Mulvaney 1969: Fig. 35.
2. Sai Yok 1 Cave, Kwae Noi, Kanchanaburi Province, Thailand. Redrawn from van Heekeren and Knuth 1967: Fig. 7.

although the same problems of definition and dating have yet to be resolved in all three areas (Glover, 1967; Mulvaney and Soejono, 1970, pp. 28–9; Golson, 1971b). However, since this paper is to be concerned with the earliest settlement of Australia in the Late Pleistocene, these conacts cannot be discussed here.

The distribution of early sites in Australia has little significance at this stage of research, and most are in the more accessible areas of the south and east. Where prolonged research has taken place in northern Australia though, sites of up to 26000 BP have been found which are purely Australian in their artefact traditions (White, C., 1971).

Detailed environmental evidence from the early period sites is still rare (Bowler *et al.*, 1970, pp. 52–6; White, C., 1971, p. 153) and relevant data has to be sought from disciplines such as geomorphology, geography, and metereology to fill out the meagre archaeological record (Jones, 1968, pp. 191–201).

The first settlers entered a continent differing in many respects from the monsoon islands of Indonesia, and they would have needed to make many cultural adaptations. But Calaby (1971, pp. 88–9) has argued that they would have encountered many superficially familiar elements in the fauna, and Golson (1971a) has shown that the botanical resources of northern and northeastern coasts of Australia, which were utilized by recent Aborigines, contains a surprisingly high proportion of species and genera, not only common in Indo-Malaysia, but which have similar food uses there. Of the 48 genera of food plants recorded from Arnhem Land, 42, or 87%, are found in Indo-Malaysia. For Cape York, the proportion is 89%, but drops to 57% in Central Australia (Golson, 1971a, Table 15,4). The widespread distribution in Australia of so many plants, economically important in Southeast Asia, makes Birdsell's estimation that the entire Australian continent could have been peopled within 2000 years by the descendants of a handful of immigrants, seem to be a real possibility (Birdsell, 1957).

Changing Sea-Levels Between Australia and Southeast Asia

There is yet no certain evidence to link the earliest known Australian archaeological finds with any particular region in Southeast Asia. Since it is still far from certain when the first settlement

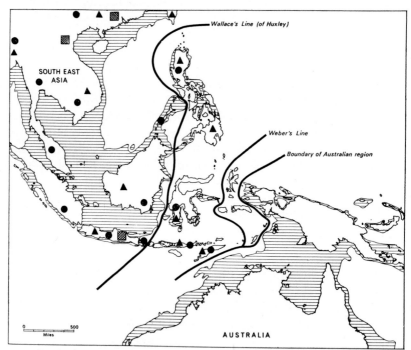

Fig. 5. Southeast Asia and Australia showing the continental shelves of Sunda Land and Sahul Land, and the main faunal barriers in *Wallacea*.

▦   Marks the locations of fossil forms of man so far discovered from the Middle and the early Upper Pleistocene.

●   Middle and early Upper Pleistocene stone industries.

▲   Extinct forms of fossil elephant derived from Asia.

took place, it is difficult to utilize the evidence of changing sea-levels, except in a very general way, in order to predict the probable location and direction of these movements. Throughout the Pleistocene, there were world wide and fairly uniform eustatic changes (Emery, 1969) and the evidence from northern Australia, scanty though it yet is (Jennings, 1971, p. 4), indicates that New Guinea and Australia were occasionally linked by a broad stretch of land across the Sahul Shelf, and the Gulf of Carpentaria to form a continent which is often called Sahul Land. This land bridge, which is shown on Fig. 5 as horizontal shading, was present perhaps from about 65 000–45 000 BP if one can directly correlate fluctuations in ocean temperatures with glacio-eustatic changes (Emiliani, 1963, p. 105), and again from about 30 000–18 000 BP. For the second period the evidence is reasonably secure (Emery, 1969, p. 114) and is supported by dated beach levels from the Sahul Shelf itself (Jennings, 1971, p. 4). During the period of maximum fall, the northern coast of Australia would have been no more than 50 miles from Timor, and a chain of islands separated by yet narrower water gaps stretched from New Guinea to Borneo, Java and Sumatra, then extensions of the Asian continental land mass – Sunda Land.

Wallacea and the Faunal Barriers

Between Sahul Land and Sunda Land lies a group of islands which include most of the Philippines, Celebes, the Lesser Sunda Islands, the Moluccas, Halmahera, and many small islands, and which is of especial relevance to the early settlement of Australia since it is through this region that the first Aborigines almost certainly came. These islands form one of the world's most pronounced zoological barriers, separating the extraordinarily different Oriental and Australian faunal regions (Darlington, 1957, p. 462). Alfred Russel Wallace, one of the earliest, and the greatest of all zoogeographers, recognized the importance of this barrier which has become the focus of attention for generations of fieldworkers after him, and it is often called *Wallacea* in his honour (Dickerson *et al.*, 1928, p. 101). Later work has shown that Wallace's original line of division between the Oriental and Australian fauna required some modifications and Mayr (1945), Scrivenor *et al.* (1943), and Darlington (1957), pp. 462–74) discuss in detail these changes and the effectiveness of the various water barriers in Wallacea to the passage of animals. It is clear, however, from both the geology (Audley-Charles, 1968, p. 1), and the distribution of freshwater fishes (Darlington, 1957, p. 463) that there have been no through land connections between Sunda Land and

E

Sahul Land since Permian times at least. Even the narrow straits separating Java from Bali have been an effective barrier for a very long time, since Bali has only a fraction of the Javan fish fauna (Darlington, 1957, p. 51). Only two placental land mammals, man and some species of rat, have successfully and independently crossed all the barriers of Wallacea to develop in the relative isolation of Australia. Within Wallacea, the larger existing mammals, with the exception of some phalangers in the Moluccas, Timor and Celebes, are all Oriental species, and good claims can be made to show that, east of Celebes, these animals (*Rusa* deer, civet cat, pig, babirusa, and domesticated cattle, sheep, goats, dogs and horses) were all carried by man within the last few thousand years (Darlington, 1957, pp. 322–4, 467; Glover, 1971, pp. 174–7).

Late Pleistocene assemblages from New Guinea, Wallacea, and Sunda Land

Archaeological material from the Pleistocene within this inter-mediate region is even less well-known than in Australia or Java. In New Guinea, the oldest material yet known is from the Kosipe site, in the Papuan highlands (White *et al.*, 1970). There, a series of well-dated volcanic ash falls from 4000 to 26 000 BP were found to contain flake and core tools of which the most distinctive elements, as known in Melanesian archaeology, are "waisted blades" (Bulmer, 1964, p. 257). These are mostly flat pebbles, with flaked notches, or waisting along the sides, and unifacially or bifacially retouched cutting edges (Fig. 6). Such tools are also known from terminal Pleistocene sites in the New Guinea Highlands (White, J. P., 1971, p. 48, White *et al.*, 1970, pp. 163–9) and there is a yet undated manufacturing site reported from New Britain (Chowning and Goodale, 1966, pp. 150–3). The antiquity of this material is really surprising, since stray finds of such tools had previously been thought to be crude forms of hoes or digging stick blades, and to belong to later, agricultural settlements. Outside parallels for these tools are found only, as far as I know, in Central Celebes at Kalumpang (van Heekeren, 1957, Pl. 47), in the Hoabinhian levels at Sai Yok, Thailand (van Heekeren and Knuth, 1967, p. 75), and in Japan (Kidder, 1959, Fig. 7a), where they are known as "fiddle-shaped" axes.

Methods of hafting axes and large flaked tools such as waisting, grooving or tanging were widely used in Asia from early times and Golson (1972, p. 544–9) has summarized most of this data. But the relationship between such flaked and hafted tools, and the various

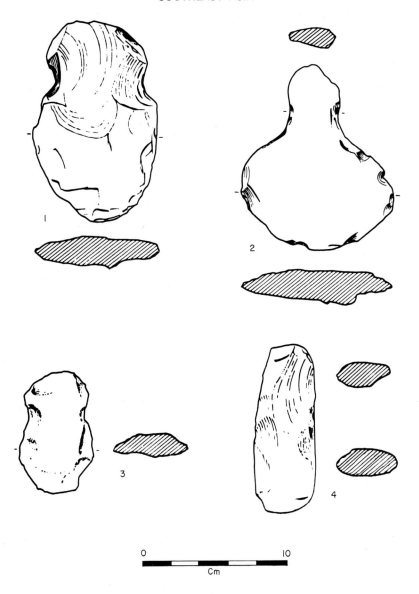

Fig. 6. Waisted blades (1–3) and a ground-edge or adze (4) from Kosipe, Papuan
Highlands. From White, Crook and Ruxton 1970: Fig. 3.
1. Unstratified.
2. Level 4, dated to between 18 000–26 000 BP.
3. Level 3, dated to between 7000–10 000 BP.
4. Level 2, dated to between 7000–10 000 BP.

forms of gripped, stepped, and shouldered, polished axes and adzes
of the neolithic cultures, which are found from Assan and Orissa in
eastern India, to the islands of Eastern Polynesia, and from Japan to
New Zealand, is not a simple one. Edge-ground, grooved axes
(Fig. 7) were found by Carmel White in sites at Oenpelli, Arnhem
Land in northern Australia, associated with dates older than 20 000
BP (White, C., 1971, pp. 148–53), and as J. P. White (1971, p. 18)
has shown, waisted-blades and ground axe-adzes were in use simultaneously in several areas of Melanesia, and for a considerable period

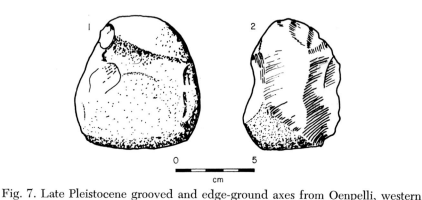

Fig. 7. Late Pleistocene grooved and edge-ground axes from Oenpelli, western
   Arnhem Land, northern Australia. Redrawn from White, C. 1971:   Fig. 12.3.
1.   Hornfels axe, grooved on one face only. From Malangangerr Cave, level IIIb,
     and dated 19 000–23 000 BP.
2.   Axe with flaked notch and one ground facet.

of time. Golson (1972, pp. 543–4) has found some internal evidence
from the inadequate excavation reports from the Niah caves to show
that edge-ground axes may appear in the sequence there by 15 000
BP, and we can expect to see the simple sequence from flaked pebble
"axes" to edge-ground and to fully polished axes, long known from
Hoabinhian deposits in Indochina (Mansuy, 1925, p. 32) to be much
complicated by present and future excavations on the mainland of
Southeast Asia.

   In cave sites in New Guinea, and all of those currently published
are in the Central or Eastern Highlands, occupation levels go back
only to about 11 000 BP (White, J. P., 1971, p. 47). At one of these
sites, Kafiavana, ground-stone axes were dated to 9500 BP, and
broken pieces of them to 10 700 BP, again testifying to the antiquity
of grinding traditions in Southeast Asia, Australia and New Guinea.
It should be pointed out, of course, that there is no evidence to show
that the makers of these tools were other than hunter-gatherers; hor-

ticulture may have come to New Guinea between 4000 – 6000 BP, and is not certainly present, on present evidence, before 2300 BP (White, J. P., 1971, pp. 48–50).

In the Philippines, flake and core tools of presumed Pleistocene Age have been recorded by von Koenigswald (1958), which may belong to the Middle Pleistocene "Chopper, Chopping-tool Complex", already known from Indochina, Thailand, Burma and the western islands of Indonesia. But our only detailed knowledge of the Pleistocene stone tool traditions of the Philippines comes from the work of the National Museum of Manila under Fox, at Tabon Cave in Palawan (Fox, 1970, pp. 1–44), the large island, which lies between Sabah and Mindoro (Fig. 1), and which was also an extension of the Asian continent. At Tabon, where a comparatively well-dated sequence now extends from about 45 000 to 9000 BP (Fox, 1970, p. 24), a single tradition of flaked stone tools was found which is also quite different from the earliest presently-known Australian material (Mulvaney, 1969, pp. 39–55) although it is difficult to characterize in any positive way (Fig. 8). Flakes are generally large (80% in one sample being more than 5 cm in length (Fox, 1970, p. 37), made from a coarse brown chert derived from pebbles whose cortex often

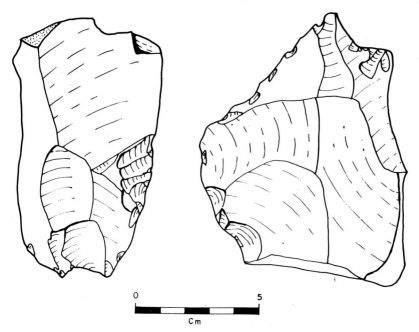

Fig. 8. Tabon Cave, Palawan, Philippines. Flake tools from Assemblage III, dated to earlier than 22 000 BP. Redrawn from Fox, 1970: Fig. 7.

remains on the flake. Although some flakes were evidently used, only about 1% show any secondary modification and these, according to Fox, defy easy classification into types based on morphology, or the positioning and nature of the retouch. Illustrations (Fox, 1970, Fig. 7) suggest that these tools can best be described as flat multi-edge scrapers, with a single implement having concave, convex and straight working edges, and occasionally prepared notches. Other, more sophisticated flaking traditions are known in the Philippines (Fox, 1970, Fig. 11) and perhaps the Tabon assemblages reflect only part of a total tool kit whose more specialized elements will be found in other sites. It is possible, however, even with this rather intractable data, to draw some parallels with the few flakes of Late Pleistocene Age found during the excavations at Niah cave, Sarawak (Harrisson, 1959, p. 3).

In the Celebes, east of Wallace's Line, van Heekeren discovered flake stone tools associated with a fauna containing a number of extinct species on a series of river terraces in the Wallanae Depression of the Soppeng district northeast of Makassar (van Heekeren, 1958). Judging from the faunal elements, it may date from between the late Middle to early Upper Pleistocene, and the stone tools, which are made of chalcedony, jasper, and other crypto-crystalline siliceous rocks, are small thick flakes with well-defined bulbs of percussion, plain platforms and, generally, an obtuse striking angle (Fig. 9). There are a few points, as well as side, end, and keeled scrapers. Some of the flakes are long and narrow, but there is no evidence for the manufacture of true blades, or Levallois flakes, from prepared cores. Van Heekeren rightly points out that this material, which he has called the Tjabengè industry after the locality of the first finds, has close morphological links with the Sangiran industry of Central and Eastern Java, which is generally believed, on the basis of the associated fauna, to be of Upper Pleistocene Age (van Heekeren, 1957, pp. 43–5). Van Heekeren, Soejono and Hooijer have undertaken further surveys and excavations in the Soppeng district in 1968 and 1970, and any further assessment of this material must await the publication of their results. We can say, however, that the Tjabengè industry shows no similarity with any of the early Australian stone traditions yet known.

In Java a number of artefact assemblages are known which are later than the Patjitanian, but whose age and associations are not at all well understood. In the 1930's excavations for fossil fauna in the Ngandong terraces of the Solo River produced, in addition to 11 skulls of the famous Solo Man, some flaked stone tools, worked bone and antler, and sharpened sting-ray spines. Nearby localities

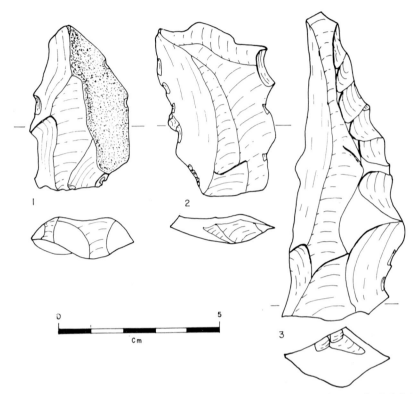

Fig. 9. Chalcedony flake tools from Berru locality, Tjabengè, South Celebes. These are surface finds on a terrace of the Wallanae River at about 50 m, and are probably of late Pleistocene Age. Occasional flakes (1) are said to have faceted striking platforms, but all are heavily rolled and the evidence for regular secondary working is far from clear. Redrawn from van Heekeren 1958: Fig. 3.

also yielded a horn chopper, a barbed bone harpoon point, and roughly worked stone balls. The associated fauna is certainly later than the Trinil and Djetis faunas of the Middle Pleistocene, for the only extinct form is *Stegodon trigonocephalus* Martin, although the elephant and hippopotamus has long been absent from Java (van Heekeren, 1957, pp. 37–46). The work at Ngandong was mostly carried out by untrained geological assistants, and subsequent information suggests that none of the associations can be relied on; even the find spot of the skulls may have been misrepresented (T. Jacob, personal communication).

In 1934 von Koenigswald found flake tools in the Notopuro Beds in the Sangiran Dome area north of Surakarta, and more were subsequently found in the Upper Pleistocene levels which are exposed along the edge of the Kendeng Hills between Semarang and Surabaja. These implements are made of chalcedony, jasper, and similar rocks, and include side and end scrapers, borers, points, and occasional blades (Fig. 10). As already mentioned, the Sangiran industry appears to be similar to that from Tjabengè in Celebes, but is yet unknown on either the Southeast Asian mainland or in Australia (van Heekeren, 1957, p. 45).

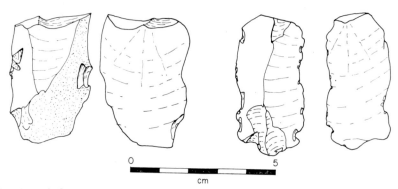

Fig. 10. Chalcedony flakes of the Sangiran industry from Sangiran, near Surakarta, Central Java. They are probably from the Notopuro Beds of the early Upper Pleistocene. From von Koenigswald 1939: Abb. 3.

Cave excavations in East Java have produced an interesting sequence of stone, bone and shell tools which van Heekeren (1957, p. 65) believes to be entirely Recent in age, since no extinct animals were present in the abundant fauna. However, as already mentioned, the Upper Pleistocene Ngandong fauna contains only one extinct species, and at Niah Cave, Borneo, only one extinct form, *Manis palaeojavanica* (a giant ant eater) occurs in the last 50000 years (Hooijer, 1961–2, p. 487). In Tabon Cave, Palawan, again only one extinct form, a small deer, was found in levels dated to between 20 000 to 30 000 BP (Fox, 1970, pp. 38–9), and at Spirit Cave, Thailand, no extinct forms appear to have been found in deposits between 7500 to 12 000 years old (Gorman, 1971). It is clear from this evidence, that the absence of extinct fauna alone is not a sufficient criterion to determine the age of archaeological deposits in Southeast Asia.

This cave industry may have developed towards the end of the Late Pleistocene, and be contemporary with the Hoabinhian culture found in Thailand, Indochina, Malaya and north Sumatra (Gorman, 1971). Unfortunately, although at least 17 caves have been excavated in Java, not one has been adequately published. Van Heekeren (1957,

p. 84) compares the material from these caves, which he calls the Sampung Bone Culture, with finds from Japan, China, Indochina, Malaya and Celebes. Certainly similar bone tools and shell ornaments are found widely distributed in Asia, but the most distinctive stone tool type (Fig. 11) is a hollow-based, or winged projectile point (van Heekeren, 1957, Pl. 44) which is not found elsewhere in Southeast Asia. And, relevant to the main problem, whatever its Asian affinities and age, the Javanese cave culture appears to be entirely unrelated to material of the early settlement period in Australia.

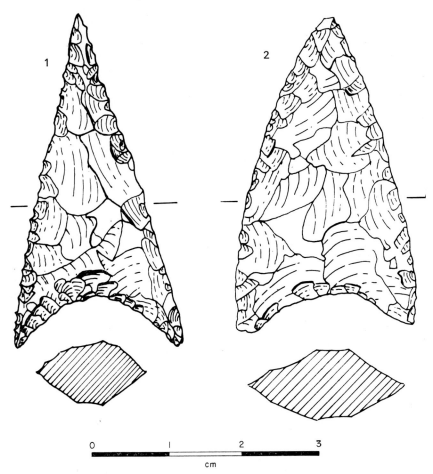

Fig. 11. Bifacial points of chert from Punung, Central Java. 1 H 945, and 2 H 882 in the Houbolt collection. These are surface finds from a factory site and although commonly referred to as "neolithic", similar points were excavated from the deepest layer at Guwa Lawa Cave, Sampung, east central Java in a deposit which contains several locally extinct animal species.

E*

I have discussed the extent of our knowledge of Late Pleistocene cultural materials from New Guinea, Celebes, Palawan, and Java. Problems and anomalies abound and at the moment make any satisfactory synthesis impossible. Palawan and apparently Borneo (Niah) share a long-lived stone working tradition where the dominant forms are large, broad, mostly unmodified flakes. In Celebes the stone assemblages can be compared to the Sangiran of Java (van Heekeren, 1957, pp. 43–5) although the associated fauna is certainly derived from South China via the Philippines and is quite distinct from that of Java (Hooijer, 1958). On the other hand, the few published tools of probable Pleistocene Age from Luzon in the Philippines (von Koenigswald, 1958; Fox, 1970, p. 43) are closer to the Chopper; Chopping Tool assemblages of Java and mainland Southeast Asia than to the Tjabengèn of Celebes. Perhaps some of these problems will be resolved when the material from each of these regions can be related to a firm chronological and geomorphological sequence.

There remains one area of Wallacea, the Lesser Sunda Islands, which has not yet been discussed, and it is with the problems and recent field work in this area that I will finish.

Nine years ago, at the 1964 ANZAAS Conference in Canberra, Soejono presented a short paper on a collection of flake and core tools collected by Father Verhoeven in the island of Flores. Soejono showed that these tools belonged to the Patjitanian tradition already known from Western Indonesia. In the same year, Verhoeven himself reported the discovery of *Stegodon* fossils and more stone tools in Timor, in addition to the earlier finds in Flores (Verhoeven, 1958, 1964). Subsequent work by Dr Hooijer on the fauna collected by Verhoeven showed that it contained two species of *Stegodon*; the same two in Flores and Timor. One was only slightly smaller than *Stegodon trigonocephalus* Martin, one of the type fossils of the Middle and Upper Pleistocene in Java (Hooijer, 1961–2, p. 486); whereas the other species was less than half the size of the Javan form, standing about four feet at the shoulder (Hooijer, 1969, 1970). Last year, Dr Hooijer visited the faunal sites in Timor and Flores and has started on an analysis of more than a ton of bones collected by Verhoeven and himself.

To date, this fauna has been found in at least eleven locations in Timor, all but one of which are situated a few kilometres east of Atambua, near the centre of the island, and in a formation known as the Ainaro Gravels (Audley-Charles, 1968, p. 1) – a stream-laid deposit almost certainly of late Middle to early Upper Pleistocene Age which is now at 400 metres a.s.l., although the marine and estuarine shells in, and immediately below the deposit indicate that it was laid down close to sea level. Work is now under way in Imperial College in London on the sequence and dating of these Pleistocene deposits in Timor, which is complicated by great tectonic movement, as well as by the normal eustatic changes (Audley Charles *et al.*, 1972).

At two locations, two bone-bearing gravel beds have been found, separated by some 20 ft of cross-bedded sands. In both cases the larger *Stegodon* form was confined to the lower bed, while the smaller one, *S. timorensis*, and a giant land tortoise are found in both (Hooijer, 1971, 1972). There is, therefore, a possibility that the smaller form of *Stegodon* is of more recent origin; the result of dwarf ing in isolation in the same way as the Pleistocene elephants in Malta, Cyprus and the Californian offshore islands. If this was the case, only one invasion of Wallacea by this giant land fauna need be postulated, and a land bridge through from Java to Timor need not be assumed.

On the other hand, there is the rather astonishing fact that in both Timor and Flores, now separated by a submarine trench which is never less than 6000 ft deep, we find the same two *Stegodon* species. It seems unlikely that these islands were as isolated from each other during the evolutionary development of the dwarf *Stegodon*, as they are today, and it is probable that tectonic movements have radically altered the land and sea relationships within Wallacea during the Pleistocene. Von Koenigswald (1967) has also reported the discovery of an Upper Eocene fossil, an *Anthracotherium*, in Timor by Verhoeven; a form previously known only from Borneo westwards.

Earlier I mentioned the finds of stone tools of an archaic type in Flores and Timor. I have only briefly examined the collection described by Soejono, but agree with him as to its similarity to the Patjitanian of Java; the most common forms being large, broad, re-touched flakes, cleavers, chopping-tools and choppers. No bifacial hand axes seemed to be present, but these are rare in any Southeast Asian collections.

The Pleistocene collections from Flores have recently been published by Maringer and Verhoeven (1970, pp. 229–47, 530–46, 636–9) and we now know much more about this important material.

At least 74 artefacts were found *in situ* in the fossil-bearing levels at Mengeruda, and a further 158 surface finds were thought to be derived from the same horizon. The commonest material used was andesite, although basalt, hornfels, quartzite and porphyry were also employed. The majority of the implements were made on flakes (85% in the surface collection, Maringer and Verhoeven, 1970, p. 531) which are usually rather thick and short with plain platforms and a striking angle around 90°. The types listed by Maringer and Verhoeven include side, end, and concave scrapers, keeled scrapers,

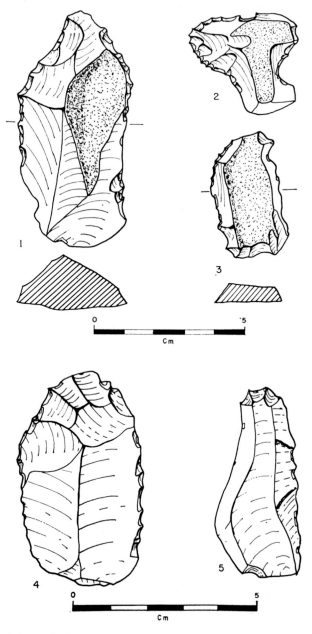

Fig. 12. Flake tools from Mengeruda, near the north coast of central Flores. 1, 2 and 3 are surface finds (Maringer and Verhoeven 1970b: Abb. 4–5), 4 and 5 are from the gravel deposits containing bones of the extinct *Stegodon trigono-cephalus florensis* Hooijer (Maringer and Verhoeven, 1970a: Abb. 2–3).

borers, points and knives (see Fig. 12). The proportion of pebble tools is surprisingly low, about 6% in the two collections, and, in addition, there are a few parallel-sided, blade-like forms; although the few cores show no signs of true blade manufacture. Maringer and Verhoeven believe that the Flores finds show greatest similarity to the Sangiran and Tjabengè industries of Java and Celebes, both of which seem to be associated with a fauna containing *Stegodon*. However, in Flores there is a core and pebble-tool element which is closer to the middle Pleistocene Patjitanian of Java, even to the extent of including occasional and rather crudely finished, bifacial hand axes (Maringer and Verhoeven, 1970, p. 238, Pl. II.4). There is a possibility, as the authors admit, that two separate traditions are represented in the Flores collections, the one Middle and the other Upper Palaeolithic and only further research at these important sites will make this clear.

The achaic tool types from Timor have not been so extensively sought nor discussed as those from Flores. Verhoeven (1964, 1968) briefly reported the finds which immediately suggested to him, as to von Koenigswald (Verhoeven, 1968, p. 402), the possibility of finding *Homo erectus* remains in Timor, and a small collection found by Verhoeven and his collaborator in Timor, Mr Domi Koten, has been described by me (Glover and Glover, 1970, pp. 188–90). Of the 17 pieces (Fig. 13), all but one are flakes 9 to 15 cms long. Secondary working is almost always unifacial; worked edges are generally convex, rather jagged and battered, but not step-flaked, or over-hanging. One artefact was a disc core, and five were choppers, using Movius' terminology. The remainder are scrapers, and are similar to the few Patjitanian flake scrapers frequently illustrated by Movius (1944, Fig. 43). Although all but one of these tools were found in the same area, near Atambua (Fig. 1), which has produced the fossils previously mentioned, they are surface finds in eroded gullies and cannot be assigned to any stratigraphic horizon with certainty. The implements are, however, quite distinct from those of the stone industry found in the cave deposits of Timor (Glover, 1971), and certainly predate this.

Finally, in 1970, Mr Tegu Asmar of the National Archaeological Institute in Djakarta, who accompanied Dr Hooijer to Timor and Flores, did find a few flakes and core tools *in situ* in bone-bearing layers in Timor; and so we have from Flores and Timor, as from Celebes, evidence to show that man, possibly a fossil form of man, was present in the islands of Wallacea in the Middle to Late Pleistocene, and was contemporary there with a now extinct megafauna derived from Asia.

I. C. GLOVER

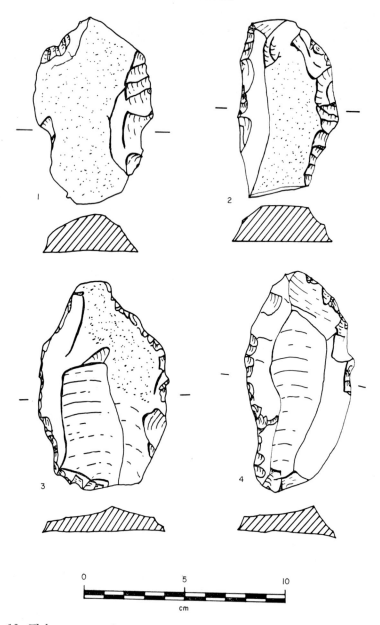

Fig. 13. Flake scrapers from Timor and Flores. 1 Namut Plain, Riung, west Flores 2 and 3 Turasmanu, Atambua, central Timor. 4 Nanekier Kefamenanu, central Timor. From Glover and Glover 1970.

Wallacea and Australia

The relevance of this for the early settlement of Australia is evident. It raises from mere speculations (Keesing, 1950) to a distinct possibility, the chance that man crossed the last of the great biological barriers of Wallacea, not a mere 30 000 years ago when he had the advantage of the most recent low sea level, but far earlier; perhaps 40 000 to 60 000 years ago, or still earlier in the late Middle or early Upper Pleistocene at a date which cannot yet be designated.

The brief survey of the archaic stone tool assemblage of Australia, New Guinea, Wallacea and western Indonesia shows that despite similarities between adjacent islands, Java – Celebes, Palawan – Borneo, Flores – Timor, it is at present very difficult to relate these traditions to the oldest Australian material. If man was in Australia by the Middle Pleistocene, as Gallus (1971) has long claimed, the answer is simple. There are still in Australia much older cultural materials which are not yet discovered; and given the relative geological stability of Australia since that time, it may be difficult to find them. On the other hand, the first colonists of the southern continent may have been few as Birdsell suggests, and in the rapid spread of their descendants into a new land which required many adaptive cultural responses, the parent culture may have been quickly lost. The first settlements were, of course, most probably on the now-drowned coasts of Sahul Land and in looking for undeniable and demonstrable links in between the material remains of the first Australians, and their ancestors in Indonesia, archaeologists may be pursuing an unattainable goal.

References

Audley-Charles, M. (1968). "The Geology of Portuguese Timor". Memoir 4, Geological Society of London.

Audley-Charles, M., Carter, D. J. and Milson, J. S. (1972). *Nature Physical Science* **239** (90), 35–9.

Bierling, J. (1969). "Migration towards Melanesia: a re-valuation", B.A. (Hons.) Thesis, Department of Anthropology, University of Sydney, November 1969 (unpublished).

Birdsell, J. B. (1957). *Cold Spring Harbor symp. quant. Biol.* **22**, 47–69.

Bowler, J. M., Jones, R., Allen, H. and Thorne, A. G. (1970). *World Archaeology* **2** (1), 39–60.

Bulmer, S. (1964). *Oceania* **24** (4), 246–68.

Calaby, J. (1971). *In* "Aboriginal Man and Environment in Australia", (Mulvaney, D. J. and Golson, J. eds.), A.N.U. Press, Canberra.

Chowning, A. and Goodale, J. C. (1966). *Asian Perspectives* **9**, 150–3.

Christie, A. (1961). *In* "The Dawn of Civilization" (Piggot, S. ed.), pp. 277–300. Thames and Hudson, London.

Clark, J. G. D. (1969). "World Prehistory" (2nd edn.), Cambridge University Press, Cambridge.

Darlington, P. J. (1957). "Zoogeography: the Geographical Distribution of Animals", New York.

Dickerson, R. E. *et al.* (1928). "Distribution of Life in the Philippines", Philippines Bureau of Science, Monograph 21, Manila.

Emery, K. O. (1969). *Scientific American*, September 1969, 107–22.

Emiliani, C. (1963). *In* "Science and Archaeology", (Brothwell, D. R. and Higgs, E. S. eds), pp. 97–107. Thames and Hudson, London.

Fox, R. (1970). "The Tabon Caves—archaeological explorations and excavations on Palawan Island, Philippines", Manila, National Museum Monograph, 1.

Gallus, A. (1971). Paper presented at the Far Eastern Prehistory Symposium, 28th International Congress of Orientalists, Canberra, January 1971 (unpublished).

Glover, I. C. (1967). *Mankind* **6**, 415–25.

Glover, I. C. (1971). *In* "Aboriginal Man and Environment in Australia", (Mulvaney, D. J. and Golson, J. eds), A.N.U. Press, Canberra.

Glover, I. C. and Glover, E. A. (1970). *Mankind* **7**, 188–90.

Golson, J. (1971a). *In* "Aboriginal Man and Environment in Australia" (Mulvaney, D. J. and Golson, J. eds.), pp. 196–238, Canberra.

Golson, J. (1971b). Paper delivered to Far Eastern Prehistoric Association Symposium, 28th International Congress of Orientalists, January 1971, Canberra (unpublished).

Golson, J. (1972). *In* "Early Chinese Art and its Possible Influence in the Pacific Basin" (Barnard, N. ed.), Col. **3**, 533–95, Intercultural Arts Press, New York.

Gorman, C. (1971). *World Archaeology* **2** (3), 300–20.

Harris, D. R. (1967). *Geographical Review* **57** (1), 97–107.

Harrisson, T. (1959). *Man* **59**, 1–8.

Heekeren, H. R. van (1957). "The Stone Age of Indonesia", Nijhoff, s'Gravenhage.

Heekeren, H. R. van (1958). *Asian Perspectives* **2** (2), 17–82.

Heekeren, H. R. van and Knuth, E. (1967). "Archaeological Excavations in Thailand, Volume 1. Sai Yok: Stone Age Settlements in the Kanchanaburi Province", Copenhagen.

Hooijer, D. A. (1961–2). *Advancement of Science* **18**, 485–9.

Hooijer, D. A. (1969). "*Proc. Koninkl. Nederl. Akadamie van Wetenschappen—Amsterdam*". Ser. B, **72** (3), 203–9.

Hooijer, D. A. (1970). *Nature, Lond.* **225**, 474–5.

Hooijer, D. A. (1971). *Proc. Koninkl. Nderl. Akademie van Wetenschappen—Amsterdam*, Series B, **74**, No. (5) 504–525.

Hooijer, D. A. (1972). *Proc. Koninkl Nderl. Akademie van Wetenschappen—Amsterdam*, Series B, **75**, No. (1) 12–33.

Jennings, J. (1971). *In* "Aboriginal Man and Environment in Australia" Mulvaney, D. J. and Golson, J. eds), pp. 1–13, A.N.U. Press, Canberra.

Jones, R. (1968). *Archaeology and Physical Anthropology in Oceania* **3** (8), 186–215.

Jones, R. (1971). Paper presented to the 28th International Congress of Orientalists, Far Eastern Prehistory Association Symposium, Canberra, January 1971 (unpublished).

Keesing, F. M. (1950). *Southwestern Journal of Anthropology* **6** (1), 101–19.

Kidder, J. E. (1959). "Japan", Thames and Hudson, London.

Koenigswald, G. H. R. von (1939). *Quatär* **2**, 28–53.

Koenigswald, G. H. R. von (1958). *Asian Perspectives* **2** (2), 69–70.

Koenigswald, G. H. R. von (1967). *Proc. Koninkl Akademie van Wetenschappen*, Amsterdam, Ser. B, **70**, 529–33.

McCarthy, F. D. (1940). *In* "Proceedings of the 3rd Congress of Prehistorians of the Far East" (Chasen, F. N. and Tweedie, M. W. F. eds), Singapore.

Mansuy, H. (1925). *Sérvice Géologique de l'Indochine* **12** (1), Hanoi.

Maringer, J. and Verhoeven, Th. (1970). *Anthropos* **65**, 229–47, 530–46, 638–9.

Mathews, J. (1966). *Archaeology and Physical Anthropology in Oceania* **1** (1), 5–22.

Mayr, E. (1945). *In* "Science and Scientists in the Netherlands Indies" (Honig, P. and Verdoorn, F. eds), New York.

Movius, H. L. Jr. (1944). *Papers of the Peabody Museum* **19** (3).

Movius, H. L. Jr. (1948). *Transactions of the American Philosophical Society* (Philadelphia) **38**, 329–420.

Mulvaney, D. J. (1969). "The Prehistory of Australia", Thames and Hudson, London.

Mulvaney, D. J. (1970). *Mankind* **7**, 184–7.

Mulvaney, D. J. and Soejono, R. P. (1970). *Antiquity* **45**, 26–33.

Sauer, C. (1952). "Agricultural Origins and Dispersals", American Geographical Society, Bowman Memorial Lectures ser. 2, New York.

Scrivenor, J. B. *et al.* (1943). *Proceedings of the Linnean Society of London*, 154th session, 1943, 120–65.

Thorne, A. G. (1971). *Mankind* **8** (2), 85–9.

Vavilov, N. I. (1951). "The Origin, Variation, Immunity and Breeding of Cultivated Plants", Ronald Press, New York.

Verhoeven, Th. (1958). *Anthropos* **53**, 264 5.

Verhoeven, Th. (1964). *Anthropos* **59**, 6–34.

Verhoeven, Th. (1968). *Anthropica, Studia Instituti Anthropos* **21**, Gedenkschrift zum 100sten Geburtstag von P. Wilhelm Schmidt, 393–403.

White, C. (1971). *In* "Aboriginal Man and Environment in Australia" (Mulvaney, D. J. and Golson, J. eds), Canberra.

White, J. P. (1971). "Studies in oceanic culture history" **2**, *Pacific Anthropological Records* **12** (Green, R. and Kelly, M. eds), B. P. Bishop Museum, Hawaii.

White, J. P., Crook, K. A. W. and Ruxton, B. P. (1970). *P.P.S.* **36**, 152–70.

Sherd Weights and Sherd Counts- A Contribution to the Problem of Quantifying Pottery Studies*

J. D. EVANS

FROM THE SEVENTH MILLENNIUM BC onwards broken pottery gradually becomes the most characteristic find on the majority of human occupation sites, as chipped stone had been previously. Thereafter, in many regions a stage was quickly reached when pottery was used in such quantities that the smallest excavation on a settlement site brings to light many thousands of sherds. Such abundance is frankly embarrassing, since although there is fairly general agreement that much can be learned from the study of pottery about the people who made and used the pots, it is not so clear how this can best be done. Apart from the time-consuming and laborious nature of such work, the chief difficulty arises from the nature of the material itself. A sherd is not a complete object, like a flint or metal tool; it may be only a very small portion of the complete pot. Moreover, the number of sherds produced when a pot breaks is a matter of chance, and may be increased by subsequent trampling, and other hazards including excavation itself. If the excavator finds all the pieces, or enough of them to restore the vessel, the case is altered; but most excavation in settlements produces large quantities of sherds which do not make up in this way, and must be studied as they are, if they are to be dealt with at all.

Until relatively recently, it was generally thought adequate to classify this kind of material on the basis of ware, form and deco-

* The excavations and studies on which this article is based were carried out with the aid of grants from the British Academy, the Wenner-Gren Foundation for Anthropological Research, the Faculty Board of Classics in the University of Cambridge, the Crowther-Benyon Fund of the Department of Archaeology and Anthropology at Cambridge, the British School at Athens, the Childe Bequest Fund of the University of London Institute of Archaeology, and the Central Research and Hayter Funds of London University. I am most grateful to all of these bodies for their support. My debt to my wife for her patient toil in the drawing and sorting of sherds is beyond measure.

ration, and then describe the characteristics of each class, probably adding some indication of which types were most frequently met with, and which were relatively rare. Though these judgements were sometimes backed up by figures from sherd counts, more often they were restricted to vague comments indicating that types were "common" or "rare", or that they were more or less so than other types. Whether well- or ill-founded, such judgements are not very informative, and can only be checked or amplified by studying the original material, if this is still available, and if it contains complete samples, which have not been subjected to selection. Increasing preoccupation during the last twenty years or so with the quantification of archaeological data has, however, led to a number of approaches being made from time to time to the question of coping more effectively with the study of pottery (e.g. Solheim, 1960; Willey, 1961; Cowgill, 1964; McPherron, 1967, etc.). Having independently made attempts to grapple with the problem of recording and interpreting large pottery assemblages over a number of years, I feel that it may be worthwhile to give a brief general account of what has been done, and discuss some of the results.

In this paper I shall first describe the simple technique which I devised some years ago for the study of the sherd material from two Neolithic settlement sites in the Aegean, Knossos in Crete (Evans, 1964) and Saliagos, near Antiparos in the Cyclades (Evans and Renfrew, 1968), and then consider the results obtained at Knossos in the light of some more recent work there which provided an opportunity to check the earlier findings. The chief object in view was to facilitate the objective description of the material as a whole, though with the hope that the results might eventually prove useful for purposes of comparison between sites. For both these purposes it seemed essential first to have some standard measurement by which the amount of pottery found in each excavation unit could be shown, and which could also serve as a means of expressing the relative frequency of occurrence of particular traits. Three possible ways of providing such a standard are to count the number of sherds, to measure the area of pot surface they represent, or to weigh them. All have advantages and disadvantages. Ideally one should probably do all three, but here the factors of cost and time must be considered. In the present instance, all study of material had to be carried out in Greece, mostly during and just after excavation, or in subsequent visits of limited length. To avoid excessive delay in the publication of the results it was therefore necessary to make a choice between them.

On the whole it seemed to me that weight of sherds was the best criterion to use in this situation. It is relatively easy to measure, for one thing, and it is at least as informative as a count of sherds. One obvious objection is that a few large, coarse sherds can weigh as much as many fine ones, which could introduce a distortion into the results; also, different types of ware may have a widely differing specific gravity. While this is certainly true, the level of risk depends on the conditions of the site and the material itself. On the sites actually studied the large quantities of sherds found are virtually all from locally made pottery of very similar fabric, so that the weight factor should be reasonably constant. Proportions of coarse and fine sherds are much the same in all levels and in different parts of the site. There is no fundamental distinction in fabric between the coarse and fine wares, and in fact they grade into each other. It could there-fore reasonably be hoped that any discrepancies in individual levels would be considerably reduced in the larger aggregates (e.g. strata or groups of strata) which were normally used for estimates of the relative frequency of the various traits. At Knossos it has subsequently been possible to count the numbers of sherds from various units of the main soundings and check these against the weight of pottery found in each. The results may be seen in Tables 1 and 2.

TABLE I. Weights of sherds recovered from each stratum of AC, AA/BB, EE and FF.

Central Court (1957–60)				West Court (1969–70)			
Sounding	Period	Stratum	KGS	Sounding	Period	Stratum	KGS
AC	L.N.	I	190	FF	L.N.	—	261·50
AC	L.N.	II	305	EE	L.N.	—	165·25
AC	M.N.	III	360	AA/BB	L.N.	B	152·50
AC	E.N.II	IV	630	AA/BB	L.N./M.N.	C	60·50
AC	E.N.I	V	385	AA/BB	M.N.	D	70·00
AC	E.N.I	VI	270	AA/BB	M.N.	E	38·00
AC	E.N.I	VII	135	AA/BB	M.N./E.N.II	F	48·25
AC	E.N.I	VIII	45	AA/BB	E.N.IIA	G	89·50
AC	E.N.I	IX	10	AA/BB	E.N.IIA/B	H	23·75
AC	Aceramic	X	0	AA/BB	E.N.IIB	J	60·00
				AA/BB	E.N.IIC	K	67·75
				AA/BB	E.N.I	L	53·25
				AA/BB	E.N.I	M	71·25
				AA/BB	E.N.I	N	42·50
				AA/BB	E.N.I	P	53·50

To express the frequency of occurrence of individual traits a standard unit of 100 kg of pottery was originally chosen as being large enough to allow a reasonable number of occurrences of even the rarer traits, and at the same time smaller (often several times smaller), than the amount of pottery actually found in each

TABLE II. Correction factors used for reducing the occurrence of feature sherds to the standard unit of 50 kg.

Period	Central Court Stratum Area AC	Factor	Period	West Court Stratum Area AA/BB	Factor
E.N.I	IX	0·2 } 1·1	E.N.I	P	1·1
E.N.I	VIII	0·9	E.N.I	N	0·9 } 2·3
E.N.I	VII	2·7	E.N.I	M	1·4
E.N.I	VI	5·4	E.N.I	L	1·1
E.N.I	V	7·7	E.N.IIC	K	1·4
E.N.II	IV	12·6	E.N.IIB	J	1·2
M.N.	III	7·2	E.N.IIAB	H	0·5 } 2·3
L.N.	II	6·1	E.N.IIA	G	1·8
L.N.	I	3·8	M.N./E.N.II	F	1·0 } 1·8
			M.N. (Early)	E	0·8
			M.N. (Late)	D	1·4
			L.N./M.N.	C	1·2
			L.N.	B	3·1
				Square EE	
			L.N.	—	3·3
				Square FF	
			L.N.	—	5·2

excavation unit used in the analysis. This unit was used for the Knossos material excavated from the sounding made in the Central Court between 1957 and 1960 and for the Saliagos material. However, the smaller quantities of pottery found in the deep sounding made below the West Court of the Palace during the more recent excavations at the Knossos Neolithic settlement in 1969 and 1970 (Evans, 1971), combined with the greater number of stratigraphic units distinguished, have made the use of a 50 kg unit of weight necessary for the study of the material from this area, and hence for comparisons with the Central Court sounding of 1957–60. The smaller incidence of sherds in the West Court sounding seems to be directly related to the much more frequent occurrence of substantial building remains there than in the Central Court one, where the deposits belonged chiefly to open areas between buildings. Though in some ways less desirable and convenient, the 50 kg unit is still large enough to provide a reasonable coverage. A 20 kg unit, which was also tried, proved to be more difficult to apply, chiefly on account of the number of traits whose frequency of occurrence then fell to less than one per unit.

The incidence of any number of traits can be measured against the chosen unit. In practice, these are grouped under the general headings of Shapes, Handles and Lugs, and Decoration, with a fourth small section for Special Features (e.g. spouts, etc.). Two features of the system are important to note. First of all, it measures the occurrence of individual traits only; no account is taken of their possible relation to each other (e.g. association of a particular pot shape with a particular kind of decoration). As a corollary of this, a single sherd may be counted several times, once for shape, one or more times for lugs or handles, and one or more times for features of the decoration. There is, of course, no reason why the relatedness of particular traits should not be recorded if desired, but this would inevitably increase the complexity of the operation and slow it down. In the circumstances and in relation to the material here considered it was judged that the results likely to be achieved would not be adequate to justify the extra effort, though in fact a few clear instances of correlation were observed without counting, e.g. ripple decoration and carinated bowls (Shape 3A); *pointillé* decoration and vertical sided dishes (Shape 9). Secondly, each feature of an individual sherd is noted as an occurrence of that feature. Thus a number of occurrences in a particular stratum may all derive from the same pot (and occasionally a stray sherd of the same pot may be incorporated into a later stratum). The use of such data as these to establish patterns of popularity of various features of the pottery obviously depends first on the assumption of some measure of regularity in the breakage of the pots and scatter of their sherds, and secondly on the use of a sample large enough to allow for the inevitable variations.

The first application of this method to the pottery from the sounding beneath the Central Court at Knossos in 1962 showed up a number of patterns in the popularity of various traits through time, some of which reinforced earlier observations (but nearly always refined on them), while others had not been previously noticed at all (Evans, 1964, pp. 196–229). At Saliagos, a quite short-lived site, with an apparently very homogeneous cultural material, study along the same lines of the pottery from an area of the deepest deposit showed up some evidence of change during the life of the site, notably a striking continuous fall-off in the popularity of white-painted decoration from the earliest to the latest stratum (Evans and Renfrew, 1968, pp. 34–46). At both sites, the data permitted useful calculations to be made about the proportions of open to closed shapes, the relative popularity of individual types, and so on.

Both these frequency counts had, however, been made on material from one area of a site only. The renewal of work on the Neolithic deposits at Knossos in 1969 provided an opportunity for checking the validity of the earlier results, and also for enlarging the number of traits taken into account in the previous work at that site. A principal objective of the new work was the digging of a second large sounding comparable to the Central Court one, but situated some distance away from it, in the West Court. Though this sounding, called AA/BB, did not, in the event, provide an absolutely complete sequence, since only about 2 m of E.N.I. deposits were found, as against about 4 m in the Central Court sounding, while the latest Neolithic deposits were found to have been removed in operations to level the surface for a building of the E.M.II period, nevertheless the greater part of it was adequately represented. In particular, three very clear building levels of the E.N.II period, which had been represented in the Central Court sounding by an undifferentiated refuse deposit, were found, and two clear phases of building could also be distinguished in the M.N. levels. There were also some deposits without building remains which separated the strata with clear L.N., M.N., or E.N.II remains, though not all of these produced any large quantity of pottery, so that it was sometimes found necessary to amalgamate them with the stratum above for the purposes of analysis of the pottery content. A very useful supplement to the Late Neolithic material, which, owing to the extensive Minoan levelling operations, was imperfectly represented in both the main soundings, was fortunately obtained from two squares, EE and FF, which were dug close to Area AA/BB in the West Court in the 1970 season.

Since there is currently much discussion about the efficiency of recovery of material in excavation, it may be worthwhile to mention that during both the 1969 and 1970 seasons both wet and dry sieving and froth flotation was carried out on extensive samples of the Neolithic deposits by a team under M. R. Jarman, Assistant Director of the British Academy Major Research Project in the Early History of Agriculture. Though the main object of this work was the recovery of plant remains and small bones, the other materials recovered, including pottery, were also kept and examined. The quantitites of pottery recovered in this way proved to be negligible, and what there was came mostly as small scraps with no features. It was judged not worth while to weigh these samples separately since they would clearly have been below the minimum weight which we were recording, 0·25 kg; they were therefore simply incorporated with the rest of the material. This result contrasts sharply with that for obsidian, of which significant amounts were recovered from sieving, and also with results recently reported by S. Payne for pottery from Sitagroi and the Francthi cave (Payne, 1972, pp. 54–9). The discrepancy may perhaps be related to the employment at Knossos of very skilled and experienced workmen, whose eyes are particularly well trained for spotting small fragments of pottery.

As already mentioned above, the number of sherds found in all strata of the two deep soundings, AC and AA/BB have now been counted for comparison with the weights recorded. The results are set out in Tables III and IV. Comparison with the weights (given in Table I) seems to indicate a fairly satisfactory correspondence. The limits within which the numbers are found to vary for a given weight of sherds (in this instance 50 kg), though fairly wide, are not sufficient to upset the relationships of the figures arrived at by using weight alone in any serious measure, as can be seen in Tables 5–7, where the figures for the occurrence of various features during the four main periods are given, first as counted, then as a mean calculated for each 50 kg unit, and finally for each 1000 sherds*. The results as given for the two standards are more or less directly comparable, since it is clear from Table 4 that the ratio of 1000 sherds to 50 kg of pottery is a close approximation to the overall average for all strata of both soundings†.

In general the comparison of the results from the two soundings at Knossos for the four main stylistic periods (Tables 5–7) seems encouraging, in that it indicates that a number of the traits recorded show a similar pattern of occurrence through time in both areas, though others seem to show either no marked pattern or else differing ones. One general comment which may be made is that where the pattern is similar in both soundings, the actual number of occurrences per unit may differ widely, though each sounding maintains internal consistency (cf. the figures for Tripartite Bowls,

---

* The figures given in Section 3 of each of these tables can, of course, be read as percentages, if desired, by simply inserting a decimal point before the last digit. Those in Section 2 cannot be reduced to percentages, though the proportions could have been expressed in this way if the sherds showing the various features had been weighed instead of counted. It would clearly have been interesting to try this approach, but much additional time would have been needed.

†The greatest deviation from this mean is found in Stratum II of the Central Court sounding (Table 2) and is undoubtedly due to the conditions of preservation there. Due to the levelling operations which preceded the erection of the Palace in M.M. times, and perhaps also earlier constructions (Evans, 1971, pp. 111–112, 1972, pp. 126–127) part of this stratum is exposed on the surface of the Court. The sherds from it are small, very friable, and mostly have heavily worn surfaces. A full count of the Stratum I sherds would undoubtedly have shown a similar situation, but some of this material was mislaid when the count was made in 1971, and the results for this Stratum have therefore not been used. The estimation of frequencies for the L.N. material in the Central Court has been based on the Stratum II material alone.

TABLE III. Numbers of sherds recovered from each stratum of AC and AA/BB.

Period	Central Court Area AC Stratum	No. of Sherds	Period	West Court Area AA/BB Stratum	No. of Sherds
Aceramic	X	0	E.N.I	P	898
E.N.I	IX	156	E.N.I	N	728
E.N.I	VIII	794	E.N.I	M	1342
E.N.I	VII	2633	E.N.I	L	982
E.N.I	VI	4720	E.N.II	K	1176
E.N.I	V	7212	E.N.II	J	977
E.N.II	IV	13656	E.N.II	H	527
M.N.	III	7042	E.N.II	G	1908
L.N.	II	8224	M.N./E.N.II	F	1051
			M.N.	E	837
			M.N.	D	1277
			L.N./M.N.	C	1483
			L.N.	B	2288

TABLE IV. Mean numbers of sherds per 50 kg unit, calculated for individual strata and combinations of strata.

Area AC				
IX–VIII	863			
VII	937			
VI	874	E.N.I		
V	937	917		
IV	1084		All AC	
III	978		1038	
II	1347			

Area AA/BB				All AC+AA/BB
				1009
P	816			
N/M	900	E.N.I		
L	818	898		
K	840		All AA/BB	
J	814	E.N.II	932	
H/G	1059	956		
F/E	1111	M.N.		
D	912	1020		
C	1236	L.N.		
B	738	877		

TABLE V. Occurrence of various shapes in the main stylistic periods.

		1. Occurrences in each period				2. Occurrences per 50 kg of pot				3. Occurrences per 1,000 sherds			
		E.N.I	E.N.II	M.N.	L.N.	E.N.I	E.N.II	M.N.	L.N.	E.N.I	E.N.II	M.N.	L.N.
1, 2 Simple open bowls	AC	3997	3031	1688	1570	237	240	235	421	258	221	241	313
	AA/BB	1804	1420	1183	1637	401	290	370	381	451	370	338	331
3A Carinated bowls, straight-sided	AC	121	178	9	19	7	14	1	1	8	13	1	2
	AA/BB	72	102	1	4	16	21	0	3	18	22	0	1
3B Carinated bowls, concave-sided	AC	125	205	1215	915	7	16	169	150	8	15	174	112
	AA/BB	1	14	115	68	0	3	36	16	0	3	36	18
4 Vessels with offset rim	AC	2724	1848	186	144	161	147	26	24	178	135	27	18
	AA/BB	520	761	117	81	116	155	37	19	130	165	37	18
4A Carinated bowls with offset rim	AC	249	322	9	9	15	26	1	1	16	25	1	21
	AA/BB	50	85	2	1	11	17	1	1	12	18	1	1
5 Bowls with inturned rim	AC	24	0	1	4	1	0	0	0	2	0	0	0
	AA/BB	1	1	3	2	0	0	1	1	0	0	1	1
6 Deep bowls or jars with mouths narrower than the widest diameter	AC	308	40	9	5	18	3	1	1	20	3	1	1
	AA/BB	13	25	11	36	3	5	3	8	4	5	3	9
7 Narrow necked jars	AC	350	112	20	4	21	9	3	1	23	8	3	0
	AA/BB	24	10	11	13	5	2	3	3	6	2	3	3
8 Funnel necked jars	AC	89	42	20	14	5	3	3	3	6	3	3	3
	AA/BB	0	3	10	12	0	1	3	3	0	1	3	2
9 Straight sided dishes	AC	25	1	0	0	2	0	0	0	1	0	0	2
	AA/BB	3	0	0	0	1	0	0	0	1	0	0	0

TABLE VI. Occurrence of various handle-types in the main stylistic periods.

		E.N.I	E.N.II	M.N.	L.N.	E.N.I	E.N.II	M.N.	L.N.	E.N.I	E.N.II	M.N.	L.N.
Tubular lugs, ring handles, etc.	AC	1805	1208	627	1124	107	96	87	184	116	88	90	137
	AA/BB	401	581	378	587	89	119	118	137	100	126	115	154
As above, but with concavity or "saddle"	AC	161	73	8	6	10	6	1	1	10	5	1	1
	AA/BB	90	85	0	5	20	17	0	1	23	18	0	1
Flap handles	AC	17	10	1	1	1	1	0	0	1	1	0	0
	AA/BB	0	1	0	3	0	0	0	1	0	0	0	1
"Horned" handles	AC	31	0	0	0	2	0	0	0	2	0	0	0
	AA/BB	2	0	2	0	0	0	0	0	1	0	0	0
Wishbone handles	AC	118	42	7	0	7	3	0	0	8	3	0	0
	AA/BB	21	1	0	0	5	0	0	0	5	0	0	0
Handles with short prong	AC	16	56	7	5	1	4	1	1	1	4	1	1
	AA/BB	3	17	2	0	1	3	1	0	1	4	1	0
Handles with long prong	AC	1	10	20	5	0	1	3	1	0	1	3	1
	AA/BB	0	3	1	1	0	1	0	0	0	3	0	0
Trumpet lugs	AC	62	80	0	0	4	6	0	0	4	6	0	0
	AA/BB	8	19	0	0	2	4	0	0	2	4	0	0
Triangular "ears"	AC	162	1	0	0	10	0	0	0	10	0	0	0
	AA/BB	4	0	10	2	1	0	3	0	1	0	3	0

1. Occurrences in each period

2. Occurrences per 50 kg of pot

3. Occurrences per 1,000 sherds.

TABLE VII. Occurrence of the chief types of decoration in the main stylistic periods.

		E.N.I	E.N.II	M.N.	L.N.	E.N.I	E.N.II	M.N.	L.N.	E.N.I	E.N.II	M.N.	L.N.
Plastic	AC	266	33	1	0	16	3	0	0	17	2	0	0
	AA/BB	38	1	0	0	8	0	0	0	10	0	0	0
Pointillé	AC	233	21	16	63	14	2	2	10	15	2	2	8
	AA/BB	106	14	0	9	24	3	0	2	27	3	0	2
Incised	AC	414	1674	904	642	24	133	126	105	27	122	129	78
	AA/BB	68	494	200	251	15	101	63	58	17	107	63	66
Ripple	AC	0	238	1281	112	0	19	178	35	0	17	183	26
	AA/BB	0	39	564	88	0	8	176	20	0	8	176	23

1. Occurrences in each period

2. Occurrences per 50 kg of pot

3. Occurrences per 1,000 sherds.

Shape 4A). Decoration seems to be perhaps the most sensitive indicator of change through time, but certain varieties of handle are also very useful, (though unfortunately some of these are rarely found in recognizable form, e.g. the various types of flap, wishbone and prong handles). Certain shapes, especially some bowls, such as 3A, 3B and 4A are helpful, though the most common shapes maintain a fairly constant level throughout.

Most forms of decoration are relatively rare, as a comparison of the figures in Table VII with those for the overall sherd counts (Table III) will show. The popularity of decoration itself shows a pattern of variation throughout the life of the site (Table VIII). It is rarest during the long E.N.I period, and reaches a maximum during the M.N. period, though if only incised decoration is considered the figures for the M.N. period, and to some extent also E.N.II and L.N. are considerably altered, and Furness' claim (Furness, 1953, p. 118) that incision was at least as popular in E.N.II as at any later time is seen to be justified.

TABLE VIII. Numbers of decorated sherds and numbers of incised sherds per 50 kg of pottery in each of the main periods.

	E.N.I	E.N.II	M.N.	L.N.
All decorated				
Area AC	56	155	304	101
Area AA/BB	48	114	246	81
Incised only				
Area AC	42	124	131	86
Area AA/BB	44	110	62	68

Further breakdown of the results can serve to indicate the finer pattern of change with time. This was already evident from the earlier work at Knossos, but is confirmed in several instances by the results from the latest excavations. Table VIII shows the figures for the various forms of incised decoration found in individual strata of AA/BB. In particular the group of patterns peculiar to the E.N.II style of incised decoration, emerges very clearly on this Table, though the irregularity and carelessness of execution which is an equally marked characteristic of them, and which would enable one to distinguish easily between a piece of E.N.II barbed wire decoration, and one of the rare later occurrences if both were found out of context, obviously cannot be brought out by this kind of presentation.

As clearly hinted above, it seems unlikely that the 2 m of

TABLE IX. Incidence of various types of incised decoration per 50 kg. of pottery in the various strata of Area AA/BB, and the L.N. strata of Squares EE and FF.

Decoration	FF	EE	AA/BB	AA/BB	AA/BB	AA/BB	AA/BB	AA/BB	AA/BB	AA/BB	AA/BB	AA/BB
Period	L.N.	L.N.	L.N.	L.N./M.N.	M.N.	M.N.	E.N.II	E.N.II	E.N.II	E.N.I	E.N.I	E.N.I
Stratum	—	—	B	C	D	E/F	G/H	J	K	L	M/N	P
Cut-out triangles										1	1	
Cross hatching									4		2	5
Lines of chevrons									3	1		
Zig-zag and line								2	4	7		
Hurdle-pattern								3	1			
Tree or fishbone pattern						2		2				
Zig-zag lines						1	13	5	7	15	3	
Parallel chevrons						2	5	8			2	
"Barbed wire"	1			2	1		8	14	17	3		
Parallel lines	19	14	32	56	34	63	81	36	24	7	3	
Hatched strips	13	5	7	7	1	1	1	1	1		3	
Hatched triangles	4	3	1	3	7	7	19	2	1			
Chequerboard patterns	4	6	5	10	1				1			
Finger nail impressions	1			1								
Large crescentic dots				1								
Jabs	5	2	1				1					
"Sewing"	2	2	4								1(?)	
Ribbing	4	4										
Unburnished incised	18	19										
Lines of jabs	3											
Lines of close-set short strokes	3											

E.N.I deposits in the West Court sounding really represent a complete sequence for this period. It is more likely that the settlement only spread to this area at a relatively late date in the E.N.I period. The rather scrappy building remains found in these levels tend to confirm this, since they were constructions of *pisé* and stone, not mud brick. This suggests that the beginning of the accumulation is probably to be fixed not earlier than that of the formation of Stratum VII in the Central Court, which is the first in which *pisé* construction replaces mud brick there. The sherd analyses do not unfortunately give as much help as might have been hoped with this problem, chiefly owing to the rather small quantities of material found in the West Court sounding, I think. Nevertheless, a comparison of the figures given in Table 10 for the incidence of various pottery traits in the relevant strata of AC and AA/BB does seem to lend some support to that view, and certainly appears to show that the earlier E.N.I levels in the West Court preceded Stratum V in the Central Court.

The figures for the sherds found in the three separate building phases distinguished in the West Court sounding for the E.N.II period (Table II) are also somewhat disappointing at first sight, and for the same reason, namely the rather sparse occurrence of some of the features which might have been most diagnostic. Nevertheless, it is possible to observe some of the expected patterns, though the figures are smaller than had been hoped. Ripple decoration, for instance, is only present in E.N.IIA (Stratum G/H), which confirms my earlier observation that the rippled sherds from the unidifferentiated E.N.II stratum in the Central Court all came from the upper half of it (Evans, 1964, p. 219) and gives greater precision to it. Plastic and *pointillé* decoration were unfortunately very rare in the E.N.II levels of AA/BB, but insofar as they did occur they again tended to support the conclusions arrived at in previous work, by being concentrated in the earlier phases. Plastic decoration occurred only once, and in the E.N.IIC stratum; *pointillé* was present throughout, but only once in E.N.IIA. Their rarity itself confirms previous observation of a considerable decline in numbers relative to occurrences in the E.N.I strata. Other features, such as incised decoration, carinated bowls (3A and B), tripartite bowls (4A), everted rims (4), and "saddled" handles, also show variations within the period which can be regarded as certainly or probably significant, but these can only be fully understood in relation to longer term patterns involving both earlier and later strata. For this reason the figures for the strata immediately preceding and following those of the E.N.II period have also been given in Table II.

TABLE X. Incidence of certain traits per 50 kg of pottery in the E.N. I strata of Areas AC and AA/BB.

	Flap Handle	Horned Handle	Wishbone Handle	Prong Handle	Trumpet Lug	Plastic Decoration	Pointillé Decoration	Incised Decoration
Stratum Area AC								
IX–VIII	5	4	4	0	13	30	24	3
VII	4	9	2	0	12	29	7	5
VI	0	1	7	1	1	21	29	5
V	0	0	9	2	1	5	18	48
Stratum Area AA/BB								
P	0	2	4	1	5	29	5	5
N–M	0	0	5	1	0	3	37	14
L	0	0	5	0	0	1	15	26

F

TABLE XI Incidence of various traits per 50 kg of pottery in the E.N.II strata of Area AA/BB ⸲

		Open Bowls (1, 2)	Straight carinated bowls (3A)	Concave carinated bowls (3B)	Offset rims (4)	Carinated bowls with offset rim (4A)	Inturned rim bowls (5)	Constricted-neck jars (6)	Narrow-neck jars (7)	Funnel-necked jars (8)	Chalices	"Legged receptacles"	Tubular lugs, rims, handles etc	"Saddle" handles	Flap handles	Wishbone handles	Short prong handles
M.N. (Early)	E	331	—	34	28	0	2	2	4	3	—	—	99	—	—	—	—
M.N./E.N.II	F	385	—	24	60	2	—	5	1	3	—	—	128	—	—	—	1
E.N.II A+AB	G/H	342	14	7	220	13	—	5	4	2	1	2	152	11	1	1	5
E.N.II B	J	329	56	—	147	32	1	5	4	2	—	4	130	21	—	1	5
E.N.II C	K	407	19	1	174	27	—	11	—	—	—	5	147	43	—	1	3
E.N.I A	L	458	44	1	93	12	—	6	3	—	—	—	131	24	—	5	—
E.N.I B	M	647	18	—	159	8	1	1	12	—	—	—	148	17	—	3	2

The occurrence of features in the various individual levels composing a stratum can also show a significant patterning. A good example is the L.N. stratum of Square EE, which consists of 19 levels whose relationship to each other is generally a simple one of direct superimposition. In Table 12 the progressive decline of ripple burnish and its disappearance from Level 13 upwards is clearly seen. Deeply incised designs, which, like ripple burnish, are so characteristic of the M.N. period, are also present in the earliest L.N. levels of EE, but again disappear after Level 13. On the other hand, horizontal ribbing or fluting, and jabbing are found only in the last ten levels, and the same is true of the "sewn" patterns, though in all cases the numbers are rather small. Unburnished incised pieces, characteristic of the full L.N. period, are well represented throughout.

Finally, some rough calculations have been made of the incidence of sherds per cubic metre of deposit for all strata of the two main soundings, and for the Late Neolithic deposits of Squares EE and FF. The cubic content of each stratum was estimated from its thickness in the drawn sections of the four sides of each area, and though the results are very approximate, they are unlikely to be wildly astray. Table 13, compiled on this basis, shows that in Area AC the number of kgs of pot found per cubic metre of deposit remained fairly steady down to Stratum VII, when it began to fall off rapidly and progressively, ending with the complete disappearance of pottery in Stratum X. In Area AA/BB the variation between strata is larger, but there

…e strata immediately above and below. (Figures for G/H divided by two, rest uncorrected).

Triangular of horn-like lugs	Plastic decorations	Pointillé Decorations	Incised parallel lines	Incised zigzag lines	Incised parallel chevrons	Incised lines of chevrons	Incised zigzag and line	Incised matched strips	Incised hurdle pattern	Incised hatched triangles	Incised hatched lozenges	Incised chequer board	Incised "barbed wire"	Ripple	Jabs	Incised cross-hatching	Tree or fishbone pattern	Bowls with internally thickened rim
3	—	—	44	—	4	—	—	—	—	7	—	—	129	—	—	—	—	—
—	—	—	69	1	4	—	—	1	—	5	—	—	158	—	—	—	3	2
1	—	1	94	16	6	5	2	1	3	22	1	—	12	20	2	—	4	3
—	—	7	43	6	10	3	5	1	1	2	—	—	17	—	—	5	1	—
—	1	5	34	10	—	2	10	2	—	1	—	1	24	—	1	—	—	—
—	1	18	8	16	—	—	—	1	—	—	—	—	8	—	—	—	—	—
—	2	57	5	6	3	—	—	2	—	1	—	—	0	—	—	—	—	—

is no overall pattern. It is striking that in all but one of the strata of AA/BB the quantities are much less than in Strata I–VI of AC, generally about half. This probably results from the greater volume of building remains found in the West Court. This situation only changes in the uppermost stratum of the Neolithic, B, which contained few building remains, and which has about the same density of sherds as upper strata of AC. The same applies to the L.N. strata of EE and FF which consisted almost entirely of refuse deposits and hearths.

The emphasis in these investigations has been on the value of this type of analysis for detecting diachronic variations in the material. This is partly because the excavations have in general only explored restricted areas of a large settlement. There is no inherent reason why it should not also be of value in detecting areal differences stemming from the organization of the village itself, but this would depend on the possibility of uncovering larger surfaces. A full consideration of all the data recorded up to now must be left for the final report on the excavations, but I hope that this brief discussion is not inappropriate for a volume which honours Professor Grimes's wide-ranging interest in the development of many aspects of archaeology, both theoretical and practical, and I have much pleasure in dedicating it to him.

TABLE XII. Incidence of various traits in the L.N. levels of Square EE (uncorrected figures).

Level	2	3	4	5	6	7	8	9	10	11	12	13	14	15	16	17	18	19	20
Spouts	2							2			1								
Unburnished incised	5	1			1	1	4	2	12		2	3	1		2		1		25
Ribbing	4	4			4				1										
"Sewing"		1			1	1			1		1								
Ripple													9	1		13	4	35	103
Deeply incised decoration														1		2		2	20
Lightly incised decoration		3		2	2	3	9	1	13	5			3	5		3		1	14
Pointillé decoration		3		2		1													
Long-prong handles																		1	
Wishbone handles		1	1																
Flap handles		1										1							
"Saddle" handles		2			1	1							2						
Tubular lugs, ring-handles, etc.	27	9		7	30	14	25	2	47	5	2	9	28	14	2	8	4	10	81
Chalices (12)								1	3									6	6
Jars, all types (6–8)		5			1		1	5		3				4					1
Carinated bowls with offset rim (4A)								1											
Offset rims (4)	9	16			6		6		6	1		4	4	6			3		15
Concave carinated bowls (3B)		5						5	2			5	1		3		1		17
Straight carinated bowls (3A)		1						1										1	
Open bowls (1, 2)	116	279	2	14	74	38	88	17	172	29	2	18	82	44	5	27	5	59	307
Level	2	3	4	5	6	7	8	9	10	11	12	13	14	15	16	17	18	19	20
Weight of sherds (in kilos)	14·50	34·50	3·25	5·00	11·00	5·00	9·50	1·25	20·25	2·75	0·75	2·00	8·50	6·75	0·75	3·00	1·25	5·00	30·25

TABLE XIII. Weight of sherds per cubic metre in the various strata of Areas AC and AA/BB.

		Weight of sherds per cubic metre		
		Central Court Area AC	West Court Square FF	
Stratum	I	7·6 Kgs	L.N.	8·0 Kgs
	II	7·6 Kgs		
	III	8·0 Kgs	Square EE	
	IV	7·7 Kgs	L.N.	7.4 Kgs
	V	7·0 Kgs	Area AA/BB	
	VI	6·7 Kgs	Stratum B	8·0 Kgs
	VII	4·9 Kgs	C	3·0 Kgs
	VIII	2·3 Kgs	D	3·9 Kgs
	IX	0·4 Kgs	E/F	4·0 Kgs
	X	—	G/H	3·0 Kgs
			J	2·1 Kgs
			K	3·8 Kgs
			L	3·0 Kgs
			M/N	5·0 Kgs
			P	3·0 Kgs

References

Cowgill, G. L. (1964). *American Antiquity* **29**, 467–473.
Evans, J. D. (1964). *Annual of the British School at Athens* **59**, 132–240.
Evans, J. D. (1971). *P.P.S.* **37**, 95–117.
Evans, J. D. (1972). *Anatolian Studies* **XXII**, 115–128.
Evans, J. D. and Renfrew, A. C. (1968). "Excavations at Saliagos near Antiparos", Oxford University Press, London.
Furness, A. (1953). *Annual of the British School at Athens* **48**, 94–134.
McPherron, A. (1967) *Anthropological Papers of the Museum of Anthropology of the University of Michigan* **30**.
Payne, S. (1972). *In* "Papers in Economic Prehistory" (E. S. Higgs ed.) pp. 49–64, Cambridge University Press, Cambridge.
Solheim, W. G. (1960). *Current Anthropology* **1**, 325–329.
Willey, G. R. (1961). *American Antiquity* **27**, 230–231.

Some Light on Prehistoric Europe

J. G. NANDRIS

IT IS POSSIBLE in a short compass only to outline a theme which ranges more widely than might be supposed at first sight; but it is the purpose of this note to suggest that a certain class of lamp, which may seem initially to be an impractical device, is a basic feature in the neolithic of southeast Europe, and probably outside that area. A number of pieces of material equipment which are often explained away as ritual objects in these cultures can be much more readily seen as lamps, once the functional characteristics of the type in question are known. This does not preclude assigning to them a social meaning. Indeed, the implications of the lamp as a form of lighting should also be considered in a biosocial context, that is to say, as a part of a certain mode of behaviour; but here again it is hardly possible to develop this notion in full. It is desirable to emphasize the practicability of the kind of lamp in question, and this can be done by reference to the reconstruction and modern use of the distinctive Dacian lamp of the Roumanian Iron Age.

What can be said briefly about the bio-social aspect should perhaps first be considered. The Neolithic has in the past been defined in various ways, technologically, by reference to stonework or pottery; or in an economic sense. Essentially however, the Neolithic is a mode of behaviour characteristic of the Neothermal period. The essentials of this behaviour, let alone the psychological impact of the new conditions, have scarcely yet been assessed. Archaeology is hardly in a state to examine them, and stands in no pressing need of new fields for unfounded speculation. A scholarly example of bio-social effect is, however, provided by Angel (1972), who attributes importance to the demonstrable lengthening of female life-span (with no comparable male effect) as a response to the settled Neolithic way of life, which made pregnancy and child-rearing less arduous than under hunter-fisher conditions. The house and its appurtenances were one major feature of the new behavioural mode, and this can be detected in the obvious pride taken in the house and its elaboration, its decoration, and the models made of it, during the sixth to fourth millennia in southeast Europe. Models were also made of the contents, notably furniture, which is attested with certainty by the end of the fifth millennium. The general effect was of an increase in the quantity, specialization, permanence, and elaboration of material possessions of all kinds, to a degree impracticable under normal pre-Neolithic conditions, although paralleled in some specially favoured conditions of hunter-fisher climax. Nearly every individual aspect of the Neolithic had been previously adumbrated under such conditions, leading to some confusion in defining the Neolithic itself when only isolated aspects, such as the economic basis, have been taken into account.

In the conditions of the Neolithic house a way of life was made possible which, as far as ordinary people were concerned, was hardly surpassed for its comfort and possibilities of cultural elaboration until quite recent times. This is not to say that advantage was always taken of these possibilities, whether for reasons of external circumstance or for lack of aspiration; but to step inside a reconstructed Bandkeramik long house (such as that available at Asparn an der Zaya in the Weinviertel north of Vienna) is to realize that life in one of these houses had much the same potential as that of a prosperous modern peasant farmer; and here it is the scale of the building which is of importance and not the correctness of the detailed superstructure.

Such a behavioural mode certainly demanded lighting. Early man was not at a loss for modes of lighting before this period, and the lamps which we are about to discuss had their precursors in the Palaeolithic and Mesolithic like the other technical and economic traits of the Neolithic. There is also a whole range of other lighting possibilities which are worth bearing in mind. These range from firelight itself through spills, tapers, torches, fire baskets, candles, and the birch-bark rolls (Clark, 1965, p. 209) of the European Neolithic, passing into the even more esoteric possibilities provided by animal luminaries. Of these the fish candles of the Canadian northwest coast Indians are among the best known, with a bark wick stuck in the throat and the oily body providing the fuel. In the Orkneys and Shetlands the stormy petrel has been used in the same manner. More recondite are the uses of large luminous beetles – "rather smaller than a sparrow" – reported from tropical south America (Robins, 1939, p. 125), which were worn fastened to each big toe with a view to facilitating nocturnal perambulation, and avoiding snakes. They could also, on occasion, be worn fastened in the hair by "native women dancing the fandango".

With the specialized exception of the fish and sea birds all these are *lights*. The distinguishing features of the *lamp* are the elements of body, wick and fuel combined. There are circumstances before the Neolithic in which this combination is attested, and others in which it might have been possible. With the permanent elaboration of domestic equipment in the Neolithic however, the lamp first becomes universally practicable, and the question is what form it then took. A more difficult question is what behavioural effect prolonged and portable lighting may either have served or induced. In addition one might ask whether this form of lighting added to the possibility that a Neolithic house would be preserved for posterity by burning, or in fact lessened it. A number of examples can be adduced to answer the first question, and we may begin by classifying the early lamp form in a rudimentary way, and then describing the Dacian lamp as a relatively late but well-defined functional example. After this it may seem clearer that it is worth looking more carefully among early material for this category of lamp.

A simple classification of the earliest forms of lighting is already apparent:

a. Lights: of which various examples have been mentioned.
b. Lamps: 1. *Animal lamps*
              2. *Open Reservoir lamps*: In these the flame is not separated from the fuel by any partition, as it already is in the next development of the form – the Roman lamp. The Open Reservoir Lamp may be of shell, stone, or clay. It may also be elevated on a stand (The "Open Stand Lamp" of Robins, 1939).

In relation to these early forms Robins (1939, p. 100) has commented on a dividing line within Europe which seems to him to appear along the line north of the "Pyrenees-Alps-Balkans". Vague as the term "Balkans" is, this implies some distinction between south-eastern and central Europe. It would be of interest to follow up the European patterns of distribution through prehistory. While this cannot be done here, the stands ("altars") of the southeast European Neolithic are a rather distinctive feature which does not occur in northern and central Europe.

Some early examples of what seem to be Open Reservoir lamp bodies in stone are known from the Magdalenian, e.g. Grotte de la Mouthe (Rivière, 1901). They occur at Pekarna, and later in flint mines, such as Grimes Graves, or from Causewayed Enclosures such as Cissbury (Clark and Piggott, 1933, Fig. 6). The decorated stone bowls from Khirokitia on Cyprus, many of them with spouts, are also very likely lamps, and most of these possibilities have been recognized as such by Robins (1939). The possibility also arises that the large stone basins found in the megalithic chambers of New

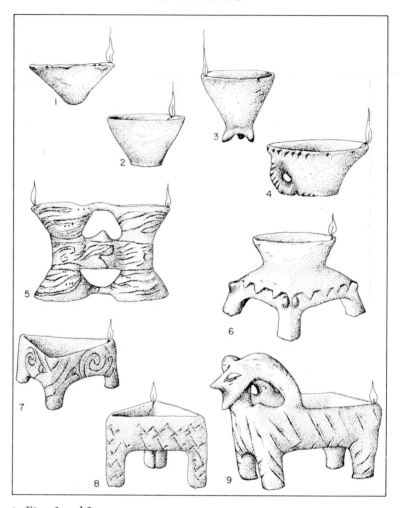

Key to Figs. 1 and 2

SUGGESTION OF POTTERY FORMS SUITABLE AS OPEN RESERVOIR
LAMPS, FROM VARIOUS NEOLITHIC CONTEXTS

1. Conical vessels from *Izvoare*, Level II (*"Proto-Cucuteni"* and *Cucuteni* A)
   contexts with rim diameters of *c*. 12 cms (Vulpe 1957: Fig. 209). These
   belong to a category of porous monochrome pottery burnished only inside
   and on the rim.
2. *Middle Minoan Knossos*. Wheel turned (see text).
3. *Porodin* or *Nea Nikomedeia*. Macedonian early neolithic contexts.
4. *Dacian*, from *Židovar*, Yugoslav Banat (Gavela, 1952, Fig. 17/1). The form
   is widespread in Dacian contexts, including burials, and is generally agreed
   to be a lamp.
5. From *Truşeşti*, Moldavia. Cucuteni A_2 context. A tentative suggestion for
   the function of this Cucuteni-Tripolje form.

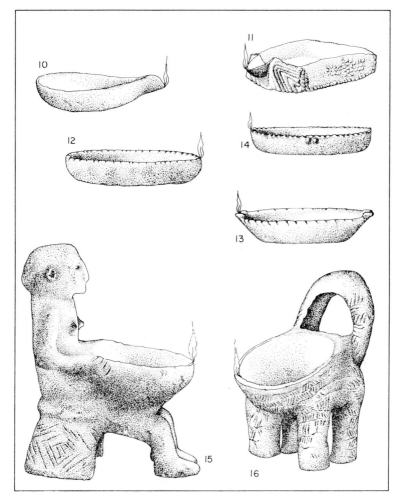

6. Stand form from *First Temperate Neolithic* contexts, mainly the Starčevo, Körös or Cris areas.

7 and 8. From *Karanovo*: triangular stands from the more southerly FTN contexts. Four-cornered shapes are also found.

9. Four cornered stand of *Vinča* type, with animal head elaboration. The example from the base of the Rudna Glava copper mine (Jovanović, 1971, Pl. III/3–4) has two such heads.

10 and 11. From *Khirokitia*, Cyprus. Stone vessels from "PPN" contexts.

12. *Ertebølle* lamps (Mathiassen, 1935), generally agreed as such and with analogies in Eskimo culture.

13. *Lengyel* contexts, Nowa Huta, S. Poland (Buratynski, 1971).

14. *Rzucewo* contexts, S. Baltic coast (e.g. Wislanski Ed., 1970, Fig. 125/48).

15. *Bordjoš*, Yugoslav Banat contexts. 19·5 cms high (Grbić, 1954).

16. *Danilo, Elateia, Reštane* contexts (Adriatic coast, central Greece, Kosovo and Metohija). E.g., Smilčić (Radovi, Zadar, 10, 1963; 105 and Pl. VIII/4).

Grange and Knowth in Ireland were lamps, analogous in conception to the great stone "thousand-year lamp" found in the remarkable tenth century AD tomb of Wang Chien in Szechwan. (Sullivan, 1948).

The other elements of the lamp, the fuel and wick, can also be categorized, but seldom definitely assigned in the prehistoric context. The fuels were either *vegetable oils* or *animal fats*, the use of mineral oils being associated with a later stage of developed lamp morphology. Caribou fat and blubber were used in North American and Eskimo contexts, and blubber has been proposed for the oval open reservoir lamps of the Ertebølle (Mathiassen, 1935) which so closely resemble the stone lamps of the Eskimos. Mutton or beef tallow was more universally available, and it is thought that the soft stone lamps of the Eastern Gravettian (e.g. at Timonovka, Clark, 1965, p. 133) used an animal fat, possibly mammoth. The rectangular houses of this Gravettian, which reached such a degree of sophistication that they had bark and clay chimneys, emphasize the association between lamps and a certain level of domesticity, whether in an early hunting context or not. Another rudimentary usage is demonstrated by the oyster shell lamps filled with tallow which were apparently in use in the Gower Peninsular (Glamorgan) at least as late as the end of the 19th century AD (Robins, 1939, p. 40). This exemplifies the shell form of the open reservoir lamp. Convolute shells, in which the wick could be aptly laid along the curved "spout" provided by nature at the base of the shell, were used at Ur (Robins, 1939, Pl. VIII).

As regards vegetable oils, a wide range of these will provide an adequate fuel. A people so sophisticated as the Minoans were still using open reservoir lamps, whether of clay or stone, and in this case olive oil is the most likely fuel. Castor oil and linseed oil were also used; it is worth remembering that the flax of the Bandkeramik could have been used for oil (or indeed for wicks), and that we have as little good evidence for weaving as we do for lamps from this context. Herodotus refers to the mixing by the Egyptians of salt with castor oil, and their use of a floating wick. The possibility of using a floating wick, rather than one which lay on the rim of the lamp, is of importance since no trace of burning would remain for the archaeologist to detect. This practice is not necessarily associated with glass vessels, although the sinking wick would tend to fall below the rim of a pottery vessel as the oil became lower. It was much used by the Egyptians (Hayes, 1953, p. 260), and indeed perhaps originated with them. Robins (1939, p. 45) comments that the Egyptian hieroglyph.

꜀ (Gardiner, 1957, R7) is usually interpreted as a bowl with incense rising, but could be a floating wick. It is however, of some interest that this Middle Kingdom hieroglyph supersedes an earlier one: ⊔ (Gardiner, 1957, W10*) which much more closely resembles a flame standing on the rim, in a manner comparable to that on the Dacian lamp.

While wicks may therefore be divided into the floating and the more universal direct forms, they could actually be made from a wide range of vegetable fibres. *Verbascum*, tow, papyrus (Robins, 1939, p. 55) or braided lint (Hayes, 1953, p. 260) are all mentioned, and there are many other possibilities. Nor is formally spun fibre necessary. The Eskimo lamps used simply an elongated heap of chopped moss along one edge of the lamp (Mathiassen, 1935, p. 146); bark can be used, and the author has observed strips of tinder (a fibrous bracket fungus) in use as wicks in Open Reservoir lamps on Mount Athos.

The Dacian lamp, and some features it shows in use, help us to understand not merely the limitations but the advantages of the Open Reservoir Lamp. This form belongs to the Roumanian Iron Age during the two or three centuries both before and after 1 AD, and is found, with other Dacian remains over a wide area extending into eastern and northern Hungary, Slovakia and north of the Carpathians, as well as present day Roumania. The "Dacian Cup" (Crişan, 1955) has long been recognized as a lamp, and has a distinctive flaring, everted conical shape with one, or sometimes two, thick handles low down (Fig. 1, 4). Traces of burning have been found, and this is in fact an Open Reservoir lamp, with direct wick lying on the rim. The fabric is usually coarse and well tempered, and significantly enough continues to be hand made throughout the period, even though the Dacians had well made wheel-thrown pottery from the third century BC. Some wheel-made ones are rare and late. This lamp seems to have been made in and for the individual home, not by professional potters. The coarse fabric allowed for heating by the wick, which is in any case only local at the rim and does not constitute a problem with such a fabric. The outside (which is in darkness when the lamp is lit) was decorated, if at all, only in a rudimentary manner with cordons. The lamps are found quite regularly in Dacian burials.

A small reconstruction of such a lamp was made of grit-tempered unburnished clay and fired in a bonfire, in order to test some of the functional characteristics, since complete original examples are not available in Britain. Several varieties of vegetable cooking oil were used as fuel, while for the wick a woven cotton bootlace proved quite satisfactory. The low-placed handle is well suited to carrying while alight. The flame perches on the rim of the bowl and can be finely adjusted by altering the length of projecting wick, which lies on the flaring side of the vessel with the lower end in the oil (Fig. 3). A further point of interest is the possibility of increasing the light available by using several wicks, and later on in the closed Roman clay lamp, examples with several nozzles attest to this practice. It is worth mentioning that among the considerable evidence of exchange between the Dacian and Graeco-Roman world (which probably included olive oil) there is a three-spouted hanging bronze candelabrum from Piscul Crașanilor.

Fig. 3. Reconstruction of Roumanian Iron Age (Dacian) open lamp.
Rim diameter 10·5 cms.

The light given by such a lamp is very effective and requires little attention. Another point of functional interest is the oil-seepage which takes place through porous fabrics. This is known in Egyptian cases of soft stone lamps to have been countered by soaking the stone in water, for which purpose a channel round the top of the lamp was made (Hayes, 1953, Fig. 167).

The three- or four-cornered stands of the early southeast European Neolithic acquire a new significance in relation to this factor of oil-seepage. These objects have been called altars, and also lamps, but usually in inverted commas. It seems possible to be less equivocal now, and to claim them definitely as Open Reservoir lamps, probably with direct wicks. Signs of burning are not usually present, nor have they been sought for, and it remains to assess experimentally how much trace would remain from the low degree of heating involved. Elevation on high feet would counter oil-seepage and bring them into the stand category of Open Reservoir lamps. The recent discovery of such a stand from the base of a copper-mine shaft attributed to the Vinča culture (Jovanović, 1971, Pl. III/3–4) lends credibility to their use as lamps.

It is possible to take the further step of suggesting that some other objects from Neolithic contexts may not be "ritual" or non-functional, as is sometimes suggested, but suitable as functional lamps. It may also be possible to identify less striking vessels as lamps. Individual cases have to be individually substantiated; but the initial criterion is that all should be morphologically suited to a role about whose practical aspects we now have a clear idea. It is recognized that Neolithic pottery assemblages contained a range of different shapes in both fine and coarse wares, with a series of functions which were defined to much the same extent as those of the various shapes we ourselves use. It is suggested that more of these assemblages contain a lamp form than has been usually allowed for. Their distinct function is often emphasized both by distinctive decoration, and by their form – especially in southeast Europe by elevation on feet.

The "stands" from First Temperate Neolithic contexts, such as Karanovo I, Kremikovci, the Starčevo or Criş; or from Boian, Vinča, and other early Neolithic contexts in southeast Europe are well enough known, and too numerous to be cited individually here (Fig. 1,6–9). The incised zig-zags on the Starčevo examples are rather distinctive of this particular type of shallow bowl on high feet (although occurring on, for example, the Ludvar house model), and the exised "Kerbschnitt" decoration on the alternative stand form, with three or four corners, is also distinctive. From Porodin and Nea Nikomedeia come little conical bowls on three feet which may be lamps (Fig. 1,3). Analogous small conical cups from Cretan Middle Minoan contexts, standing some 4–5 cms high and c. 8 cs across the mouth, with flat bases, certainly are Bronze Age lamps. They are carelessly thrown, occur in large numbers, and are of porous clay with lumpy inclusions, cut off the wheel with a cord (Fig. 1,2). Some have a red slip, but many are natural buff in colour, and the most plausible fuel here is certainly olive oil.

In the Lengyel material from Nowa Huta in Southern Poland (Fig. 2,13) there are shallow oval vessels, comparable to the Ertebølle lamps (Fig. 2,12) even to the extent of being decorated by nicks along the rim, and with the additional refinement of two small lugs on the rim at each end between which the wick could be laid (e.g. Buratynski, 1971, Pl. XVI,12). A more widely known form from the Lengyel is the solid clay block, with a depression at the top and perforated corners, sometimes claimed as a hanging lamp. This remains to be convincingly demonstrated. Of great interest however is the further occurrence, even to the sparse decoration, of the Ertebølle/Lengyel type of oval lamp in Rzucewo contexts on the south Baltic coast (Fig. 2,14). What we know of this culture makes it very likely that seal blubber was the fuel used. These occurrences are very suggestive of the way in which the Neolithic mode of behaviour penetrated to the south Baltic, just as the Satrup type of axe has been used to suggest a mechanism for its derivation in more westerly areas (Schwabedissen, 1967).

Two remarkable pottery types should finally be cited, since they have in the past been unhesitatingly claimed as non-functional objects of a ritual nature. Both could without a doubt be used as Open Reservoir lamps, and when we consider the imaginative and indeed often humourous use of anthropomorphic figures in the Neolithic, as well as the functional criteria of this lamp type, it seems possible to claim them as such. The first are the four-legged vessels (Fig. 2,16) with mouth rising steeply from the front legs, and a handle above, which Weinberg successfully reconstructed from Elateia and Corinth and linked with those found in Danilo on the Adriatic coast (Weinberg, 1965, p. 41). They also occur in Yugoslav Metohija (Reštane).

The second example is more isolated; but in the figure found on the surface at Bordjoš, near Bečej on the Tisza in the Yugoslav Banat (Grbić, 1954). We may just possibly find one of the greatest expressions of this imaginative faculty (Fig. 2,15). This figure is seated on a seat of the type found in figurines from Tisza and Lengyel contexts in the fourth millennium, decorated on the sides, and holds before it on its knees a shallow bowl, or Open Reservoir lamp. Both these types are functionally suited to this role.

With these few examples in mind it would be possible to continue towards a more systematic examination of the occurrence of lamps in European Neolithic assemblages. On our present view of the hunter-fisher mode of behaviour the lamp was an inessential and occasional adjunct, but with the formal and regular exclusion of the sky at night by the Neolithic house, and the greater specialization of material possessions made possible by that mode, it acquired greater importance. The transition from form to function is by no means a simple one; but the mode of behaviour in question seems to demand a form to fulfil this function. Certain practical requirements also rule out a wide range of forms. Tests being carried out in the Department of Chemistry at University College London by Dr P. J. Garratt to establish the extent and nature of hydrocarbons present in some of this material have produced very promising results, but no conclusions can be put forward until the programme has been extended.

Acknowledgements

I am grateful to Prof J. D. Evans for lending me a Middle Minoan clay lamp and to Dr Ian Cornwall for commenting on traces of burning thereon. Mr H. M. Stewart gave invaluable help with Egyptian material, both lamps and hieroglyphs. Miss S. Lunt drew Figs. 1 and 2. Mr Peter Dorrell kindly took the photograph for Fig. 3.

References

Angel, L. (1972). *World Archaeology* **4/1**, 88–105.
Buratynski, S. (1971). *Materialy Arch. Nowej Huty* **IV**, 7–66.
Clark, J. G. D. (1952, reprinted 1965). "Prehistoric Europe, The Economic Basis". Methuen, London.
Clark, J. G. D. and Piggott, S. (1933). *Antiquity* **VII**, 166–183.
Crişan, I. H. (1955). *Studii şi Cercetari Ştiinţifice, Cluj, Ser III.* **VI**.
Gardiner, A. H. (1957). "Egyptian Grammar". Oxford University Press, Oxford.
Gavela, B. (1952). "Keltski Oppidum Židovar." Naučna Kniga, Belgrade.
Grbić, M. (1954). *Arch. Iugo.* **I**, 15–18.
Hayes, W. C. (1953). "The Scepter of Egypt". Harvard University Press. Cambridge, Mass.
Jovanović, B. (1971). *Metalurgija eneolitskog perioda Jugoslavije.* Arh. Inst. (Belgrade): Posebna Izdanja, Belgrade.
Mathiassen, T. (1935). *Acta Arch.* **VI**, 139–152.
Rivière, E. (1901). *Bull. Soc. Anthrop. Paris*, 1901.
Robins, F. W. (1939). "The Story of the Lamp". Oxford University Press. Oxford.
Schwabedissen, H. (1967). *Palaeohistoria* **XII**, 1966 (1967).
Sullivan, M. (1948). *Transactions Oriental Ceramic Soc.* **23**, 1–11.
Vulpe, R. (1957. "Izvoare". Editura Academici R.P.R. Bucarest.
Weinberg, S. S. (1965). The Stone Age in the Aegean *C.A.H.* **36**.
Wislanski, T. Ed. (1970) "The Neolithic in Poland". Zaklad Narodowy Imienia Ossolinskich Wydawnictwo Polskiej Akademii Nauk. Wroclaw.

Bronze Age and Earlier Languages of the Near East: an Archaeological View

J. MELLAART

THIS HUMBLE OFFERING presented in honour of Professor W. F. Grimes is concerned with a somewhat controversial subject; the age and origin of a number of language groups in the Near East and their association with various cultures and civilizations. Admittedly this is a field full of potential and actual traps and pitfalls where most archaeologists fear to tread. When and where the texts fail and only archaeological evidence is available, usually of a somewhat uncertain kind, many philologists also draw in their horns. *Errare humanum est* and I suspect that in the course of this essay a few plunges into hidden pits and traps are somehow unavoidable.

When one looks at the linguistic pattern of the Near East today and compares it with the pattern at the end of the Bronze Age one is struck by a great amount of continuity. The old lands of the Fertile Crescent still speak Semitic tongues and though Arabic, one of these, now also reigns in Egypt, Coptic, the last descendant of Ancient Egyptian, is not yet extinct. Iranian, a newcomer of the Late Bronze Age, flourishes as ever from the Zagros Mountains eastwards and in the west, Greek persists with undiminished vigour. The main difference is the prevalence of Turkish in Anatolia and Northwest Iran, which has supplanted both the old Indo-European Hittite, Luvian and Palaic west of the Euphrates, and the non-Indo-European Hurrian of Eastern Anatolia and Transcaucasia. Yet, in the many languages and dialects of the Caucasus and Georgia pre-Indo-European languages continue to be spoken to the present day. Further south, however, the old languages of the Zagros, including Elamite, which lingered on into the tenth century, are now extinct, supplanted by Iranian.

Whether one looks at the large pattern in 1973 AD or that of circa 1250 BC the coexistence of languages of different types and ages is a normal phenomenon, which would have encouraged the exchange of some vocabulary in the form of loanwords. To this should be added the use of place and personal names, many of which derive from linguistic substrata, frequently the only source of information about long since vanished populations of prehistory.

The archaeologist's interest in the remains of prehistoric languages, frequently confined to onomastica and toponyms, is obvious, for it may be possible to associate them with distinct archaeological groups, cultures, pottery distributions and the like from which something might be learned about migration patterns or autochthonous origins, as the case may be, as well as their antiquity.

In the third millennium BC of the Near East, for example there is abundant evidence for migrations of ethnic elements associated with the appearance of various Indo-European languages (Greek, Hittite, Luvian, Palaic) attested at a later date in writing in the same territories where there is good archaeological evidence for disturbance before, i.e. the Aegean and Anatolia west of the Euphrates. There is similar evidence in the Fertile Crescent for the movements of mountaineers or nomads, that can be linked directly or indirectly with the spread of non-Indo-European Hurrian or Semitic (Akkadian and Amorite). The archaeological evidence provides the basis for a discussion of where some of these new people came from and not infrequently it rather circumscribes the areas from which they probably did not come. On archaeological grounds e.g. it is extremely unlikely that the language known as Linear A ("Minoan") was Semitic!

Through the association of archaeological material with the remains of language it can frequently be determined how old some of the languages must be, even if only minimum ages can be defined. In terms of longevity Ancient Egyptian takes pride of place, for in its descendant, Coptic, it is still with us after a minimum age of about 5500 years, and probably more. Ancient Egyptian appeared fully fledged at the very beginning of the First Dynasty, at a date that with calibration is something like 3500 BC. By this period, the language already had both a hieroglyphic and a cursive (hieratic) script, which presupposes earlier beginnings during the Gerzaean period circa 4000–3500 BC, which has not yet yielded remains of writing. Now Old Egyptian, as this language is called, is distinguished by a Semitic type of grammar, but a Hamitic vocabulary (Albright, 1970). Emery (1961) concluded that the formation of the Egyptian monarchy in both Upper and Lower Egypt in the period preceding the unification was due to an influx of foreigners, the so-called "Dynastic Race", whose presence in Egypt was due to infiltration into Egypt during the Gerzaean period. This theory finds confirmation in different physical types as well as different burial habits, compared to those of the older native population, practised by the new ruling class. There is further support for this theory in the increasing amount of contact shown by the Gerzaean graves (no settlement has yet been excavated) in which unmistakable imports (and more numerous copies) of Late Chalcolithic Palestinian pottery occurred. The exact nature of relations with Palestine and Syria is still disputed, but the fact remains that Semitic elements of grammar entered into the structure of the Egyptian language, probably at this period. This simple fact is frequently ignored by the historian and archaeologist alike, when they favour the theory of Sumerian participation in the rise of Early Dynastic Egyptian culture reaching Egypt by the long route around Arabia and the Wadi Hammamat. But the Sumerians did not speak a Semitic language and the Semitic elements in Egyptian rather seem to demand the presence of invaders reaching Egypt from the Levant through Sinai. The presence of Lower Mesopotamian features in the Late Gerzaean could have reached Egypt just as easily from North Syria, where new excavations have shown Mesopotamian culture of the Uruk-Jemdet Nasr type well established on the Euphrates, the more so as Egypt was already engaged in the timber trade with the Levant coast.

The implications thus seem to favour Semitic speaking immigrants during the Gerzaean period, from circa 4000 BC onwards, who left their mark on the presumably Hamitic speech of the native Egyptians, developed during the preceding Amratian and Badarian periods in Upper Egypt, and the Fayum neolithic in Lower Egypt. On the calibrated time scale, these neolithic cultures date back to circa 5000 BC. Ancient Egyptian could therefore be described as a "neolithic" language in origin. Whether it was native to the Nile valley or was introduced with the techniques of neolithic farming from Asia, remains however unknown.

In Lower Mesopotamia, the language of the earliest clay and stone tablets, which date back to the Late Uruk period (calibrated date circa 38–3700 BC) is Sumerian. This was a non-Semitic language which dominated until the end of the Third Dynasty of Ur, to survive only as a dead language, read, copied and spoken? by *savants* during the second and first millennium BC in Mesopotamia. Already from the beginning of the Early Dynastic period, circa 2900 BC, Akkadian, an East-Semitic language was spoken side by side with Sumerian. It is not at present known how far back Sumerian extends in time and though all scholars agree that it must go back to the Middle Uruk period circa 4000 BC it may have arrived much earlier. There are two theories; the one maintains that Sumerian is autochthonous in

Lower Mesopotamia and linked with the Ubaid culture and its earliest phases, Eridu and Hajji Muhammed – the first settlers on the Mesopotamian alluvium (Albright, 1970) whereas the other assumes that the Sumerians came in considerably later, perhaps with the Red and Grey Uruk wares (in the Late Ubaid period, circa 5000 BC on calibrated C–14 date of circa 4200) and already found a Pre-Sumerian (Ubaid) culture and language fully established (Landsberger, 1944; Nagel, 1964). Upholders of the Sumerian immigration theory point out that the names of Euphrates (Buranun) and Tigris (Idigna) as well as those of all the chief Sumerian cities (Ur, Uruk, Nippur, Kish, Eridu, etc.) are not clearly Sumerian in origin (Kramer, 1957 against Albright, 1970). Whereas the philological argument of the Sumerologists appears rather strong, archaeological evidence for a Sumerian takeover is by no means conclusive and it is by no means inconceivable that the Uruk culture developed out of the Ubaid. There is one further point of interest; the Uruk culture is as well developed in Northern Mesopotamia and North Syria as it was in the south, but it would appear extremely unlikely that Sumerian was ever spoken in those parts. This same argument also holds for the Ubaid culture in the north and it is rather doubtful if one can link pottery distributions to linguistic patterns in Mesopotamia. Whether Sumerian was autochthoeous or not, its origins ultimately would seem to go back to the cultures of the Zagros zone before the establishment or irrigation agriculture in Mesopotamia in the 6th millennium BC.

A Zagros home is also indicated for the Proto-Elamite language of Khuzistan, an area that shared the same economic development as Lower Mesopotamia after mountain tribes established agriculture on the alluvial flats. As this language has not yet been deciphered it is unknown whether it contains a possible linguistic substratum.

Evidence for the antiquity of various Semitic tongues in the Near East is less explicit and apart from a number of Pre-Semitic topographical terms in North Syria and the Lebanon, (both Lebanon and Hermon are said to be non-Semitic names) there are only minimum dates for the first appearance of Semitic. East Semitic Akkadian is attested by circa 2900 in Sumer and along the Middle Euphrates (Mari) as well as in Accad (Kish). The evidence of Semitic grammar in Old Egyptian suggests that West Semitic was spoken from at least 4000 BC onwards, in territories adjacent to Egypt such as Sinai, Palestine and Syria during the Late Chalcolithic period (Byblos Enéolithique and Amuq F). Beyond this one can not say anything for certain, but it would cause little surprise, in my opinion at least, if the preceding Ghassulian culture (including its first Proto-Ghassulian phase) with its pastoral aspects, its desert habitats and its early metallurgy, intrusive in Palestine and South Syria from areas further to the north and northeast might not have been heralded in by the first Semites after the collapse of the Halaf culture of north Syria and north Mesopotamia. There appears to be a gap in the archaeological record on many sites and it would not be impossible that new elements filtered in from the desert to fill the cultural vacuum left at the end of the Halaf period. On numerous later occasions this same pattern of immigration from the desert pasture lands was followed by other Semitic speakers; the Akkadians in the Sargonid period, followed by the Amorites, Hebrews, Arameans and Arabs. If this hypothesis is acceptable, and the evidence on which it is based is admittedly very slender, West Semitic may have been predominant in the Levant from circa 4500 BC and the Syrian Pre-Semitic place names (Drower, 1971) may go back to the Halaf period. It would mean that the entire cultural development of the Levant from the Late Palaeolithic to the Halaf period was the achievement of Pre-Semitic populations of whose language (or languages) only a few place names have managed to survive. If this line of argument is correct, the rise of Semitic speech might be linked with the vigorous development of the "Chalcolithic" period in the Levant and North Mesopotamia, which put fresh blood into the decaying "neolithic" communities at the end of the Halaf period. Semitic speech would thus be a relative newcomer to the Near East.

The highland zone of Eastern Turkey and Transcaucasia formed a stronghold of conservative non-Indo-European languages like its southern extension, the Zagros zone. Our earliest textual evidence, dating from the Sargonid period points to Hurrian as the language of the area, but nobody knows how old Hurrian is. An Indo-European language of the kingdom of Mitanni in the second millennium BC, attested in a number of glosses, and numerous names of nobles, kings and deities shows that the area was penetrated by newcomers (from beyond the Caucasus?) but the Mitannian kings used Hurrian, the language of their subjects, in administration and foreign correspondence, and with the extinction of the Mitannian kingdom the Indo-European language seems to have got lost. Hurrian, on the other hand, survived into Urartian and Indo-European languages such as Armenian and Kurdish did not gain a foothold in this area until the Medic conquest. Many archaeologists think that the Early Bronze Age culture of this vast region (the Kur-Araxes or Karaz culture) may have been the work of the Hurrians and there is good evidence to suggest that this culture was rooted in those of the preceding neolithic e.g. the Shulaveri culture of Georgia. Do the origins of Hurrian take us back to the 6th millennium BC?

Anatolia, west of the Euphrates, and the Aegean show a different cultural and linguistic development. As far as we know these were the first territories in the Near East to be affected by Indo-European invaders, arriving at the end of the Troy I, or during the Troy II period by a northwesterly route that brought them along the western shores of the Black Sea, between circa 2900 and 2600 BC (calibrated C–14 dates). At the beginning of the Early Helladic III period (circa 2350 BC) the first Indo-Europeans also entered main and Greece, apparently from the northeast through Bulgaria and Thrace. The first group of Anatolian Indo-Europeans may have developed in Anatolia into the three related languages known as Hittite, Luvian and Palaic, and those who entered Greece are generally thought to have been the first speakers of Greek. In both areas the invaders found a numerous population and they encountered considerable resistance. In the Aegean they apparently failed to overrun the Cycladic islands and Crete, which became relict areas of the earlier non-Indo-European language. As these islands were not apparently taken over by the Mycenaean Greeks until circa 1450 BC, nearly a thousand years after their first arrival in the country and as the Minoans in Crete (and the islands under their dominion) had developed a greatly superior culture, there was evidently plenty of time and opportunity for a great enrichment of Greek with loanwords from the earlier language, which is called "Pre-Greek". In a recent study, which also summarizes the various problems and interpretations connected with this language, Furnée (1972) estimates the number of Pre-Greek words at between 5000–6000, the largest body of words from a substratum language preserved in the Near East. The distribution of Pre-Greek covers the entire Aegean and Asia Minor, especially its western and southern parts, where Pre-Greek was still known in Hellenistic times. In Central and north Anatolia, however, Hattic, a non-Indo-European language preceded Hittite (Nesite) and was still recorded by the Hittites for the cult of Hattic deities, absorbed into the Hittite pantheon. As a spoken language Hattic may have been extinct by this period, i.e. the Late Bronze Age.

Although there do not appear to be any close relationships between Hattic and Pre-Greek, toponyms of the Pre-Greek type also occur in Hattic territory as Laroche (1957, 1961) has shown e.g. Zippalanda, a famous Hattic and later Hittite cult centre. This well known group of toponyms (Pre-Greek -nthos and -ssos and Anatolian -nda and -ssa) including such names as Corinthos, Knossos, Puranda, Apassa, etc. had generally been regarded as Pre-Indo-European until Laroche suggested an Anatolian Indo-European origin, quoting several examples with good Indo-European morphologies like Wiyana-wanda "Wine-town". The presence of vast numbers of similar place names in Greece, the Cyclades, Crete and Anatolia could then be linked with Anatolian Indo-European elements also in Greece. According to this theory the Greeks only arrived in Greece at the time of the Shaft Graves (sixteenth century) as a second wave of Indo-Europeans, preceded by an Anatolian Indo-European group (often loosely called Luvian) with the -ssos and -nthos names in Early Helladic I (Laroche, 1961, Palmer, 1965), circa 2350 BC. In that case Pre-Greek was not a Pre-Indo-European language, but Anatolian Indo-European, a conclusion that few linguists are prepared to accept (Furnée, 1972). He has shown that the structure of the Pre-Greek words is quite unlike that of the Indo-European. Attempts to read the Minoan Linear a language as Luvian (Palmer, 1965) are not convincing and Furnée points out that comparison with Pre-Greek may offer better chances of success.

The recent calibration of C–14 dates now allows one to date the Indo-European incursions into Anatolia at a considerably earlier period than those of Greece, destroying the previously acceptable synchronization circa 2300 BC (end of Troy II period). There are no events in the Early Bronze Age development in Greece comparable to the cultural break between the Troy I and II periods and the wide-spread signs of disturbance in Anatolia between circa 2900 (end of Troy I) and circa 2600 BC. With the calibration the suggestion that the destruction of the EB2 culture of the Konya plain was somehow linked to Sargon's campaign against Purushanda becomes chrono-logically impossible, as it would have taken place several centuries before his birth. In the same way, the new dating leaves the theory of a Luvian invasion of Greece hanging in mid air, and it will have to be abandoned on chronological grounds. These new developments tend to dissociate the dates of Indo-European arrivals in Anatolia and Greece and they clearly represent separate and unconnected events; an earlier movement into Anatolia and a later one into Greece, each associated with a different and unrelated language.

The existence of Pre-Greek in both areas, Greece and Anatolia, suggests a Pre-Indo-European common substratum language, swamped earlier in Anatolia than in Greece. There is good evidence that it originally covered even wider areas (Schachermeyr, 1954), including e.g. Macedonia and Thrace. How old was this language when the first Indo-Europeans arrived? Few scholars now believe that the Early Bronze Age cultures of Greece were the result of an immigration from Southwest Anatolia, complete with the Pre-Greek language (Haley and Blegen, 1928). There is steadily increasing evidence that the Early Bronze Age cultures of Greece and Anatolia as well as those of the Balkans had their roots in a more remote past, whether this is called neolithic as in Greece, eneolithic as in the Balkans or chalcolithic as in Anatolia. For all its novelty, there are many features that can only be derived from earlier cultures, and nowhere is this more clearly seen than in the continuity of religion and religious practices.

The distribution of Pre-Greek place names extends from Thrace and Macedonia to Crete and the islands and from the Ionian sea to the Konya plain and Cilicia on the border with Syria, an area of many local cultures at all periods from the neolithic till the Early Bronze Age, yet exactly the area in which the Anatolian neolithic developed and to which it was first diffused in southeastern Europe.

If the geographical names illustrate the distribution of the Pre-Greek language, the contents of the vocabulary are equally revealing; Mediterranean trees, plants, flowers, herbs; the various members of the fauna, the sea and its creatures, foodstuffs, various rocks, artefacts of leather, wood, straw and basketry, pottery? drinking vessels, etc. There are Pre-Greek words for stone and mudbrick, for cave, sickle, knucklebone, for portable tables, for city and burg, temple and shrine and a word for the steering of a ship. There are hundreds of adjectives, a fine selection of pejoratives, many terms for lascivious behaviour, etc. But there are remarkably few words for metal or metal objects. Although the contents of a Pre-Greek vocabulary can not give one a precise date for the period in which it was formed – there must have been additions from time to time as new products appeared or were invented – it would not seem out of place in a neolithic agricultural community (Schachermeyr, 1954). It is in fact just the sort of "inventory" one would have expected the first farmers to have made of their environment.

If Pre-Greek then represents the remnants of the language of the first Anatolian farmers to cross the Aegean circa 6000 BC and of their descendants in southeastern Europe, I venture to suggest that it was mainly transmitted to the Greeks, by their descendants, the Minoans of Crete.

The preservation of remnants of substratum languages is of course very much a question of chance and Furnée estimates that even in Pre-Greek the 5–6000 words may represent only one-half of the full vocabulary. Outside the literate Near East the chances of preservation of substratum languages were considerably reduced, yet it is fairly obvious that they once existed. A West-Mediterranean substratum (or several) has been recognized in Italy, southern France and the Iberian peninsula and a number of words are close to those

of Pre-Greek (Furnée, 1972). Are these the result of Greek and
Etruscan colonization of the Western Mediterranean or do they go
back to the neolithic secondary diffusion from Greece and the Balkan
peninsula, the so-called Impresso-wares of the earliest West-
Mediterranean neolithic of the sixth and fifth millennia? I do not
feel qualified to comment on such issues, but it should not be
forgotten that the introduction of agriculture, whether brought by
actual settlers from the Near East, its homeland, or acquired through
contact by the former hunting and gathering populations of Mesolithic Europe (and North Africa) from those Near Eastern settlers
had an extraordinary powerful effect. It ensured a regular food
supply, greater stability, an increase in the birth rate, a decline in the
death rate and hence a general increase in population, which then
stimulated increased agricultural activity involving emigration into
new territories. In this way, neolithic populations spread and with
it their attitudes towards life, and its conservation, the cult of the
"Mother Goddess" and of course the ritual and technological
processes necessary to ensure its continuation and the means to
communicate – the language. The tremendous increase of neolithic
populations carried certain languages or groups of languages over
vast areas of territory: Semitic spread throughout the Arabian
peninsula, Hamitic reached from Egypt to the Atlantic; Pre-Greek
from Cilicia to the Danube, and Indo-European once spanned nearly
the whole of Eurasia, from the Atlantic up to the frontiers of China.
All apparently developed in what may *lato senso* be called neolithic
communities and all knew agriculture. As the bearers of these various
cultures are ultimate descendants of Palaeolithic hunters, some
elements of speech may conceivably have been preserved from that
remote period.

References

Albright, W. F. (1970). *C.A.H.*, **1**, (1), pp. 122–55, esp. 147–9.
Drower, M. S. (1971). *C.A.H.*, **1**, (2), pp. 320–21.
Emery, W. B. (1961) "Archaic Egypt", pp. 30–31, 38–42.
Furnée, E. J. (1972). "Die wichstigen Konsonantischen Erscheinungen
    des Vorgriechischen." p. 399, Mouton, The Hague.
Haley, J. B. and Blegen, C. W. (1928). *AJA*, 141f.
Kramer, S. N. (1957). *Scientific American, October*, **1**, 46.
Landsberger, B. (1944). *DTFF Dergisi*, **2**, 435ff.
Laroche, E. (1957). "Gedenkschrift P. Kretschmer" **II**, 1–7.
Laroche, E. (1961). *R.H.A.*, **69**, 57–98.

Nagel, W. (1964). *B.J.F.* **4**, 1–9.

Palmer, L. (1965). "Mycenaeans and Minoans., (2nd edn), pp. 348–9. Faber and Faber, London.

Schachermeyr, F. (1954). *R.E.* **XXII**, **2**, 1494–1548.

The Origin of the Canaanite Jar

P. J. PARR

BY NO MEANS THE LEAST important (or the least troublesome) of the duties of the Director of the Institute of Archaeology is that of assuming ultimate responsibility for the well-being of what is surely one of the most comprehensive collections of Palestinian antiquities outside the museums of Jordan and Israel. As is well known to students of Levantine archaeology, the nucleus of this collection is formed by the mass of objects (pottery and small finds, especially scarabs) brought back to England by Sir Flinders Petrie from his excavations at Tell el-'Ajjul, Tell el-Far'a and Tell Jemmeh, to which have been added over the course of the years large groups of material from Tell ed-Duweir, Jericho and Samaria, as well as smaller groups. The collection is particularly rich in pottery of the Middle and Late Bronze Ages and the Iron Age; the Early Bronze and preceding periods are not, at present, so well represented, though it is hoped to rectify this in time. Although meticulously catalogued and admirably arranged as a teaching and research tool by Dame Kathleen Kenyon, the collection contains much material, particularly that from Petrie's work, still very inadequately published, and it is gratifying to report that in recent years there has been an increasing number of students, both from the Institute and elsewhere, who have been prepared to devote themselves to the task of re-publication. Professor Grimes deserves the thanks of all Near Eastern archaeologists for the encouragement he has given such students, and for the sympathetic concern he has consistently shown with regard to the problems arising from the Institute's guardianship of this important material.

In terms of actual bulk, the most imposing part of the Palestinian collection is unquestionably made up of the hundred or so examples of the so-called "Canaanite jar" – that large ovoid or piriform, pointed based vessel, used for the storage and transport of wines and oils, which first appeared in the Levant around the beginning of the second millennium BC and which, having become widely popular throughout the Eastern Mediterranean region during the following two thousand years, is the direct ancestor of the Greek and Roman amphora. It is doubtful whether any other ceramic type has had such a long history, or has preserved its original form so faithfully. Some aspects of its history were reviewed several years ago by Miss Virginia Grace, in an essay dedicated to another distinguished scholar (Grace, 1956), but the questions of the origin of the type and of the implications of its appearance have not, so far as the writer is aware, been discussed. It is the purpose of the present short paper to make some preliminary remarks in this connection.

The most remarkable thing about the Canaanite jar, when it first appears in, for example, the Courtyard Cemetery at Tell el-'Ajjul (Tufnell, 1962) or the Royal Tombs at Byblos (Tufnell, 1969), is the complete novelty of its shape and method of manufacture when compared with previous vessels of similar function from the same region. The standard Early Bronze Age storage jar of Palestine and coastal Syria, from Arad in the south to the 'Amuq in the north, is a flat based vessel, the body always hand-made, but the rim sometimes wheel-made or at least wheel-finished*. Only in the very north of the region, in the 'Amuq, are large round based jars found, and they are not common (Braidwood and Braidwood, 1960, p. 268 and Fig. 203). The Syrian vessels are handleless, and have a more-or-less vertical neck, high or low, with an out-turned rim (for examples from the 'Amuq, see Braidwood and Braidwood, 1960, Figs. 203, 207, 211; from Ras Shamra, see Schaeffer, 1962, Fig. 16). Identical jars are known from Palestine†, but probably more common in this country are handled jars, with either vertical loop handles or (more frequently, judging from the numbers published, though no quantitative analysis has been made) horizontal ledge handles. Another feature apparently confined to Palestine during the Early Bronze Age is the hole-mouth rim; Hennessy (1967, p. 40 and Plate XXXIII) draws attention to some hole-mouth jar rims from Qal'at er-Rouss on the Syrian coast, but these are of Proto-Urban date, and the type does not seem to be represented in the published Early Bronze Age pottery from Byblos, Ras Shamra or the 'Amuq.

In Palestine, at least, these various types of flat based jar continue, with only minor modifications, into the following EB – MB (MB I)

* The rims of the Plain Simple Ware storage jars of 'Amuq Phase G are explicitly stated to be wheel-made (Braidwood and Braidwood, 1960, p. 264), while regular horizontal striations suggestive of some sort of turning process can be seen on many rims of Palestinian jars in the Institute's collection.

† Individual references to these and the following Palestinian jars are not given, since they are well known. For convenient illustrations see Hennessy (1967).

Fig. 1. M.B.I. storage jar from Tell el'Ajjul Courtyard Cemetery, T.1417 (Inst. of Arch. Reg. No. E.XII 3/4).

period. The only exceptions are the relatively uncommon globular round based jars of Amiran's Group B (Amiran, 1960), largely confined to the north of the country, and these seem to be not so much a new type as a local variant of the flat based jar, many of which are also now more globular than ovoid. Little is known of the corresponding period in coastal Syria, but it can be safely assumed that the predilection for flat based storage vessels continued here also. In the north the large jars of 'Amuq Phases I and J are very little different in shape from those of Phases G and H, though they do differ in that they are now entirely wheel-made (Braidwood and Braidwood, 1960, pp. 406, 408 and 446, and Figs. 114 and 345, for example). Further south, nothing is known of the large jars of the period until Byblos is reached, but here such specimens as that of the "Montet deposit" (if it really is of EB – MB date; see Tufnell and Ward, 1966) is also in the Early Bronze Age tradition as regards shape and method of manufacture. It is interesting to note that, judging from the only relevant material presently available from further inland in western Syria, that from Hama, it is only at this time (Hama J) that the flat based jar becomes popular away from the coast, being completely unrepresented in the preceding Level K. The close relationship of the Hama J jars with those of the Palestinian EB – MB period, which are themselves a development of the earlier Early Bronze Age vessels, provides an important link, the cultural and historical implications of which the writer hopes to pursue on another occasion.

In striking contrast to the types of jar so far considered, the Middle Bronze Age "Canaanite" jar has a pointed base*, and, in contrast to all but the 'Amuq I and J vessels, they are entirely wheel-made. Miss Tufnell (1958, p. 220) has referred to the impracticability of the round or pointed base as compared with the flat base, and surprise is often voiced that the more stable flat based jar should have gone completely out of use at this time, never to be revived. Miss Tufnell postulates a change in function to explain the change in shape, and suggests "the arrival of a wine-drinking instead of a beer-drinking community", without elaborating her reasons. It is much more likely that any change in function was connected with the very great superiority of the pointed based jar as a means of conveyance, as distinct from stationary storage. For, except in the one particular of stability, the pointed jar is technically a much more advanced and

---

* There are, of course, degrees of "pointedness", and the earliest MB I (MB HA) jars have, in fact, a slightly flattened base. Base and walls are, however, conceived and constructed as an entity, and not as two separate elements, as they were in the EB and EB–MB vessels.

successful vessel than its flat based predecessor. The point of greatest weakness in the latter – as anyone who has excavated or restored such a jar will aver – is the junction between base and walls, a sharp change of angle vulnerable not only to internal strain, on account of the weight of the contents of the vessel bearing directly upon the flat base, but also to external damage, from inadvertant knocks and kicks, especially when the vessel is being lifted or manoeuvred. In contrast, the pointed jar, with base and walls all of a piece, and with a smooth regular profile, can be lifted (with or without the use of handles), pivoted, and generally man-handled with far less risk of damage, while the stresses emanating from the weight of its contents are more evenly distributed throughout the whole fabric of the vessel. As for stability, the pointed jar can be rested against a wall or stacked against its fellows very easily and safely, or it can be used with a separate jar stand. There can be no doubt that, in the history of the design of large containers for transport, the introduction of the pointed based vessel represents quite a technological revolution.

By reason of its shape, its method of manufacture, and its functional superiority, the Canaanite jar is thus a complete innovation to the region at the beginning of the Middle Bronze Age. In this it is no different, of course, from the majority of the other vessels in the MB I ceramic repertoire: the carinated bowls, ring based jugs, pinched mouthed juglets and piriform juglets are, as has often been pointed out, all new forms at this time. It is this new ceramic repertoire which has provided the point of departure for all discussions of the cultural, ethnic and political history of Palestine in the early second millennium, particularly by Kenyon (1966), who has concluded that the re-establishment now of urban civilization in Palestine, following the non-urban EB – MB interlude, was the result of the arrival of new groups of people most closely linked (on pottery evidence) with, and therefore probably emanating from, coastal Syria, though contacts with inland Syria also are not denied. Other scholars (e.g. Albright, 1933, p. 69; Mazar, 1968, p. 69) have emphasized more these inland, north-eastern, connections, and have linked the re-population of Palestine with the continuing expansion of the Amorites. But in none of these discussions has the course of events in coastal Syria itself been adequately described, or the suddenness with which the new MB I pottery appears here, no less than in Palestine, explained. It is not the purpose of the present paper to deal with this broader question; the Canaanite jar is its sole concern. But, in view of the sometimes injudicious manner in which archaeologists tend to equate changes in material culture with historically significant

G

events, it is perhaps worth stressing that at the beginning of the second millennium in the Levant the changes in the pottery repertoire are so complete that here, if at all, we are surely justified in interpreting them as reflecting some rather drastic developments in the political and ethnic situation. Thus, a search for the origin of the Canaanite jar must be made and, if successful, cannot help but throw light on wider historical matters.

In view of the close commercial connections known to have existed during the Old Kingdom and again at the beginning of the Middle Kingdom between Egypt and the Levant, it is only natural that we should look first to the Nile Valley in our search for possible antecedents of the Canaanite jar. The analogies we find are, in fact, not unimpressive. The pointed based ovoid storage jar is a type with a long history in Egypt; Petrie (1953) illustrates a range of Early Dynastic forms, while similar vessels are shown on reliefs from, for example, the Fifth Dynasty tomb of Ti (conveniently illustrated in Vandier, 1964, Fig. 128) and the Eleventh Dynasty tomb of Aashayt (Michalowski, 1968, Fig. 271). The type is straighter and narrower than the Canaanite jar however, has a lower neck, and is always without handles. It is this lack of handles on the native Egyptian jar which Grace (1956, pp. 82–3) suggests was the reason for the later popularity in the Nile Valley of the handled Canaanite jar; though it should be noted that not all of the latter, at least in their homeland, did have handles (e.g. Tufnell, 1958, p. 221 and Plate 87). Despite these differences, the Egyptian third millennium jar is sufficiently close to the jar appearing in the Levant at the beginning of the second millennium to suggest some relationship. Moreover, some of the later third millennium Egyptian jars seem to have been made in much the same way as the Canaanite vessels; to quote Hayes (1953, Part I, p. 147): "in addition to having been turned on the potter's wheel, [they] have had their lower parts scraped or whittled to shape with an edged tool – a technique especially common during the First Intermediate period and the Middle Kingdom". Many of the Canaanite jars in the Institute's collection exhibit vertical scorings on their lower parts which testify to a precisely similar technique of "whittling" after being thrown on the wheel.

Tempting though it may be at first sight to see an Egyptian origin for the Canaanite jar, however, the truth seems to be otherwise, since by far the closest analogies to its form come from the other end of the Fertile Crescent, from southern Mesopotamia. At Nippur the jar designated Type 19B in the Oriental Institute's publication (McGown et al., 1967, Plate 87) is extremely close in general shape, especially in having a pronounced neck and thickened, sometimes profiled, rim.

The type is always handleless, however, and is somewhat smaller than all but the smallest Canaanite vessels. It is not clear from the accompanying descriptions whether the Nippur jars are wheel-made; the drawings suggest that they are. The Mesopotamian parallels cited in the report are all from sites in the southern part of the country (the Diyala, Kish, Tello, Warka, and Ur), and nothing as close seems to be published from the north. An identical jar form is known at Mari, however, from the palace (Parrot, 1959, p. 122 and Fig. 87, nos. 895 and 897). In the north, large round (rather than pointed) based jars are found at Tepe Gawra Level VI (Speiser, 1935, Vol. I, Plate LXX, no. 142, etc.) and Tell Billa Stratum V (Speiser, 1933, Plate LV, no. 3). The Nippur jars are shown on Table II in the publication (McGown *et al.*, 1967, opposite p. 77) to have a chronological range of from sometime after the beginning of the Ur III period until well into the Isin-Larsa period, with the greatest number of examples apparently coming from towards the end of Ur III; approximate dates would thus be c. 2075 – c. 1850 BC, with a concentration in the final few decades of the third millennium. The basis for this dating is, to be sure, fragile; McGown *et al.*, (1967, p. 74) notes the inadequacies of the relevant epigraphic evidence, while a glance at the sections published on Plates 66, 67 and 78 of the report is enough to illustrate the inadequacies of the stratigraphic control of the excavations. In the absence of anything better, however, the Nippur evidence must be accepted, and – if a date of sometime after 2000 BC for the beginning of the MB I period in the Levant is also accepted* – then it would seem that the southern Mesopotamian

* Mazar (1968) and Wright (1971, p. 289) suggest a date in the twentieth century, Kenyon (1966, p. 13) a date in the second half of the nineteenth, and Albright (1965, p. 57) circa 1800 BC. All of these dates are open to criticism, since they are based on a number of wholly unproven assumptions: first, that the revival of urban life in Palestine and coastal Syria was a reflection in some way of Egypt's renewed vigour at the beginning of the Twelfth Dynasty; second, that the Palestinian MB I pottery is chronologically closely linked with that of the Byblos Royal Tombs; and third, that the amount of material known from the MB I period does not allow for its constituting more than a short prelude to the following MB II (MB II B–C) period, commencing in the eighteenth century. Each of these assumptions can be contested, and in view of the increasing evidence that Byblos was in contact with both Egypt and Mesopotamia during the EB–MB period (corresponding to the First Inter-mediate and the Ur III periods) (e.g. Ward, 1971; Tufnell and Ward, 1966) and of the fact that the metallic version of the MB I carinated bowls was already in use before the end of the third millennium (Tufnell and Ward, 1966), it might be suggested that 2000 BC is by no means too early a date for the commencement of MB I, at least on the coast. However, it remains true that the earliest dated Canaanite jars are those in the Royal Tombs, which Albright has convincingly shown to be of the eighteenth century.

pointed based storage jar appeared at least seventy-five years or so earlier than did the Canaanite version, while the Gawra and Billa jars (if they be related) suggest that the Mesopotamian type had roots going back even earlier, into the Akkad period.

The Canaanite jar thus seems, on present evidence, to be derived from a very similar type of vessel in use somewhat earlier in southern Mesopotamia. This conclusion agrees with the view expressed years ago by Albright (1933, p. 69) that the carinated bowls of the Palestinian Middle Bronze Age were also of Mesopotamian origin, and it strongly suggests that a good part of the cultural, and probably ethnic, stimulus which was felt in the Levant at the beginning of the second millennium and which soon resulted in the revival of town life in Palestine came from this direction. It may well have been, as Kenyon supposes (1966, pp. 7–9), that the immediate source of the influences bearing on Palestine was the Syrian coast, but the roots of the new civilization, and the original homes of the new immigrants, are more likely to have been in the east. For this reason it would, perhaps, be more accurate to refer to the "Canaanite" jar as the "Amorite" jar.

Yet the conventional term is in fact the more appropriate, since it was, after all, the Canaanites who carried the new pointed based jar around the Eastern Mediterranean in their ships, and were thus responsible for its wide popularity and its long life. Its popularity was no doubt due to its functional excellence (as we have seen) and to the fact that in Egypt, at least, one of Canaan's most important customers, the vessel was of a familiar and well-proved design. What is perhaps surprising is that the pointed based jar, in its new Canaanite form, did not apparently spread eastwards, back to its original homeland, despite the close commercial contacts between the Levant and Mesopotamia during the second millennium. It may have been that the jar was considered particularly suitable for sea-transport; but it would be interesting to know what containers were used for the well documented trade in wine and essences from Syria to Mesopotamia, especially in the Old Babylonian period. This, and other problems concerning the use and development of storage vessels remain to be investigated, and no better place for the start of such an investigation could be found than in the Palestinian collection of the Institute of Archaeology.

References

Amiran, R. (1960). *Israel Exploration Journal* **10**, 204–25.
Albright, W. F. (1933). *Annual A.S.O.R.* **XIII**, New Haven.

Albright, W. F. (1965). *In* "Chronologies in Old World Archaeology" (R. W. Ehrich, ed.), pp. 47–60, University of Chicago Press, Chicago.

Braidwood, R. J. and Braidwood, L. S. (1960). "Excavations in the Plain of Antioch" Vol. I. University of Chicago Press, Chicago.

Grace, V. G. (1956). *In* "The Aegean and the Near East. Studies presented to Hetty Goldman" (S. S. Weinberg, ed.). Augustin, New York.

Hayes, W. C. (1953). "The Scepter of Egypt" Part I. Harvard University Press.

Hennessy, J. B. (1967). "The Foreign Relations of Palestine during the Early Bronze Age". Quaritch, London.

Kenyon, K. M. (1966). "Palestine in the Middle Bronze Age". *C.A.H.*, (revised edn, fascicle 48).

Mazar, B. (1968). *Israel Exploration Journal* **18**, 65–97.

McGown, D. E., Haines, R. C. and Hansen, D. P. (1967). "Nippur" Vol. I. University of Chicago Press, Chicago.

Michalowski, K. (1968). "The Art of Ancient Egypt". Abrams, New York.

Parrot, A. (1959). "Mission Archéologique de Mari. Le Palais: Documents et Monuments" Vol. 11/3. Geuthner, Paris.

Petrie, W. F. (1953). "Corpus of Proto-Dynastic Pottery". British School of Egyptian Archaeology, London.

Schaeffer, C. F. A. (1962). "Ugaritica IV". Geuthner, Paris.

Speiser, E. A. (1933). *Museum Journal*, **23**, 249–83.

Speiser, E. A. (1935). "Excavations at Tepe Gawra", Vol. I. A.S.O.R., Philadelphia.

Tufnell, O. (1958). "Lachish" Vol. IV. Oxford University Press, London.

Tufnell, O. (1962). *Bull. Inst. Arch.*, **3**, 1–37.

Tufnell, O. (1969). *Berytus* **XVIII**, 5–33.

Tufnell, O. and Ward, W. A. (1966). *Syria* **XLIII**, 166–241.

Vandier, J. (1964). "Manuel d'Archéologie Egyptienne" Tome IV. Picard, Paris.

Ward, W. A. (1971). "Egypt and the East Mediterranean World, 2200–1900 BC". A.U.B., Beirut.

Wright, G. E. (1971). *J.A.O.S.* **91**, 276–93.

Early Vaulting in Mesopotamia

E. E. D. M. OATES

ELEVEN PAST AND PRESENT members of the Institute, from three Departments, have served at various times during the past eight years on the excavations at Tell al Rimah in Northern Iraq. This note concerns one aspect of our discoveries that is of more than local Mesopotamian interest, and is offered to Professor Grimes in recognition of the help and encouragement that he has given to both staff and students to undertake fieldwork overseas.

The Site and its Buildings

The site of Tell al Rimah was chosen for excavation in the hope that it would throw light on the history of Mesopotamia in the second millennium BC; it has in fact proved to be a city, Karanā, that played some part in the complex politics of Hammurapi's time, and has yielded a sequence of material covering much of the second millennium. Preliminary reports have been published in *Iraq* (Oates, 1965, 1966, 1967, 1968, 1970, 1972). An unexpected result has been a considerable addition to our knowledge of architecture and building techniques in the traditional Mesopotamian material, unbaked mud-brick.

About 1800 BC the site, hitherto a large village or small town, was deliberately enlarged, surrounded by fortifications and endowed with a monumental temple. This building programme must have been sponsored by some outside patron, probably the contemporary king of Assyria, Shamshi-Adad I, for it required not only a large labour force but the services of skilled architects trained in the Babylonian tradition. The earlier settlement, which stood on a mound some 100 m in diameter and 6 m high – the débris of occupation from at least 5000 BC onwards – became the platform on which the great temple was founded. It was approached by a free-standing stair carried on vaults, and from its roof further stairs or ramps led to a high terrace, perhaps surmounted by another shrine; the whole three or four-tiered structure must have resembled a ziggurrat. The temple itself, on its platform high above the city, was laid out on the Babylonian plan and decorated in a style that also has southern parallels, although as a complete system of ornament it is unique. All the external and the courtyard façades were adorned with engaged columns, set singly or in groups, 277 in all; the 50 large columns were built of carved bricks, laid in complicated patterns to represent spirals or palm trunks. Although the temple and high terrace were eventually completed, minor aspects of the scheme were not and it seems that subsequent maintenance was beyond the means of the community. Substantial repairs were carried out on one occasion, probably about 1700 BC, but thereafter the buildings decayed slowly, although the shrine remained in use until the town was abandoned about 1200 BC. The rise in floor levels that took place with the accumulation of débris over the centuries helped to preserve the lower parts of the temple and it still stands in places up to 10 m high, thus affording us a unique opportunity to observe the method of roofing employed, at least in the lower storey.

The presence of this massive complex effectively prevented any investigation of the earlier settlement beneath, but the edge of the third millennium deposit was visible at several points on the southern and western slopes of the mound where caves had been dug early in this century to provide seasonal shelter for herdsmen and their flocks. In 1968 we decided to investigate these levels by cutting a trench through two caves on the south slope; against the disadvantage of working in disturbed ground we expected the benefit of a large stratigraphic exposure for comparatively little time and money. We found ourselves in the heart of an elaborate structure of at least three storeys, built against the slope of the mound, which even in the third millennium had a relatively steep profile. It was evidently designed to support a terrace or building on the edge of the settlement. No trace of the superstructure remained, but it is the building techniques used in the foundations that are of interest here; they are dated by associated pottery to the end of the third millennium, two or three centuries earlier than the Great Temple.

Building Techniques

The most startling feature of the construction of the Great Temple was the widespread use of vaulting. The stair that led up to it from the city was carried on three vaults of progressively increasing height (Oates, 1968, Plate XXXI), and within the building vaults were employed to roof many if not all of the ground floor rooms. In some cases the evidence is lacking, notably in rooms approached through wide doorways in one or both of the long walls; these doorways were almost certainly arched, and we may suspect that the builders preferred to avoid the problems of intersecting arches and vaults by using the traditional Mesopotamian flat ceiling of mud and matting supported on timber in these chambers. We cannot assume, however, that any problem was beyond their capacity, for they displayed considerable virtuosity in the use of vaulting to support the upper flight of stairs within the temple that led to the second storey (Oates, 1967, Plate XXXIV). Here, spanning a ground floor room some 8 m long, we found a series of eight transverse vaults of increasing height, each supporting two treads of the mud-brick stair above.

The construction of these vaults requires little comment, for they were all of the familiar pattern with voussoirs laid radially. The bricks are of the standard size (33–34 cm^2, and averaging 9 cm thick) employed in the temple walls, and are not tapered, the interstices being filled with mud mortar of the same composition as the bricks. The unusual feature of the vaults to a modern eye is their high-pitched profile, of which a characteristic example is shown on Fig. 1. The first few courses above the spring are gradually corbelled outwards, and thereafter the voussoirs are turned at an angle which permits each to be supported by its predecessor and the adhesion of the mud mortar until the gap has narrowed to approximately half its original span; thus only the crown of the vault needs the support of scaffolding. This was obviously intended to economize in the use of timber, but the shortage of timber is a fact of Mesopotamian life that probably dictated the adoption of this method long before we find it at Tell al Rimah. In general, the builders of the temple display a familiarity with their techniques and material that can only derive from a long tradition. An example of this, particularly convincing because it occurs in an inconspicuous position, is the head of an internal doorway that still stands to its full height (Fig. 1). Doorways of this size in ancient and modern buildings are usually spanned by timber lintels, often of poplar which is readily available in the locality. Here, however, the mason has chosen to build a flat arch, a feature which one would have thought impossible to execute in unsupported mud-brick but which has survived for almost four thousand years.

Radial brick vaults were standard throughout the buildings of the original complex, and were also employed in the only major reconstruction about a century later. Clearly the structural tradition that they represent continued at Tell al Rimah for a few generations

G*

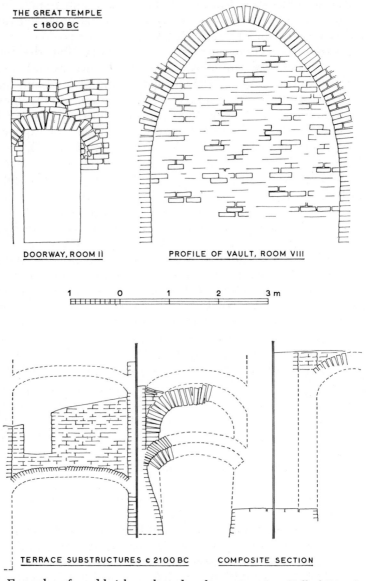

THE GREAT TEMPLE
c 1800 BC

DOORWAY, ROOM II   PROFILE OF VAULT, ROOM VIII

1   0   1   2   3 m

TERRACE SUBSTRUCTURES c 2100 BC   COMPOSITE SECTION

Fig. 1. Examples of mud-brick vault and arch construction, Tell al Rimah, late
third and early second millennium BC.

after its brief moment of grandeur. There was, however, another
tradition of vault construction used in work that is more likely to
have been executed by local masons, and our earliest example of this
is found in the terrace substructures in the south slope of the mound;

a composite section through this building is illustrated at the bottom of Fig. 1. It was a honeycomb of small vaulted chambers, accessible through low doorways opening off narrow passages, and at least three storeys high. The plan (Oates, 1970, Plate VIII) lacked regularity, since the builders obviously laid out the main lines of the supports required at the upper level and filled in the intervening space with a series of more or less flimsy structures erected by rule of thumb and taking advantage of earlier masonry where it existed. We were immediately reminded of the substructures of the Great Palace of the Byzantine Emperors in Istanbul (Talbot Rice, 1958, Fig. 14 and Plates 5–7), where a very similar though much larger system of vaulted chambers was employed to terrace the slope of the site over-looking the Bosphorus in the fifth century AD. The resemblance, moreover, extends beyond the common feature of terracing by a system of vaults to the detail of the distinctive method of vaulting employed.

This is commonly known as "pitched-brick" vaulting, in which the need for wooden centring is virtually eliminated by laying successive rings of bricks with their edges across the long axis of the vault; the laying starts from both ends simultaneously, and each ring is inclined at a slight angle to rest on its predecessor, which supports it during construction. When the rings meet in the middle, there remains a lozenge-shaped gap in the crown of the vault that is then filled with ring segments of diminishing size and finally plugged with brick fragments. This is the method employed in the Great Palace, but at Tell al Rimah there are significant refinements. Whereas the Byzantine builders began their construction by carry-ing the end walls of the chamber to a greater height than the side walls and resting incurving triangles of brickwork against them to support the first complete ring, their Mesopotamian predecessors started from the same level on all four walls and built shallow pendentives to carry the ends of the vault. One complete example of this type has survived and is illustrated in plan and section on Fig. 2. In another version (Oates, 1970, Plate VIa) which survives only in an incomplete form, the pitched-brick rings were apparently omitted and the pendentives were continued inwards until they met and interlocked. In both types the vaulting bricks are much smaller (24 cm² by 4 cm) than those in the walls and arches, and in some cases are keyed with diagonal finger grooves. Most of the vaults in our structure were surprisingly flat in profile, and were presumably not required to carry heavy loads although the spaces between them were certainly accessible and may have been used for storage. But

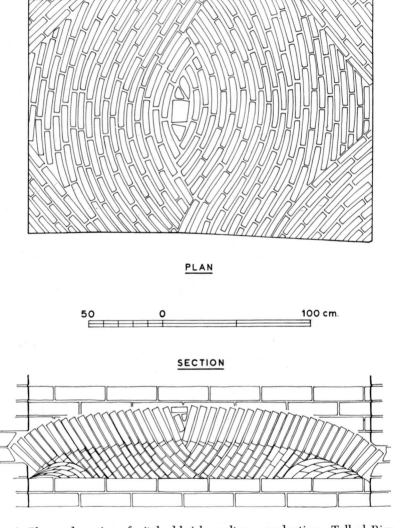

PLAN

50   0   100 cm.

SECTION

Fig. 2. Plan and section of pitched-brick vault on pendentives, Tell al Rimah,
late third millennium BC.

on occasion the builders had to employ a higher curvature to over-
ride an arch at one end of a passage and the pendentives then
assume the familiar modern profile. It is worthy of remark that the
arches used in walls that presumably outline the load-bearing structure are of the conventional radial type (Fig. 1, Section).

Historical Connections

We cannot yet place these discoveries in historical perspective, since we have no evidence from the great cities where major developments in architecture are likely to have taken place. The Great Temple at Tell al Rimah was a derivative building, following in ideal form a plan which had been developed in the cities of Sumer and Babylonia under the Third Dynasty of Ur, and probably designed by southern architects. We may reasonably assume that the radial brick vaults employed in it were a common feature of late third and early second millennium construction wherever these architects worked, and that the unique evidence for them at Tell al Rimah is an accident of survival attributable to the fact that the town, when thrown back on its own resources, could not afford to maintain – still less to replace – its principal temple as was the custom in wealthier and more populous centres. It is unlikely that any major architectural innovation would have been tried for the first time in a country town, and the wide variety of uses to which the radial vault was put argues that the builders had a long familiarity with its potential. With this in mind we may even postulate a continuous tradition of vaulting in free-standing structures – there are many examples of its use below ground – that goes back at least to the earliest known example at Tepe Gawra in the fourth millennium (Speiser, 1935, Plate XXIVa). There is no doubt that in the third millennium three techniques of vaulting were in simultaneous use – radial, pitched-brick and corbelling – and it may be that the adoption of radial vaults in monumental architecture should be attributed to the school of architects that arose under the patronage of the kings of the Third Dynasty of Ur and perhaps their Akkadian predecessors, from about 2350 BC onwards.

The later history of radial vaulting is not well documented. We know that it was employed in the reconstruction of the Rimah temple in the early seventeenth century and in the store-rooms of the Kassite palace at Aqar Quf some two centuries later (Baqir, 1945, Figs. 18, 19), though in this instance the vaults are much lower in pitch. We may assume that the technique was not lost, since many Late Assyrian reliefs of the ninth to seventh centuries BC show the characteristic high-pitched profile on the gate arches of besieged cities. But the vault was not extensively used in the great palaces and temples of this time, in which the main reception rooms were up to ten metres wide and massive timbers, often cedars of Lebanon, were available to the builders as part of the tribute of the Assyrian Empire. By the sixth century the radial vault had been translated into baked brick, probably in Babylonia where the use of this material as a structural element, rather than a protective surface, seems to have originated; both arch and vault now approximate to the classical semi-circular profile (e.g. the "Hanging Gardens" at Babylon, Koldewey, 1914, Fig. 62).

On the subject of pitched-brick vaulting we are little better informed. Again the variety and familiarity with the technique evinced in the terrace substructures at Tell al Rimah argue a considerable period of development but, as we have already pointed out, the pitched-brick vault appears to have been used above ground not in monumental buildings designed by architects, but in more flimsy structures that would have been erected by local builders. This is borne out by the later evidence from Tell al Rimah (Oates, 1970, p. 21), where pitched-brick vaults are found from the seventeenth to the fourteenth centuries BC, always in contexts that suggest the obvious and easy method of roofing a small room. It is especially revealing that when, in the fifteenth century, it was found necessary to replace the radial vault in one of the rooms of the temple, now sadly diminished in size and importance, a pitched-brick vault was inserted at a lower level (Oates, 1966, Plate XXIa). The only technical change that took place during the second millennium was, as far as we know, a simplification; the use of pendentives was abandoned in favour of the simple vault in which the rings of brickwork rested against the end walls. It would not be safe to assume that the earlier expertise had been lost. Very few of the relatively unimportant buildings that might have been roofed in this way would survive to the height from which the vault sprang, and the residential areas of Mesopotamian sites on which they could occur have been largely neglected by excavators concerned to justify their expenditure by more spectacular discoveries. We certainly cannot claim that the Mesopotamian invention of the pendentive in the third millennium BC influenced its use as the standard method of supporting a dome in later Roman and Byzantine architecture. On the other hand the simple version of the pitched-brick vault, for which there is no evidence in Mesopotamian buildings of the Late Assyrian and Neo-Babylonian periods, clearly survived as a domestic building technique that was later translated into baked brick and employed in monumental architecture. Ward Perkins (1958) has shown that its use in Constantinople in the fifth century AD derived from earlier Near Eastern prototypes, and the classic Mesopotamian example is the Arch of Ctesiphon, the principal reception hall in the winter palace of the Sassanid kings, built in the sixth century AD. There can be no doubt of a continuous tradition in the basic technique, and it

is doubly interesting that one of the parallels cited from Roman
Egypt by Ward Perkins (1958, Fig. 20B) shows a pitched-brick vault
in mud-brick, supported on shallow pendentives and virtually
identical with the late third millennium example illustrated in Fig. 2
from Tell al Rimah.

Obviously we cannot suggest a direct tradition linking these two
structures, so far apart in time and space. The common factor is the
use of sun-dried, moulded mud-brick as a building material which is
both cheap enough to replace timber for roofing, especially in arid
regions, and far more flexible in the shapes that can be achieved. It
lacks the structural strength of mortared rubble or concrete, but its
durability is remarkable. Both its characteristics and its place in the
history of architecture deserve more study than they have yet
received.

References

Baqir, T. (1945). "Iraq Government Excavations at Aqar Quf", *Iraq Sup-*
plement, London.
Koldewey, R. (1914). "The Excavations at Babylon", Macmillan, London.
Oates, D. (1965). *Iraq* **27**, 62–80.
Oates, D. (1966). *Iraq* **28**, 122–39.
Oates, D. (1967). *Iraq* **29**, 70–96.
Oates, D. (1968). *Iraq* **30**, 115–38.
Oates, D. (1970). *Iraq* **32**, 1–26.
Oates, D. (1972). *Iraq* **34**, 77–86.
Speiser, E. A. (1935). "Excavations at Tepe Gawra", Vol. 1, University of
Pennsylvania Press, Philadelphia.
Talbot Rice, D. (1958). "The Great Palace of the Byzantine Emperors,
Second Report", Edinburgh.
Ward Perkins, J. B. (1958) in "The Great Palace of the Byzantine
Emperors, Second Report" (D. Talbot Rice, ed.), pp. 52–104, Univer-
sity Press, Edinburgh.

Preliminary Report of the Environmental Archaeological Survey of Tell Fara, 1972

D. PRICE WILLIAMS

THE FOLLOWING REPORT is a preliminary statement of the findings of a largely British team working for the month of July 1972, in the area around Tell Fara South, Sharuhen, in the Nahal Basor (Wadi Ghuzzeh), Israel. (Fig .1).

Theory

In principle, it was intended to undertake an interdisciplinary study of a specific area, to examine its ancient and modern topography, its present and its past botanical material, the chemical and mechanical construction of its soils, its hydrological and erosional history and the extent, distribution and dates of its ancient sites. The aim of such a study would be to provide a background, in depth, to the ecology and positioning of archaeological sites in the area, to try to understand their inter-relationship and their economic potential.

The Tell Fara region was chosen for a number of reasons : (a) It lay in a truly marginal agricultural area, evidenced by its annual rainfall and the unwillingness of the Israeli authorities to consider giving drought insurance for annual crops at this point. As such, minor fluctuations of climate or local problems of land utilization would have a critical effect upon Neolithic and post-Neolithic man and undoubtedly have affected the usage of the area by pre-Neolithic populations. (b) Geologically the area was interesting from its exposures as part of the wadi drainage system, and afforded opportunities for study of the stratigraphy of geological material and the construction of terraces. (c) Botanically it would be possible to make a collection of material both of the wadi flora and that of this semi-arid zone. Only the time of year here would affect the result. (d) It is dominated by a major Bronze Age site, Tell Fara (Petrie, 1930), but earlier sites

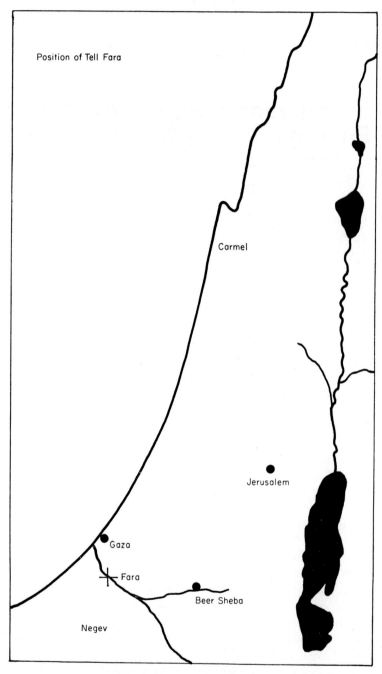

Fig. 1. Position of Tell Fara.

in the form of Chalcolithic (Macdonald, 1932), and later in the form of Roman and Byzantine have previously been reported; even pre-historic material was suspected by people such as Petrie, who had recovered such material from the wadi.

It became obvious during the survey that in every respect the area was both filled with data of every discipline and that this was the sort of data necessary to conduct the proposed study. As a result, only a small area has been imperfectly surveyed. While it had been hoped to cover an area from Tell Fara north-west along the wadi to the Shellal Bridge, an area some 1·5 km square was thought by all disciplines to be sufficiently absorbing.

Geomorphology

Aims

The geomorphological work of the survey was more general and preliminary than detailed and quantitative. The intention was to examine the landforms and sediments and their relationship to ancient sites in the vicinity and to see whether such a study might contribute to an understanding of the distribution, siting or environment of ancient settlement. Even in the short time during which we have been working this proposition has been amply proved and, indeed, it is now difficult to see how settlement could be studied in the area except on such a basis.

The area which it was originally intended to survey included the Tell and its immediate environs, and the riverine slopes as far north as the Shellal Bridge. This area was walked over in the search for sites, but the complexity of the landforms and of the sediments meant that only a very much smaller area was studied in any detail.

Geology

The lowest exposed rocks in the neighbourhood comprise a series of cross-bedded and loosely cemented fossil dunes. These emerged on headlands on both sides of the wadi and appear to underlie at least part of the loess. Along the right bank of the wadi for a distance of approximately a kilometre opposite and north of the tell, they are very much lower and covered by a bed of gravel and cobbles. This bed slopes down to the present wadi level almost without interruption and appears to form a slip-off slope in one of the inside bends of the wadi's incised meander system. Both the sandstone and the gravel contains rocks of many different lithologies; some of the cobbles of harder rock show signs of beach-battering and may there-fore be of marine origin. Overlying all except the highest sandstone is a thick deposit of loess the upper levels of which form the country surface throughout the area, (Fig. 4). Loess deposition appears to have been discontinuous and there are several phases of reworking and of soil formation within the column (Reifenberg, 1947).

Drainage and Erosion

In the region as a whole there is said to be a general westward migration of wadis, but little evidence of such a movement can be found near Tell Fara. Early sites were found undisturbed fairly close to its eastern bank and the Roman revetment wall (Petrie, 1930) which runs along the eastern foot of the tell slope has nowhere been seriously breached by the wadi nor, interestingly enough, does the present level of the wadi lie anywhere more than a metre or so below the lower courses of the wall, indicating that there has been little general down-cutting since its construction.

There is one well-marked terrace some 500 m north of the tell, at present covered by dense growth of tamarisk. It stands about 2 m high and consists entirely of fine sand and finer grade material. Its position and height at first suggest that it belongs to the group of "Mediaeval" terraces commonly found along Mediterranean rivers, but since it stands at the focus of a number of actively eroding side wadis, and since its composition includes no gravels, it seems more likely that it is in the nature of an alluvial fan, partly dissected by the main wadi.

Some 500 m north of the tell, on the right bank, lies an extensive area of "badlands" caused by linear erosion of the loess surface down to the wadi level, (Fig. 4). This area, rather more than 500 m square, comprises a tangled morphology of great complexity and appears to represent several phases of erosion (Evenari et al., 1971). It is in this area that the history of loess deposition, erosion and reworking is more clearly demonstrated, and the presence of several sites of differ-ent ages enables a picture to be built up, however incompletely, of the relationship between settlement and landforming processes over a considerable period of time. The lowest series of the loess appears to consist of some metres of more or less homogeneous silts, fairly horizontal in the north-south plane and dipping very gently to the west. Within this series, or more likely upon a surface cut in this series, lies Site B, (Fig. 5) described elsewhere. It lies in the lower levels of an east-west ridge and the strata both below it and above run more or less parallel with each other. Although extensive excavation and redeposition of the strata is conceivable, there are no obvious signs of processes nearby, and the simplest explanation of its position is that it occupied a fairly temporary surface of accumulation formed when the loess stood at that level. There are no signs of deep weathering or of soil formation on this surface so it is unlikely to have been of very long standing. The general horizontality and lack of filled gullies at these levels seem to indicate a depositional rather than an erosional phase. The contemporary position of the wadi, assuming that it existed, is more speculative. The indications are that it must have followed more or less its present course, i.e. south-north. There is no wadi trace running in any other direction than the present unless it ran through the badlands themselves. Elsewhere the gravels are unbreached (and these underlie the loess) and within the badlands the general agreement of the loess strata in dip and position make such a course unlikely. The westward limit of the ancient wadi line is limited by the position of the Tell with its Roman revetment and MB II remains, and the eastward by Site B itself (which is certainly undisturbed Middle Palaeolithic). There need, of course, have been no wadi at all, but the presence of the latter site and its neighbours indicated some nearby source of water, and the sorting and redeposition of strata close above the site horizon indicated a drainage pattern of some sort. Above the site deposition continues and there are exposures of undisturbed, resorted and weathered aeolian material. At a very few places towards the bottom of the column there are lines of gravels in depositional channels, indicating that at those levels some higher source, presumably the gravel beds or the sandstones, were available. In a number of horizons there are heavily oxidized and weathered bands, some apparently *in situ* and others derived. Samples from these and other strata have been taken though not yet analysed, but superficially at least these bands are very similar in texture and appearance to seasonally arid weathered tropical soils. At all events they seem to represent considerable pauses in the process of loess deposition.

Within the badlands area there are several residual blocks rising almost to the elevation of the surrounding country surface. On a number of these grouped approximately 400 m east of Site B lie traces of an extensive Roman/Byzantine settlement, Site C. There are no signs of stratification apart from a cistern, described elsewhere, but many sherds occur on the upper surface and down the slopes showing that the site originally stood at least as high as that surface.

Limits were thus set by the two sites to the major part of the period of loess deposition.

A striking feature of the area is that nowhere, at least on a super-

ficial examination, could be found any trace of erosion channels subsequently re-filled by loess. The pattern of deeply eroded channels
and gullies existing at present is therefore either very modern, comprising only a single phase, or else very enduring. In other words,
ancient gullies lay approximately along the tracks of modern gullies.
Since there are many traces of terraces and benches within the system
this explanation is far more likely. It is not yet possible to define with
certainty the limits, let alone the ages, of erosional and depositional
phases, but some pointers do exist. The earliest phase of erosion
following the deposition of the country surface remains as an accord-
ant bench running across the whole area apart from the residuals. It
is now represented by the tops of ridges running down to focus on
the wadi. The slope and direction of a number of these ridges were
measured and by constructing overlapping profiles, or by computing
regression surfaces, it may be possible to estimate within reasonable
limits the height and position of the wadi floor during this erosional
phase. Below this is one, and probably more, surface running up to
residuals in pediments, lightly coated with subsequent deposits.
Much detailed levelling will be necessary before it is possible to
say how many phases are represented by these pediments. It is interesting to note that these suggest, on a miniature scale, an inselberg-
and-pediment morphology of the sub-Saharan type. These pediments
were breached by a gulley system which has also cut through depositional levels left by earlier phases, and this system, now represented
by fairly wide, steep-sided gullies with depositional floors, has in
recent years been intensively gullied by the present phase of severe
linear erosion. The present phase cuts not only through previous terraces and benches but is now excavating deeply into the country
surface and into undisturbed basal levels, (for a section through the
whole area, see Fig. 3). The history of the more recent phases is
rendered more difficult of interpretation by the presence of silt dams
across the mouths of several of the side wadis. These have all been
breached by the most recent erosional phases and their contained
deposits deeply gullied, but great caution is necessary in measuring
wadi-floor deposits because of these man-made features.

Prognosis

From the samples and measurements which have been taken this
year it should be possible to determine the size, distribution and
chemical composition of the more obvious deposits, and especially
to estimate the degree of leaching, oxidation and soil formation
within the apparent "buried soils". Since there is a vertical series of

these deposits, comparison of one with another might give a valuable insight into the different climatic and surface conditions through the period of their formation. Pollen analysis and the examination of macroscopic plant remains may prove to be the most valuable means of reconstructing the ancient environments, although great caution will be necessary in the interpretation of the results both because of dearth of comparative material and because of the inherent distortions in the pollen spectrum of sub-arid deposits.

Much could be learned from the careful measurement of the slope and areal extent of fossil erosional and depositional surfaces in the area. It might be possible to reconstruct the erosional and depositional history of the wadi and perhaps to throw some light on the vexed question of the different conditions necessary for lateral and linear erosion. Comparison with present-day conditions, on which much work has been done, might also help to evaluate past regimes, as might lithological examination and stone-counts of the present wadi-gravels and the upper slip-off slopes.

Botanical Work

Aims and Methods

The main object of the botanical work was to make as complete a qualitative collection as possible of the surface flora of the survey area. The area south-east of the tell to the Shellal Bridge was first examined in order to ensure that the plants collected were representative. Plants were pressed in the field wherever possible, using lattice presses supplied by the Herbarium at Kew, and records were kept of their habitats. Where the material was considered unsuitable for pressing it was preserved in airtight containers in a solution containing 50 parts alcohol (metholated spirits), 50 parts water, 10 parts glycerol and 30 ml formalin per litre. A comprehensive collection of fruits and seeds was made to enable comparisons between these and plant remains found during the course of excavations. When dry, the material was collected in airtight tubes; when moist, the preserving fluid was again used. Small samples from the secondary wood of branches of trees in the area were taken, both for diagnostic purposes and for comparison with excavated charcoal fragments. All plant material was then classified.

During the course of this work, it became evident that there was distinct vegetation zoning, as shown on the map (Fig. 2). In an attempt to provide some explanation for this, soil sampling was carried out as follows :

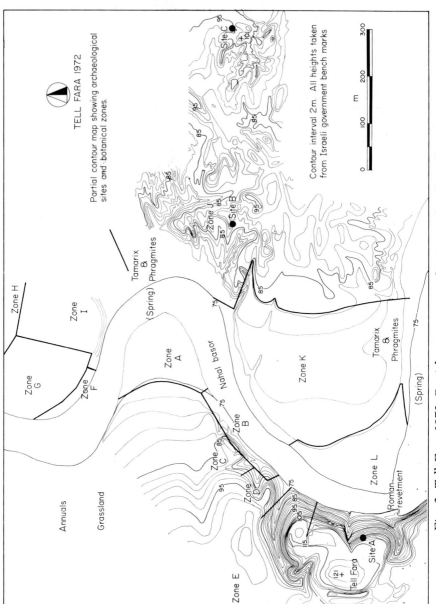

Fig. 2. Tell Fara 1972. Partial contour map showing archaeological sites and botanical zones.

At least three points within each zone were randomly selected and recorded on the area survey map. At each of these approximately 8 ounces of soil was removed, at a depth of 10 cm, and stored in air-tight bags. These were then analysed for the following components:

   i. % coarse material   v. % magnesium oxide
  ii. % fine material   vi. % iron
 iii. % suspended material   vii. % salinity
 iv. % calcium carbonate

Quantitative assessments were made of the vegetation by random sampling of the areas adjacent to the three selected archaeological sites, using a 60 × 60 cm quadrant.

Portions of the laminae of each of the following six grasses were cut and preserved. These were the only undesiccated Gramineae in the area:

Phragmites communis   *Aristida ciliata*
Cynodon dactylon   *Polypogon monspeliensis*
Aristida plumosa   *Echinochloa colonum*

It was hoped that by the later use of sectioning and differential staining techniques the silica in the cellulose cell walls of the epidermal cells could be examined and compared with any silica skeletons appearing in ash layers at the three sites.

Finally, microscope slides covered with a thin film of Vaseline were left exposed for 5½ hours at two selected sites where soil samples had been taken for future palynological studies. Each sample was then sealed with another slide and it was hoped that these would provide a record of aerial pollen grains.

Botany Results

One hundred and seven plant species were collected. This figure was far higher than expected since the rainfall had been high and many annuals, which included a large number of segetal and ruderal species, still survived. Two algae were present; a filamentous species in the spring north of the Tell and *Chara* sp. (Chlorophyceae) – apparently an indication of nitrogen lack – in the spring south-east of the Tell. Four species of lichens were collected, three of which occurred on sandstone outcrops and one on woody caducous *Lycium shaui*. No Bryophytes or Pteridophytes were found. The Gymnosperms were represented solely by *Ephedra campylopoda* (Gnetales). Among the Angiosperms many species of annuals occurred along the edge of the wadi bed where there was still some residual moisture. On the more exposed upper slopes, farthest from the wadi, these plants were quite dead and here accurate identification was impossible. Woody and herbaceous perennials were well represented throughout the area and the majority of these were Irano-Turanian species (Zohary, 1962). Of the woody species chamaephytes were dominant and some of these, particularly plants of *Noëa mucronata* and *Lycium shaui*, appeared dominant and were caducous, apparently to withstand desiccation. Three trees appeared in the area; *Tamarix nilotica*, *Acacia raddiana* and a palm. The *Tamarix*, in conjunction with *Phragmites communis*, apparently formed a vegetational climax along with erosional banks of the wadi. The Angiosperms were classified as follows:

Compositae	20 spp	Geraniaceae	2 spp
Gramineae	11 spp	Hypericaceae	1 sp
Chenopodiaceae	9 spp	Primulaceae	1 sp
Leguminosae	7 spp	Portulacaceae	1 sp
Solanaceae	6 spp	Orobanchaceae	1 sp
Cruciferae	4 spp	Malvaceae	1 sp
Rosaceae	3 spp	Amaranthaceae	1 sp
Scrophulariaceae	3 spp	Zygophyllaceae	1 sp
Boraginaceae	3 spp	Resedaceae	1 sp
Liliaceae	3 spp	Thymelacaceae	1 sp
Caryophyllaceae	3 spp	Plumbaginaceae	1 sp
Ranunculaceae	2 spp	Rutaceae	1 sp
Polygonaceae	2 spp	Aizoaceae	1 sp
Labiatae	2 spp	Ephedraceae	1 sp
Tamaricaceae	2 spp	Plantaginaceae	1 sp
Cyperaceae	2 spp	Cucurbitaceae	1 sp
Euphorbiaceae	2 spp	Dipsaceae	1 sp
Umbelliferae	2 spp		

Both horizontal zones, parallel to the wadi, and vertical zones, at right angles to it, were found to occur. Within each zone dominant species could be clearly distinguished as shown (Fig. 3):-

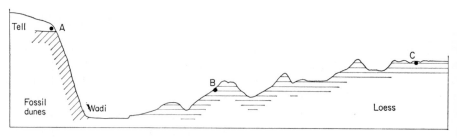

Fig. 3. Schematic section west – east from Site C through B to the Wadi – and from Wadi to south of Tell to A. (Vertical distortion × 4).

ZONE A AND ZONE L
(Both areas sub-   Sandy soil   *Artemisia monosperma*
ject to back   *Achillea fragrantissima*
eddying from   *Phagnalon rupestre*
the wadi.)

ZONE B
Horizontal zone   Sandy Soil   Fairly dense ground cover of
                                         annuals and grasses. *Alhagi
                                         maurorum* was the dominant
                                         perennial

ZONE C
Marginal zone   Sandy soil   *Helianthemum, Aristida,
between B and   Echium angustifolium*
D

ZONE D
Vertical zone   Sandstone   *Helianthemum* with *Noëa,
                                         Ephedra, Retama, Aristida*
                                         and *Echiochilon*

ZONE E
Vertical zone   Greyish spill   *Lycium shaui, Salsola vermi-
                    and mudbrick   culata* and *Mesanbryanthe-
                    débris   mum* where mudbrick débris
                                         occurs

ZONE F
Horizontal zone   Sandy soil   Fairly dense cover of annuals
                                         and grasses with *Haplophyl-
                                         lum* and *Helianthemum*

ZONE G
Vertical zone   Sandstone   *Helianthemum* with *Noëa,
                                         Ephedra, Retama, Aristida*
                                         and *Echiochilon*

ZONE H
Horizontal zone   Sandy loess   Dense cover of annuals and
                                         grasses

ZONE I
Vertical zone   Silt–apparently   Halophytes – *Salsola inermis,*
                      saline   *Anabasis articulata, Atriplex*
                                           halimus

ZONE J
Vertical zone   Silt–apparently   *Salsola* and *Anabasis* and a
                      saline   few grasses

ZONE K
Vertical zone   Sandy soil   Annuals and grasses with
                                           Alhagi and some *Thymelaea*

The pH of the soil in all areas was approximately 8. The other components analysed showed great variation between the zones.

Conclusions

Whilst the large number of plant species was encouraging, since it enabled a fairly comprehensive collection to be made, this was an atypical year with high rainfall and the vegetation would presumably show a marked variation in drier years and in different seasons. A study of the flora earlier in the year would give an indication of the distribution of Monocotyledons other than grasses and it would also enable the many species of grasses and annuals in areas of dense ground cover to be identified. The almost complete lack of lower plants was surprising since in temperate regions Bryophytes and lichens are almost invariably initial colonizers. The scarcity of algae may have been due to the use of Lysol for the control of mosquito larvae. The wadi was sprayed heavily during the course of the survey and may also have had earlier treatments. Presticide residues and detergents were reported previously along the wadi banks and the effect of these, although impossible to evaluate, may have been considerable. The distribution of the trees was unexpected. Most of the Tamarix, with the exception of a few trees at the top of the badlands, were probably not more than 25 years old. *Acacia raddiana,* often recorded as a dominant in reports from the Northern Negev, was represented by only one mature tree to the south of the tell. A possible explanation for this may have been their use for fuel by the Bedouin. A very large number of *Acacia raddiana* seedlings were found on the right bank of the wadi near the South Spring and around the Shellal Bridge. These presumably grew from seed deposited by the wadi and suggested that under natural conditions the tree might still have been a dominant, as it is in the more arid areas to the east (Evenari, 1971).

The vegetational zoning was very marked, probably because the area is one supporting a marginal environment. The horizontal zoning was clearly due primarily to water availability but this did not appear to be the sole nor even the most important factor in the case of the vertical zoning. Here there was apparently an interaction between the mechanical properties of the soil particles and the availability of minerals, since there was a great variation between the amounts of coarse and fine particles, calcium carbonate and magnesium oxide between the zones. Magnetic iron also varied considerably although this would probably not be a major factor affecting plant cover. Zones I and J apparently had a comparatively high saline content (up to 2%), hence their dominant vegetation was halophytic and the plant cover was sparse. These preliminary findings would certainly justify further investigation. Initially, the mineral requirements of the dominants within each zone could be determined by water culture techniques and, subsequently, the capacity of each soil type to adsorb selectively the required ions, could be measured.

Prognosis

Palynological studies in the area seem to present two main problems. Firstly, some of the plants are representatives of families unknown in Britain; thus, a complete collection of present-day pollen should be made as a prelude to pollen analyses of fossil soils. Secondly, in such an area of marginal environment, plant cover is comparatively sparse. Of this cover, two of the families most commonly represented, the Chenopodiaceae and the Gramineae are entirely aneomphilous, as are several of the local Compositae. Any estimate of the actual plant cover at different periods in fossil soils will therefore be impossible, as any results obtained will be very misleading and can only be used for comparative studies.

The quantitative assessment of vegetation must be regarded as very approximate, since at all three sites the plant cover was sparse and largely dead, and the results could not therefore be subjected to analysis.

Archaeology

Site Survey

From material gathered, a number of periods are represented in the area, from Middle Palaeolithic to the present day.

Middle Palaeolithic. Five concentrations of material were found in the area. Of these, three were non-nucleated and probably lowered – *i.e.* their surface had been eroded away – either in antiquity or recently. Two were thought to contain sufficient faunal remains with charcoal to have been *in situ*. Horizons for these could be identified. One of these, Site B, (Fig. 5), was examined in more detail topographically, geomorphologically, botanically and archaeologically in a more detailed surface survey. It appears at this time to be a Levalloisian/Mousterian site typical of Palestine and is comparable to the Levalloisian material found previously in the Negev near Avdat (Marks *et al.*, 1971). The deposit, however, is heavy and apparently stratified and looks more like a living area than a tool manufactory, possibly a semi-permanent butchery-site.

Upper Palaeolithic. Lithic material has been found, never in concentration and never in context, which is Upper Palaeolithic.

Chalcolithic. Despite the heavy concentration of Chalcolithic sites in the region (Macdonald, 1932), many of which were found and recovered, little Chalcolithic material is evident in the 1·5 km square. Certainly none has appeared in context and none of the deposits are in any way comparable to those north-west on the residual loess spur.

Bronze-Iron Age. The Tell itself, from MB II onwards, provides the focus of Bronze Age attention. Early Bronze material also was found, but in no way intact as at Petrie's Site H at the Shellal Bridge (Macdonald, 1932). A step trench was cut into the wadi side of the Tell, Site A (1972) to redefine its stratigraphy, to examine the wadi edge of the Tell to determine erosion and to sample the immediately pre-tell surface.

Roman/Byzantine. Besides the Roman material on the Tell, the remains of an extensive settlement was found, high up above the wadi and about 1·5 km to the east on the country surface. In extent it covered an area about 100 m × 50 m (Site C). All the material had been lowered on to the residual eroded pinnacles, and only the intact remains of a subterranean cistern illustrated the integrity of the deposit. Lower down, in the deep erosional gullies leading to the wadi, the remains of a series of large silt dams were found and are presumed to date to this period because of their size and extent.

Arab. A variety of surface material was noticed from mediaeval Arab pottery to quantities of twentieth century Gaza Black Ware strewn over the whole area. On the topmost scarps of the wadi Bedouin burials were seen to be extruding into the surrounding gullies. They were cut into the country surface to a depth of 1·5 m and covered with flat stones. As this country surface is now being rapidly cut away, they are seen as it were in section.

Modern. The whole area is littered with military débris from Turkish, Mandate and Israeli periods, both in munitions and simple fortifications.

The wealth of material in this apparently barren area is most surprising. There seems no square metre of its surface that is quite sterile.

Site A—Tell Fara

In order to evaluate the Tell deposits, their relation to the wadi and to examine the pre-tell surface, a 75 cm wide stepped trench (four steps) was excavated on the wadi face of the Tell, towards its southern end, (Fig. 2). The total vertical section represented is 5·50 m but in no place do the steps cut vertically more than 1·6 cm into the Tell face.

The Tell face at this point is at an angle of 45° and is covered by an homogeneous diagonal overburden some 60 cm in thickness. This is either the upper Tell deposits sliding over the edge or the remains of Petrie's dump. Eighteen layers of débris were defined above natural, though some late ones have been grouped together for convenience.

The layers are, to all intents and purposes, horizontal and illustrate thus that the Tell has been truncated. Strangely, no structural remains at all were present, all the layers being of ash and mud brick débris, many no more than 10 cm in thickness. Whilst then the Tell deposit may have been curtailed by erosion into the wadi, it seems that structures were never placed as far to the east as this edge, unless the deposit has been removed or replaced by horizontal wash layers, which seems unlikely.

Ceramic was common, though mostly of undiagnostic body sherds. Rims and bases do provide a fairly reasonable record of the construction of these non-occupational layers, from Roman through Iron Age to MB II. This requires more study to determine with certainty, but it would accord with the findings of Petrie (1930).

The Tell site, at this point at least, lies directly upon a sandstone bluff 109·91 m above sea level. The transition between Tell and natural is uninterrupted by any obvious soil layers, fossil or otherwise. A sample of this layer was taken at its upper surface. It was homogeneous to a depth of at least 1·5 m. The prognosis of pollen within this layer is better than at first thought, since a similar sandstone bluff, on the other side of the wadi and directly north of it, now lies fully exposed, yet exhibits considerable plant cover (Botanical Zone B).

As an adjunct to the Tell work, the Roman revetment at the Tell on its south-east corner was examined, and illustrates that the wadi has not seriously undercut the bluff since that period.

Site B—Middle Palaeolithic

During the course of a site survey of the area a certain amount of material of palaeolithic type was found in units over the surface. Upon close examination of the outfall areas of this material it was possible, in at least two cases, to determine its stratigraphic integrity and that it was a primary deposit. This was based upon the evaluation of extruded materials from the eroded slopes of the gullies running down to the wadi, in particular the colocation of flint artefacts, bone and charcoal. Three other sites proved to be less authentic and consisted only of flint débris in washed layers. The overburden, however, implied that this dissemination had taken place in antiquity. Nevertheless it was one of the two *in situ* sites that was chosen.

Site B lies some 10 m above the wadi floor (83·8 above mean sea level) and 120 m away from its present course, just above the north spring, (Fig. 2). It lies at the base of a recently eroded scarp, running west-east. Along the face of this scarp was a heavy covering of washed out débris, particularly flint, although close to the true deposit there were also bleached fragmented bones and teeth. In length the surface deposit covered at least 18 m. Upon examination it appeared to be emitted from more than one horizon; at least two if not three were readily visible once the scarp was brushed. They were apparently covered by an overburden of sterile débris 3½ m in height at the east end of the deposit and 3 m at its west end. It was assumed that this height in no way represented the total overburden, but only a residual spur.

SURFACE MATERIALS

The lithic material is mainly of brown flint, the raw material being manifestly locally available wadi cobbles, since no tabular flint was found. The cobbles, of banded flint and chert, have no true cortex but a battered and rolled surface. The combination of banding and battering results in the cobbles being badly stressed externally and internally. The flakes and blades are still extremely sharp; no sign of patination was observed, implying that the exposure is recent (Stekelis, 1952). Those eventually found *in situ* were similarly unpatiated.

About 1000 pieces were collected, varying in size from 3 × 2 cm and smaller to 8 × 5 cm. Larger objects were rare and no obviously heavy tools were found. As expected the greater part of the collection was made up of irregular trimming flakes. Small tools, however, were found, but cores were rare.

In order to test the validity of the deposit horizontally and vertically, four small soundings were made into the eroded scarp face to remove the surface drift more carefully and hence expose the true lithic surface in section. The total lateral distance sampled was 7 m. (Fig. 5).

In all four cases material was found *in situ* in a concentrated layer, c. 5 cm in thickness. Each displayed bone, flint, charred bone and charcoal mixed together in a heavy deposit. In each case, below this layer by some 20 cm, was a second horizon apparently even more filled with charcoal. This second layer was not investigated further.

With regard to the breadth of the deposit a stepped soil section was cut, 1 m wide, through the sterile soils above the deposit, to ascertain the soil stratigraphy. This illustrated a number of features: (a) the material above the site seems to be a series of sand, soil and loess in washed layers ; (b) one flint of indeterminate typology occurred *in situ* in locus 1, layer 2, 3 m above the deposit described above; (c) in locus 1, layer 12, a hard packed loess layer immediately overlying the artefact layer exposed in the other three sections, contained bone and flint at 1·3 m north from the east-west scarp face. Once this was reached the section was closed to leave the deposit covered.

Three-dimensionally, then, it seems that the deposit runs for at least 7 m × 1·3 m and from an examination of the scarp face at least two horizons are visible.

Flint Remains

The excavated artefacts number 182, made up of three cores, 141 flakes and 48 pieces in the tool category. These are mostly Levallois flakes, the next most common type being the "cortex" backed knives. Some of the most common pieces are the Levallois points which were well made, and some had "chapeau de gendarme" butts.

The surface collection of 900 pieces is essentially similar with 160 pieces in the tool category, also many levallois flakes and points and "cortex" backed knives. The Levallois index was 40·2, fairly high; the facetting index was 54·8 (I.F.1.) and the laminar index was 15·5.

The material bears strong relationships to that published by Neuville (Neuville and Vaufrey, 1931) and also to the Mount Carmel material (Garrod and Bate 1937).

Mammalian Remains

Bone was obviously extruding in equal quantity with the flint.

H

Fig. 4. View North East from top of Tell (Site A). Left foreground, fossil dunes; Centre, Wadi; Right foreground, cobble slip off slope; middle distance, Loess "badlands"; far distance, country surface of Negev. Site B lies in the right ⋯⋯ ⋯⋯⋯ N.P. The large stands of Tamarix and Phragmites on the

Long bone remains seem large, perhaps those of Bos or some form of large deer. The bone itself is found mainly unchanged but mineralized. Occasionally, charred bone was in evidence. In particularly good condition were several large teeth, probably those of *Cervus* (?) *elaphus*.

Site C—Byzantine

The position of Site C was 1 km north-east of the Tell (Fig. 5); in extent it was c 100 m × 50 m. While material was distributed over this area, the surface had been eroded into a series of residual pinnacles, none of which rendered an original horizon of the period. The material itself consisted of large amounts of ceramic, some glassware and a scatter of stones with mortar still adhering.

On an eroded gulley below the country surface was what appeared to be a Byzantine cistern, at one time subterranean but now partially eroded away. A 75 cm wide sounding illustrated its plaster facings and a certain quantity of Byzantine ceramic. The exposed exterior of the cistern was sounded and appeared to be sitting in natural ground, thus providing a terminus for the country surface.

The ceramic recovered was uniformly of the Byzantine period attributable to the time of the Emperor Justinian (circa 550 AD). The provisional typology indicated two-handled, elongated, cylindrical jars with a pointed base with heavy rouletting and light combing in zones as at Ashdod (Dothan, 1967). The rather shapeless shoulder and neck had in each case been daubed before firing with a slurry, similar to those found at Bethany where also occurs the second storage jar of the more common globular type with rounded base, two handles and zones of rouletting (Saller, 1957). Other types included late Roman cooking pot wares. A full exposition of the typology will appear at a later date.

Glassware appeared only in fragments on the surface. All pieces showed heavy irridescence and were not recognizable.

Conclusions

General

Three conclusions relating to method are at once apparent:

1. It is possible to combine a number of scientific disciplines in a field survey of this nature without isolating each subject. The mutual leavening of ideas was found to be most valuable. Further, the eventual archaeological focus of these disciplines was always present.

Fig. 5. View 60 metres South West of B, looking North East, showing loess "badlands" in horizontal bands up to the country surface, and the numerous radial gullies. Middle left, Site B step trench; Middle right, linking soil sections.

2. The data were more complex than had been anticipated and, at the same time, were potentially more rewarding. The concentration of archaeological material of varying periods was unexpected. The botanical collection is much larger than was at first thought possible, and the uniformity of ground cover was very localized. Geomorphologically, the "badlands" area provided much more scope for the reconstruction of the depositional and erosional history of the area than had been expected, but, correspondingly, the data were present in greater bulk.

3. At this preliminary stage, and without the laboratory work being brought to bear upon the problem, it is difficult to imagine how an excavation of any site in this area can be undertaken with any hope of successful interpretation until the topographical and ecological history has been understood in its relationship to the archaeological sites. This was adequately illustrated by Site B, the Middle Palaeolithic site, whose present position now bears no relation whatsoever to its original position or topography. But the same argument might equally be applied to any site here.

Soils

The numerous soil samples that were taken are being analysed according to the following programme :

1. The samples in the sequenced column are being analyzed for their mechanical and chemical properties to discover which, if any, are true palaeo-soils and also to determine the method of deposition of the material, particularly any original loess which may be present.

2. Particular samples are being examined exhaustively for fossil pollens. There have been variant views regarding both the availability of this data and also its value as primary evidence. As to availability, preliminary tests indicate the presence of pollens in the geological deposits, but no qualitative analysis was attempted in the field. Subsequent tests have revealed quantitatively significant ancient pollen in at least one sample which lies stratagraphically half way between the palaeolithic site and the Byzantine site; except for an increase in arborial pollen the sample is apparently similar to the present day flora quantitatively and qualitatively. Regarding its value, it is hoped to understand more fully the complexity of this evidence by controlling the result with modern samples compared to the modern floral position.

3. Certain surface samples were taken in each botanical zone, to try to explain the anomalous zoning. Again, from a mechanical and chemical evaluation of these samples, it may be possible to draw conclusions on this point.

Botany

A large botanical collection was made, both of pickled and pressed material. This will be kept as a reference collection and the following work will be conducted:

Plants will be sampled and sectioned and epidermal strips made so that phytolithic material in the soils might be compared and, hopefully, evaluated.

Environment

It is not possible at this early stage to say very much about the changing face of the Negev throughout the 50,000 year period now defined. However, a simple example has already emerged to illustrate the potential of the work. It has always been recognized that anthropogenic influences play an important part in the alteration of the economy of this and other areas. Three "economic" periods can be witnessed during the last 1500 years at Fara which are briefly described here.

The Late Roman/Byzantine period provides evidence if not of urbanism at least of widespread farming around Fara and elsewhere in the Negev (Avi-Yonah, 1958). The Nabatean exploitation is well attested in the Avdat area (Evenari *et al.*, 1958–67). At Fara, Site C illustrates a farm of some size and extent, gleaning its crops by damming the surrounding gullies for silt and probably utilizing the upper country surface also. Such occupation would imply relatively stable, though precarious, agricultural conditions. Either through economic or political necessity, this type of farming came to an end with the Islamic invasion in the 7th century, and has never reappeared.

It was following this time that the Bedouin, no doubt omnipresent in the desert fringes, took over the area. These were roving pastoralists, not so much pure nomads, whose economy was based upon scant farming and upon sheep and goats. More than 1000 years of subsequent over-grazing and tree-felling appears to have decimated the vegetation of the area, illustrated now by the lack of mature examples of the apparently dominant trees *Acacia raddiana* and *Tamarix nilotica*. These no doubt were cut down for firewood, etc. An incipient erosional phase at this time may be evidenced by the severe dendritic erosion of the Byzantine farmstead alluded to above, which has left only remnants standing upon pinnacles – this at least illustrates that no deposition seems to have taken place in post-Byzantine times.

During the past 25 years, Bedouin have been discouraged from using this area as part of a resettlement scheme. The resulting new lush vegetation in and around the wadi at Fara is well attested by the large stands of young tamarisk and the multitudinous acacia seedlings. A comparison today with photographs taken by Petrie (1930) shows a dramatic reversal of the barren landscape here. This is also true of the nearby area around Tell Jemmeh (Petrie, 1928). Whilst garden escapes now present in the flora of the wadi make a return to pure pre-nomadic vegetation impossible, the new period certainly presents an interesting picture of change based largely upon man's own behaviour.

Proposals for Future Work

The full report of the archaeological soundings, together with the results of the analysis now being conducted will be published shortly.

The Environmental Survey of this specific area is far from finished. It is already known that the soil samples are incomplete, the botanical and archaeological understanding of the area requires more work still. Undoubtedly when the samples that have been taken are analysed, more problems and questions will arise. Subject to confirmation, then, Fara would require more work after a period of consideration and the rephrasing of the question. Also, it may have great relevance to Fara to study, if only partially, another area to add a control to the methods employed. The opportunities here are legion.

Acknowledgements

To The Team

I am deeply indebted to the following members of the team for the immense amount of work carried out: Dr Juliet Prior (Botanist), Dr Hans L. Lehmann (Chemist), Mr Brian Feldman (Surveyor), Miss Peggy Nuttall (Editor), and to Messrs. Jonathan Tubb and Martin Bidmead (Site Supervisors), and Fr Robin Duckworth (Coordinator) as well as to the remainder of the volunteers.

For Additional Help

The team is grateful to the following Institutions and individuals:
EEI, Leonard Street, Belmont, Mass, USA.
Department of Antiquities, Jerusalem
Negev Institute for Arid Zone Research, Beersheba
The Royal Botanical Gardens at Kew
Professor Hayn, Dr Dannin and Dr D. Yallon, Hebrew University, Jerusalem

Desmond M. Collins, MA, University of London
Professor G. W. Dimbleby, Dr I. Cornwall and Mr P. G. Dorrell,
Evironmental Department, University of London
Dr William Melson, Department of Petrology, Smithsonian Institu-
tion, Washington DC, USA.

References

Avi-Yonah, M. (1958). *Israel Exploration Journal,* **8**, 40.
Dothan, M. (1967). "Atiqot, **VII**", p. 69.
Evenari, M., Shanan, L. and Tadmor, N. H. (1958–67). "Runoff farming
in the Negev desert of Israel". I–IV. Rehovot.
Evenari, M., Shanan, L. and Tadmor, N. H. (1971). "The Negev". Harvard.
Garrod, D. A. E. and Bate, D. M. A. (1937). "Stone Age of Mount Carmel",
Vols. I and II, Oxford University Press, Oxford.
Macdonald, E. (1932). Prehistoric Fara, *In* "Bethpelet II", Quaritch, Lon-
don.
Marks, A. E., Phillips, J., Crew, H. and Ferring, R. (1971). *Israel Explora-
tion Journal,* **21**, 13ff.
Neuville, R. and Vaufrey, R. (1931). *Archives de l'Institut de Paléon-
tologie,* **24**, 1–270.
Petrie, F. (1928). "Gerar". Quaritch, London.
Petrie, F. (1930). "Bethpelet I". Quaritch, London. *and* p. 21, pl. lxii. 6.
Reifenberg, A. (1947). "The Soils of Palestine". Murby. London.
Saller, S. J. (1957). "Excavations at Bethany, 1949–1953". Jerusalem.
Stekelis, M. (1952). *Israel Exploration Journal,* **2**, p. 19.
Zohary, M. (1962). "Plant Life of Palestine, Israel and Jordan". Ronald
Press Co., New York.

The History of the Fiblua

J. A. ALEXANDER

THE CUSTOM OF USING long straight solid pins of bone or metal was widely established in Western Asia and Europe in the fourth millennium BC and may well, like the thorns and slivers of wood still used in many parts of the world, have been clothes fasteners. In the third millenium BC, side by side with the solid pins, pins with perforations in their shanks or heads are found, and some of these in Western Asia, were used to fasten clothes (Woolley, 1934, p. 239

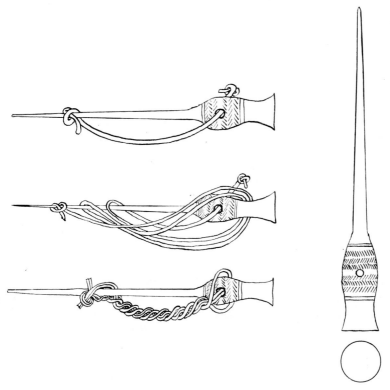

Fig. 1. The "Eyelet-pin" fibula with a bow of organic material. Three alternative ways of fastening the bow.

and Plate 231). The perforations have been interpreted as anchorings for one or more threads, cords or thongs which could be tied to hold the cloth or leather garment securely in place on the pin (Fig. 1).

These two-piece fasteners have generally been called "toggle or eyelet-pins" but the former is a misnomer, for a toggle should have a near-central perforation and a pin blunt at both ends.* The prehistoric pins are long and pointed and are meant to be fixed to clothes so that "fibula" a general term for fasteners, is perhaps a better name.† A full description of them in a recent morphological analysis was "Two-piece-fibulae-with-organic-bows-and-metal-pins", (Alexander, 1973) and from them undoubtedly descend the modern safety pins.

This summary of the fluctuating fortunes of the fibula during three thousand years is offered to Professor Grimes as a tribute to his interest in fashion and status-indication in archaeology.

Early in the second millennium BC "eyelet" pins (Gewandnadeln) were widely used in Western Asia where rod-, bulb- and flat-headed forms were found. By the middle of the millennium they are characteristic of the Middle Bronze Age of Central Europe where they have been studied by Lissauer. He has shown that they fall into five main regional groupings and they were probably used for clothes fasteners (Lissauer, 1907). Regional and sexual distinctions already seem to be shown by them.

In this paper interest is centred upon the type which has cast, often ornamented, swelling beneath a relatively small, and usually flat-topped head; the cast perforation is through the centre of the swelling. This is Lissauer's type II.2 which he shows to have a South Central European distribution with a concentration in the Upper Danube Basin. The whole type belongs to the Middle Bronze Age (Reinecke C-D) and to the earlier phase of the Late Bronze Age (Hallstatt A) (1450–1000 BC. Fig. 2).

In two regions peripheral to the main concentration, N. Germany-S. Denmark and E. Austria-N. Italy, bows of metal wire begin to appear early in this period. In the north the wire is stout enough to swivel on the pin and is secured by bending the wire back upon itself (Fig. 3). This defines the "Urfibeln" of earlier writers and is securely dated to Montelius II (Sprockoff, 1938). In the south the bow seems to have been of finer, more pliant, wire or metal strip. In one case at

* "Togglepin" is not accepted by the Oxford Dictionary. A toggle, usually made of rope, was a nautical term.

† "Fibula" was, in Latin, so vague a term (clasp, buckle or brooch) that its restriction by seventeenth century antiquarians to specific kinds of safety pin was arbitrary.

least (Unterradl) it appears (Fig. 3) when not in use to have been twisted around the pin. Since "trade" connections right across Central Europe at this time have long been assumed, the northern and southern developments from a common ancestor are natural enough but it is surprising that it did not happen as well in the ancestral area further west.

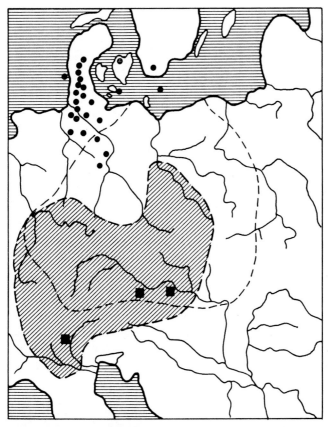

Fig. 2. The origins of the Fibula. Hatched area: Eyelet or Toggle Pins (after Lissauer's type II.2) Eyelet-Pin fibulae with metal bows of (a) Stiff wire: dots (after Beltz), (b) Flexible wire: squares.

The use of metal for the bow as well as the pin was an invention capable of many adaptations and the direct cause of two long series of undoubted and efficient clothes fasteners (fibulae) in the first millennium BC. In the north and centre the two-piece form was retained for nearly a millennium and was linked with a strong preference for the bow to stand away from the cloth. A distinctive form of bent wire safety catch was also invented (Fig. 4Sa). In Eastern Germany, Poland, Denmark, and Scandinavia generally, fibulae of this "spindelsfelden" type may be traced through to the third century BC, and in their shape and style left their mark upon the succeeding "brooches". The type did not spread far outside Central Europe although Hungarian and Italian versions had some temporary popularity (Fig. 2).

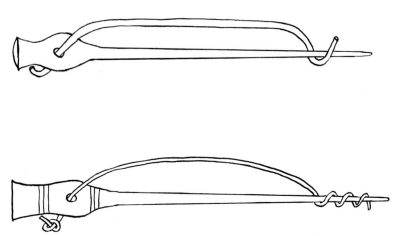

Fig. 3. Two ways of fastening "Eyelet-pin" fibulae with metal wire bows. Top: With stiff wire (Northern Europe). Bottom: With flexible wire or strip (Central Europe).

In the south in Austria and N. Italy a one-piece form relying on the tensile qualities of bronze coiled into a spring to hold the pin in a guard of sheet bronze was invented in the thirteenth or twelfth century BC. This is the "safetypin" of more recent terminology (Childe, 1930, p. 112). It was, in most of its early forms, meant to be worn with the bow hanging downwards (Fig. 6Fa) and as the more popular and long lived form its history can be traced further (Fig. 5).

Within a century this invention had been taken to Greece and Cyprus, although it was not until after the collapse of the Mycenaean kingdoms that it became widely used (Pittioni, 1954; Desborough, 1964, p. 25; Birmingham, 1963). From c. 1100 BC onwards however it gained so greatly in popularity that by 700 BC, five separate provinces stretching over 2500 miles from Iran to the West Mediterranean can be recognized (Fig. 8). In the first, Western Asia, a series derived from Aegean forms flourished from the ninth into the fifth century (Stronach, 1964; Girshman, 1964) and must be seen as a spread due to fashion and the acceptance of a useful invention. They were worn as dress fasteners by both men and women and some forms can be seen to have indicated special, even divine, status (Musca-rella, 1967). In the second province, the Aegean Coastlands and the Greek settlements overseas, a bewildering variety of forms and styles are found between 1000 and 400 BC. Some were certainly worn to indicate status as well as being simple clothes fasteners (Blinken-berg, 1926; Lorimer, 1950). Although many of the earlier forms were

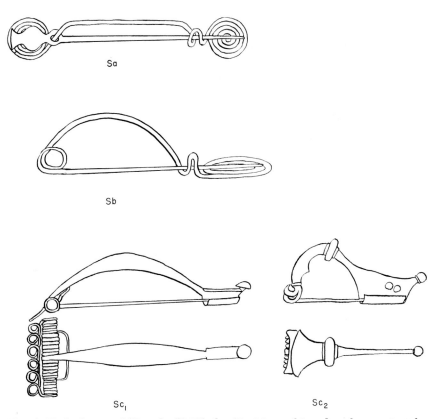

Sa

Sb

Sc₁   Sc₂

Fig. 4. Early forms of "Stand-off" Fibula. (Position achieved without using the bow.)

meant to be worn with the bow hanging downwards, the popularity of forms in which the bows were designed to stay flatly above the pin, especially derivatives of the spectacle type (Alexander, 1961) (Fig. 6Fa), gradually increased and developed into "brooch" forms with ivory, metal and bone ornamental plaques in the sixth to the fifth centuries. The third province in Italy was in part, in the Po Valley, within the area of original discovery and a series of forms quite as distinct and as inventive as the Aegean series developed (Sundwall,

1943). Here as well as in the two regions just discussed, the forms with the bow hanging downward were predominant and remained popular into the fifth century. In Tuscany, in particular among the Etruscans, extremely elaborate and costly forms suggest that social as well as sexual status was indicated by them. The fourth province was in South Central Europe in the Alps, their northern and western foothills, Czechoslovakia, Silesia and in the North Balkans. Here, in the original area of discovery, influences from further north and south were received and incorporated into existing forms between 1000 and 500 BC (Beltz, 1943). A preference for low-bowed forms which did not hang bow downwards but which the bunching of the cloth held erect, persisted throughout. There is evidence that different types were worn by either sex and that some indicated social distinction (Kramer, 1960).

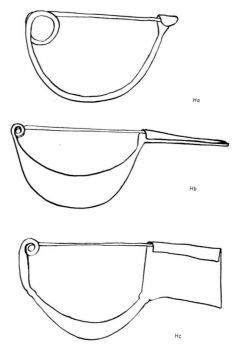

Fig. 5. Early forms of Hanging Fibulae.

In the fifth province, North Central Europe, two-piece "Spindels-felden" fibulae remained in common use until after 400 BC. The many varieties have been studied by Sprockoff and all preserve the discs on either side of the bow which kept it standing out at right-angles to the cloth (Sprockoff, 1938; Schlabow, 1961; Hald, 1962). An increasingly small bow, which allows little room for cloth, is often compensated by a curved pin. Larger than their predecessors these fibulae seem to have served mainly as cloak fasteners.

During these five hundred years the safety pin spread relatively slowly into Western and Northern Europe and it is only from the middle of the first millennium BC onwards that it became popular.

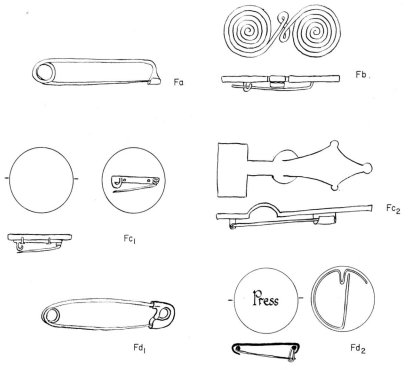

Fig. 6. Types of "Flat Lying" Fibulae.

By 500–400 BC the first climax of popularity of the fibula was over and during the next six hundred years it was only in Northern and North Western Europe that it spread and developed many new forms. In the Mediterranean coastlands and in Western Asia its use declined rapidly, and under the Hellenistic kingdoms and the Roman Republic it was little used except to mark specific and relatively minor status (such as soldiers on active service) (Lorimer, 1950, p. 402). Presumably the fashions for unpinned garments (like the toga) or for tailored clothes were partly responsible for this. Further east in Asia beyond Iran, fibulae never seem to have been accepted nor were they in Africa south of the Mediterranean coast lands (Figs. 8 and 9).

In Central and, for the first time, in North Western Europe, the safety pin developed new forms and flourished between 500 BC and AD 50. These "La Tène" forms were based on North Italian and Alpine styles of the sixth century and seem a response to the demands of Celtic taste (Barfield, 1972, p. 151). The newest element was the use of enlarged, and often crossbow-like springs to hold the bow at right-angles to the cloth, which brought them nearer to the northern two-piece fibula tradition. Many different sizes were made, both plain and elaborate, and were worn by both men and women as fasteners and apparently as tribal, sexual and social status indicators. Common at first in Central Europe, they spread slowly into the British Isles, where early La Tène fibulae are rare, across the North European Plain and into the Lower Danube Valley (Fig. 4.Sc).

Fibulae of "La Tène" types remained popular in Western Europe until after the Roman Conquest and a modified series, influenced by Roman Military forms continued to be worn.* By the second century AD they had, however, disappeared from general use, the final blow perhaps being Caracalla's decree of AD 212 which gave Roman citizenship (which of course included the right to wear the toga) to all free men in the Empire.

In Northern Germany, Poland and Scandinavia, during the period 500 BC–AD 300, the one-piece fibula gradually replaced the two-piece form, presumably under the influence of western fashions (Almgren, 1895).† The popularity of the crossbow spring, which allowed the safety pin to be worn like the old two-piece form (with the bow at right angles to the cloth) possibly aided the change-over (Fig. 4.Sc). Disc-brooches (violin bow fibulae with large discs mounted on their bows) also spread into this region. Fibulae continued to be worn by men and women and their elaboration suggests that they were worn as status symbols as well as external fasteners.

By AD 300, the use of fibulae in the world had shrunk, except for a few specific status roles in the Roman Empire, to the northern and eastern parts of Europe. Its role as a useful fastener was neglected and almost forgotten elsewhere. This marks the end of its first cycle of popularity which had spanned a thousand years and had been largely concerned with the visible wearing of the pins. Whilst several local spreads of specific types can be related to the tribal movements (e.g. the movement of Celtic speaking peoples into the Balkans) many other distributions must be due to fashion or political and religious influence (Fig. 10).

The second spread of the safety pin both to the east and west began

* M. R. Hull, personal communication.

† Most recently discussed in "Les Celtes et Les Germains a l'èpoque paienne", Eggers et al. (Eds.), Paris, 1965, p. 32.

after AD 300. In Western Europe, fibula-wearing North Europeans and their women-folk can be recognized in the third and fourth centuries and with the collapse of the Western Empire, fibulae of North European type spread wherever Teutonic peoples wandered. Only, however, where the settlement largely displaced the previous populations did fibulae become popular (Fuchs and Werner, 1950; Leeds, 1949). The northern fibula types signally failed to stimulate southern imaginations in the way the earlier forms had done, and no popular local derivative series arose. Most of the fibulae were large and ornamental and were meant for male and female display.

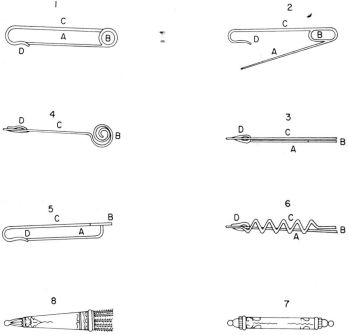

Fig. 7. The rediscovered "safety pin" (1849 patent).

Well before AD 300 fibula wearing had begun to be popular among the Slavic-speaking peoples of Eastern Europe (Cofcianka, 1949). The forms were related to those of Northern Europe, the pins sitting flatly on the surface of the cloth. With the movements of some Slav tribes southwards, these new types appear in the Balkans and Southern Russia.

Elaborate fibulae derived from earlier Mediterranean forms also continued to be used as status indicators, and especially as cloak fasteners, in the East Roman Empire. The use of them does not seem to have spread to neighbouring peoples and in Asia east of the

Euphrates and in Africa south of the Sahara no examples are known from this time.

By c. AD 800 the role of the fibula, (or brooch to give it the north European name)* seems to have been set in the form it was to hold until the nineteenth century AD. Restricted almost entirely to Europe it was to be a status indicator whilst serving as an external (and therefore visible) fastener. In particular, in rich and elaborate forms it was to be worn through mediaeval times by aristocrats and royalty and to be restricted by sumptuary laws in many countries†. One of its few common mediaeval uses seems to have been in non-clothes-fastener roles, as for example, in the hat badges of religious pilgrims. By the sixteenth century, as the sumptuary laws lapsed, it had certainly begun to show financial status, and to indicate wealth. Costly forms were worn by the womenfolk of the merchant classes as ornaments more than as fasteners. In much of Europe this non-clothes fastening role was greatly developed by the eighteenth century when French courtly fashions seized upon it and it became common for women to wear many purely ornamental (simulated bows, etc.) brooches (Planché, 1876, p. 60). This usage spread to many neighbouring countries, and with Europeans, to many parts of the world. The use of the safety pin in parts of Western and Southern Asia to fasten "aigrettes" and other headdress ornaments was presumably due to this influence. In the nineteenth century this non-functional use, often linked with status indication (for example, when mourning), continued and elaborate brooches were widely worn. This continues today for disc brooches (often of cardboard) distinguished by colour, size, inscription and shape can indicate membership of societies, conferences and similar bodies (Fig. 6.Fd$_2$).

In the early nineteenth century the discovery that the safety pin has much wider usefulness and versatility than its uses as a status indicator suggests, seems to have been made for the first time in North America. Many of those responsible for the developing Industrial Revolution were conscious of and affected by, the styles of the classical world of Greece and Rome, and collections of objects from the Mediterranean were being amassed in Western Europe and North America. Among them were certainly safety pins of Italian type, and it is tempting to speculate that the simple violin bow types from the Alps or the Mediterranean caught the eye of an enterprising American inventor. Whether as the result of having seen these or

* The term "Brooch", meaning an ornamented fibula, is used across Europe from Spain to Sweden.

† In England, for example, in the fourteenth–fifteenth centuries, brooches of gold, silver or gilt were forbidden to all under the rank of knight or bishop.

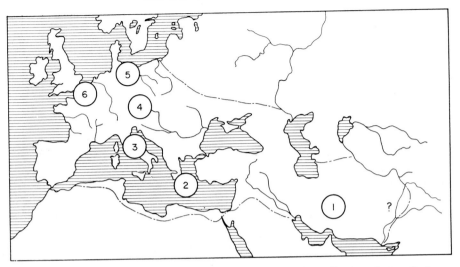

Fig. 8. Limit of distribution of the fibula at its first climax of popularity (700–300 BC). Main schools of fashion thus.

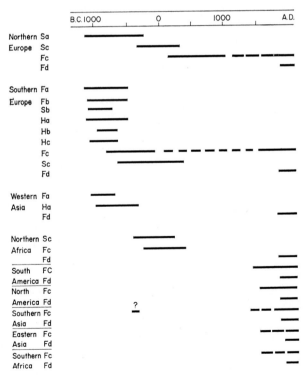

Fig. 9. Geographical and Chronological Distribution of Fibulae.

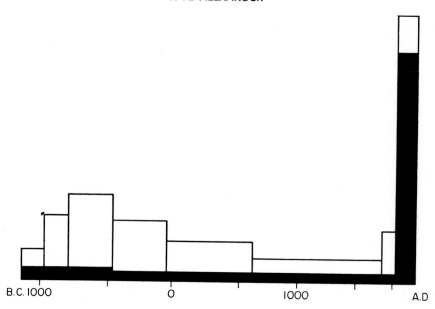

Fig. 10. Relative Popularity of Fibulae in the World. Their use as Status
Indicators (White) and as Simple Fasteners (Black).

through a completely independent invention, a fibula surprisingly like
the Alpine form of the twelfth century BC was patented in the USA
in 1849 by Mr Walter Hunt of Connecticut* (Fig. 8). Mr Hunt was
much concerned with new ideas, in the previous years he had registered nine other inventions†. Since he at once sold his "safety pin", as
he named it, for £300 he was possibly a professional inventor. The
idea, and the name, appeared six months later (12 October 1849)
among the English patents when it was registered by Mr Charles
Rowley of Birmingham.‡ Its manufacture now commenced and it
was made, in a variety of sizes, for purely functional use. It was in no
way a status indicator or even necessarily a clothes fastener since it
was used for blankets and beds (Fig. 6.Fd₁).

    *U.S. Patent no. 6281 of 10 April 1849, J. Eldridge's patent of 1857, which
is quoted by the Oxford Dictionary as the earliest use of the "safety pin", refers
to an ordinary pin.

    † "List of Patents for Inventions and Designs 1790–1847." Washington, 1947.

    ‡ British Patents Journal 9·30. It was first publicized in the Mechanics Maga-
zine, 52. 318. The term "safety pin" does not seem to have been used by
archaeologists until the 1880's.

In its new and strictly functional form it was exported and soon became popular in Europe from France to Russia, and in both those countries the name "English pin" was given to it. In most cases "safety pin" was translated into each language (spilla di sicurezza, etc.) but in no case was "brooch" or "fibula" used. During the last hundred years it has increased in popularity in Europe and has spread widely through the world. It now seems well established in its dual function as a strictly functional violin bow fastener, and as a non-functional status indicator in various brooch forms, but elaborate functional forms remain rare.

It would seem from this summary that both of the cycles of popularity of the safety pin, whose beginning in c. 1200 BC and AD 1850, commenced in periods of industrial development (or revolution?) in areas at the centre of current inventiveness and enterprise. It would seem that in a general atmosphere of change and discovery this simple and useful idea could be widely adopted.

References

Alexander, J. (1973, In Press). In "The Explanation of Cultural Change" (C. Renfrew, ed.), Duckworth, London.

Alexander, J. (1961). A.J.A. **69**, 7–23.

Almgren, O. (1961). "Nordeuropäische fibelformen" Haeggeström, Stockholm.

Barfield, L. (1971). Northern Italy before Rome" Thames and Hudson, London.

Beltz, R. (1943). Zeitschrift für Ethnologie **45**, 313.

Birmingham, J. (1963). P.E.Q. pp. 80–112.

Blinkenberg, C. (1926). "Fibules grècques et orientales" (Lindianka V) Høst, Copenhagen.

Childe, V. G. (1930). "The Bronze Age" Cambridge University Press, Cambridge.

Cofcianka, A. (1949). Przeglad Archeologiczny **8**, 38–46.

Desborough, V. (1964). "The Last Mycenaeans and Their Successors" Clarendon Press, Oxford.

Fuchs, S. and Werner, J. (1950). "Die Langobardischen fibeln aus Italien," Berlin.

Girshman, R. (1964). Iranica Antiqua **4**, 90–107.

Hald, M. (1962). "Jernalderens Dragt", Copenhagen.

Kramer, K. (1960). "Das Gräberfeld von Hallstatt", in Vienna, Sansoni, Florence.

Leeds, E. T. (1949). "A Corpus of Early Anglo-Saxon Great Square-Headed Brooches" Clarendon Press, Oxford.

Lissauer, A. (1907). *Zeitschrift für Ethnologie* **39**, 51.

Lorimer, H. (1950). "Homer and the Monuments" Macmillan, London.

Muscarella, O. W. (1967). *J.N.E.S.* **26** (1), 82–6.

Pittioni, R. (1954). "Urgeschichte des Oesterrichischen Raumes" Franz Deuticke, Vienna.

Planché, L. (1876). Cyclopaedia of Costume", London.

Schlabow, K. (1961). "Trachten des Eisenzeit" Wachholtz Neümünster.

Sprockhoff, E. (1938). "Marburger Studien" Darmstadt, Wittich.

Stonach, D. (1954). *Iraq* **21**, 181–206.

Sundwall, J. (1943). "Die älteren italischen fibeln" de Gruyter, Berlin.

Woolley, L. (1934). "Ur Excavations Vol. II", British Museum, London.

Roman Soldiers in Roman London

M. W. C. HASSALL

IN THE FIELD of Romano-British studies, Peter Grimes has played a full and distinguished role, from the publication of the important military tile works at Holt (Grimes, 1930) to the excavation of the London Mithraeum and fort in the fifties (Grimes, 1968). The first two are almost type-sites of their kind – a legionary industrial establishment, and the shrine of a group of wealthy Mithraic worshippers in the most cosmopolitan city of the province. Both are presented complete and entire to students of Roman military antiquities on the one hand and to those of Roman religion and art on the other. But the surprising discovery of the fort prompts further speculation: Professor Grimes has given us its size, 11 acres, and the approximate date of its foundation, about AD 100, but who were the troops who were stationed within its walls and what was their function? This note offered to a distinguished scholar and a good friend reviews the possible answers.

Ralph Merrifield (1969) suggested that the fort was garrisoned by men seconded from the different British legions – the presence of men from all three II, VI and XX is attested by their tombstones, while Professor Frere (1967) thinks of an urban cohort – "the police force of a provincial capital" – which explanation is likely to be correct – or can a third hypothesis be advanced?

The 'Urban Cohort'

The question of urban cohorts is a complicated one but since it has been studied fully by Freis (1965, 1967), no prolonged treatment is given here.

It is enough to say that the absence of such a unit at London in the historical or epigraphic record need not in itself be significant. Only a handful of tombstones survive from Roman London and the unit itself would not be included in the lists of alae and cohorts given in the half dozen or so military diplomas that survive from Roman

Britain. These were issued to veterans of auxiliary units who received citizenship on discharge. Each diploma gives in its preamble a list of *all* units from which discharges were being made at a particular time, not only the unit to which the veteran actually receiving the document belonged. But the soldiers in urban cohorts were already Roman citizens and will have been treated differently on completing their military service. Though they did receive a diploma on discharge as the surviving diploma issued to a veteran in coh. XIII Urbana at Lyons shows (*CIL* XVI 133), these merely confirmed, if necessary retrospectively, the legality of marriages they might contract or have contracted with citizens (female) and peregrines. The chances of finding a diploma issued to a veteran in any particular unit are very remote. If veterans in a hypothetical London Urban cohort had special diplomas issued to them, one would be fortunate indeed to find one. However, though this negative evidence is hardly significant, there are strong *a priori* grounds for thinking it extremely unlikely that a unit of this type was ever stationed in London, or indeed that an urban cohort was the normal "police force" of any provincial capital. Apart from Rome, and occasionally other places in Italy, such as Puteoli and Ostia, urban cohorts are known only to have been stationed at Lyons (variously XIII, XVII, XVIII and I) and Carthage (XIII and I). Lyons was not only the capital of Gallia Lugdunensis, but the venue for the annual meeting of the *Concilium Galliarum*, the provincial council representing all three Gallic provinces. It was also the centre of the road system in Roman Gaul and in the first century housed an imperial mint. Carthage was, after Rome, one of the most important cities in the West and the seat of the Proconsul of Africa, one of the two most senior governors of senatorial provinces. However, Gallia Lugdunensis had no permanent military establishment while Africa, after the creation of a separate command in Numidia under Caius, was likewise devoid of troops. In both cases the importance of the towns concerned coupled with absence of troops in the vicinity entailed taking special measures and the posting of urban cohorts was the solution adopted. This was not just a matter of prestige: the Lyons cohort also provided the personnel for the governor's staff (normally seconded from legions stationed in the province) and that at Carthage a proportion of the staff of the proconsul of Africa, the rest being supplied by men from III Augusta in Numidia. London did not compare in status with either Lyons or Carthage and Britain with three or four legions was not short of men for the governor's staff, while the shadowy existence of a mint which may on occasion have been temporarily set up in the province under the Flavians (Mattingly, 1967) or during the reign of Antoninus Pius (Askew, 1951; Todd, 1966) will hardly have been permanent or important enough to warrant the creation of a special British urban cohort. The only possible candidate for such a unit is coh. XVI, attested before AD 66 (*ILS* 2648), whose whereabouts is unknown. The unit however is not mentioned again and probably only existed under Claudius and Nero, long before the construction of the Cripplegate fort.

Seconded Legionnaries

On the analogy of other provinces, soldiers will have been supplied by all three British legions for service at the provincial capital. The ranks and functions performed by these soldiers serving on the *officium* of the governor have been reconstructed by von Domaszewski (1967) and summarized by Jones (1960) and it would be out of place to reiterate their conclusions here. It is enough to say that the total number of such men must have been very large – 200 or more for the *officium* of the governor of a three legion province (Stein, 1932) – though scarcely large enough to form the major element in the garrison of the Cripplegate fort, and that they ranged in their duties from clerks and grooms, to prison guards and executioners. The largest group were known collectively as *beneficiarii consularis*, sixty, or perhaps thirty, being detached from each legion for service with the governor. None are known from Roman London and many will have been detached for service elsewhere in the province where they are in fact attested. There will have been a considerable number of *stratores* too, nominally grooms; however, like the *beneficiarii* some at least may have been outposted, performing minor local administrative functions, at any rate the sole *strator consularis* known from the province was buried at Irchester (Northants.) (*RIB* 233). Another significantly large group were the *speculatores*, ten from each of the three legions. They were normally concerned with the custody and execution of prisoners, but like another group, the *frumentarii*, had wider duties as government agents which might take them to Rome. The Ashmolean Museum possesses a fine tombstone (*ILS* 2372) set up by a *frumentarius* of leg. XX V. V. as other inscriptions (*CIL* VI 3357, 3359) show to a *speculator exercitus Britannici*. For their existence in London we have direct epigraphic evidence too (*RIB* 19), while a reference in Justinian's Digest (XLVIII, 20, 6) may relate to one of the more ghoulish aspects of their duties in the provincial capital (see Appendix 2).

Before leaving the question of legionaries at London, it is worth noting that several do not have a specific function attributed to them on the tombstones; and there thus remains the possibility that a small legionary detachment was stationed there quite apart from those "specialists" who served on the governor's staff.

Some may have been under the command of the procurator. In an often quoted passage, Tacitus (*Annals* XIV 22) describes how, at the time of the Boudiccan revolt, the procurator Decianus Catus sent two hundred soldiers to Colchester, and it has usually been assumed that they came from London.

The Governors Guard

The guard of a governor of an imperial province consisted of both cavalry and infantry known respectively as *equites* and *pedites singulares*. Both sections were formed from picked men (hence the name "singulares"), drawn from the cavalry alae and infantry cohorts serving in the province. The *equites* were commanded by a seconded legionary centurion known as an *exercitator equitum singularium ILS* 2417) and according to Stein (1932) had a nominal strength of 500. The *pedites* were also commanded by a legionary centurion, who at least on occasion doubled up as commander of the *stratores* (*ILS* 2418). Inscriptions (*CIL* XIII 8185, 8223, 8188, 6270) suggest that guardsmen of both groups remained enrolled on the strength of the auxiliary units from which they were detached for they are described on them as being an *eques* or *pedes* of such and such a unit, followed by the words *sing(ularis) co(n)s(ularis)*. In fact we have direct proof that this was so. The annual status report of *cohors I Hispanorum veterana* stationed in Moesia, which lists a whole series of men who were out-posted though still on the rolls of the unit, includes one or more men detached for service with the legate as *singulares* (Fink, 1971, no. 63). A consequence of this is that on completing terms of service men would be discharged from their own units not from the guard, in contrast to the imperial *equites singulares Augusti* stationed at Rome who had an independent establishment and received diplomas on retirement (*CIL* XVI 144, 146, Speidel, 1965). This explains why units of provincial *equites* and *pedites* are never found on the diploma lists. The exception that proves the rule is the unit of *pedites singulares Britannici* who, as their name shows originally served in Britain and who are found on a number of second century diplomas from Moesia and Dacia. They will have been despatched from Britain under exceptional circumstances and henceforth developed an identity of their own independent of the units from which the individual soldiers were drawn. Professor E.

Birley, who draws attention to this unit and its significance, suggests (1953a) that it may have been removed as a consequence of Domitian's purge of Sallustius Lucullus, a governor of Britain suspected of tampering with the loyalty of the troops. At all events after its removal from the province, it is inconceivable that it was not replaced, while an inscription from Ribchester (*RIB* 594, cf. also 725, 1266, 1713) proves that the *equites singulares* certainly survived.

The permanent quarters of the *equites* and *pedites singulares* must have been London, in succession to Colchester, the capital of the province. Since the cohort of *pedites singulares Britannici* is not described on the diplomas as milliary, it presumably numbered five hundred, thus corresponding to the *equites*, making a total of one thousand in all. In the relatively cramped conditions of the northern frontiers (Jarrett, 1969), the thousand strong *ala Petriana*, admittedly all cavalry, occupied an area of just over 9¼ acres at Stanwix. If, at 11 acres, the Cripplegate fort is considered still too large for the governor's guard alone, it may also have housed some of the detached legionaries serving at the capital – especially perhaps the *stratores*, who as we have seen were sometimes at least commanded by the same centurion as the *pedites singulares*. However, that the guard formed the major part of the fort's garrison, seems on present evidence to be the most likely explanation of its existence.

Appendix I: Dio LXXIII (Xiphilinus' epitome)

There is one possible literary reference to the London garrison which should be mentioned. In Xiphilinus' epitome of Dio (LXXIII = Loeb, p. 88) we read how the legates in Britain, in the absence of the governor *(οἱ ἐν Βρεττανίᾳ τοίνυν ὑπάρχοντες)*, during a period of anarchy towards the end of Commodus' reign having picked a force of fifteen hundred javelin men *(χιλίους καὶ πεντακοσίους ἀκοντιστὰς ἀπὸ σφῶν ἀπολέξαντες* sent them to Italy to enforce their demands. Dio's original text could conceivably have referred to the *equites* and *pedites singulars, stratores* and others of the London garrison all of whom would have been "picked". The regular Greek term for *pedites singulares* was ἐπίλεκτοι πεζοι cf. Josephus *Bellum Judaicum* III, 5.5, and *equites singulares* ἐπίλεκτοι ἱππεις cf. Arrian *Contra Alanos* 4 and 24.

Appendix 2: Digest XLVIII 20, 6

As shown above, among the legionaries seconded to the provincial capital of London, were the thirty *speculatores* or military policemen. The text discussed here concerns the function of *speculatores* as military police and probably relates specifically to the province, although not dealt with by E. Birley in his study of Roman Law and Roman Britain (Birley, 1953b).

The passage in question contains a rescript of Hadrian, with the early third century jurist Ulpian's comments upon it, sent to a certain provincial governor, Aquilius Bradua. He had been identified with M. Appius Bradua, whose family name was Atilius for which the Aquilius of the Digest is almost certainly a corruption (*PIR*[2] A no. 1298, Thomasson, 1960). He is known from a broken inscription set up at Olympia (*ILS* 8824a, Dittenberger and Pergold, 1896, no. 620 with drawing) to have been governor of (Lower) Germany and Britain. A. R. Birley (1967) suggests that these posts were held under Trajan and that he received the rescript later as proconsul of Africa under Hadrian. Such a post would have been mentioned on the inscription which, since it describes Hadrian as *divus* was set up after that emperor's death. The only possible place for such a mention is in the lost second line together with Bradua's consulship, and the fact that he was *comes*? of Hadrian. However, its inclusion here is unlikely since this would mean that the sequence of posts held by Bradua, given in chronological order on the inscription, would be broken. Bradua's governorship of Lower Germany will have followed shortly after his consulship in 108 and before he went on to govern Britain (the British governorship regularly follows that of Lower Germany in the second century). He should then have received Hadrian's rescript while serving in Britain as one of that emperor's first governors.

The rescript – a legal ruling in answer to a question raised by a provincial governor in his capacity as judge – concerns *pannicularia* – literally "rags", a technical term for the clothes that a condemned man wore which were often considered as the "perks" of the *speculatores*. The soldiers in the gospels who drew lots for Jesus' clothes after his crucifixion were, in the eyes of the law, disposing of *pannicularia*. Bradua, who presumably had sentenced men to death in the province, was concerned with the precise definition of the term and Hadrian wrote back to say that it included besides the prisoners' clothes, any petty cash or cheap rings less than 5 *aurei* in worth, but excluded rings set with a sardonyx or other precious stones, or bonds for large sums of money. Ulpian in his commentary says that nobody, from the *speculatores* to the governor, should appropriate these trifles which like the more valuable property belonged to the imperial treasury. But since it was not worth sending the price fetched for them to the emperor, as over-scrupulous governors frequently did, it was enough that any money realized should go to the Parchment Fund of the governor's *officium*, or pay for other minor expenses.

References

Askew, G. (1951). "The Coinage of Roman Britain". Seaby Ltd., London.

Birley, A. R. (1967). *Epigraphische Studien* **4** = *Beihefte der Bonner Jahrbücher* **25**, 63–102.

Birley, E. (1953a). *In* "Roman Britain and the Roman Army". (Collected Papers). pp. 20–30. Titus Wilson and Son Ltd., Kendal.

Birley, E. (1953b). *In* "Roman Britain and the Roman Army". (Collected Papers). pp. 48–58. Titus Wilson and Son Ltd., Kendal.

Dittenberger, W. and Pergold, K. (1896). "Olympia V—Die Inschriften von Olympia". A. Asher and Co., Berlin.

Domaszewski, A. von (1967). "Die Rangordnung des römischen Heeres" (2nd edn revised, B. Dobson). Böhlau Verlag, Köln Graz.

Fink, R. O. (1971). "Roman Military Records on Papyrus". (The American Philological Association Monograph **26**, The Press of Case Western Reserve University, Cleveland).

Freis, H. (1965). *R. E.* supplementary vol. 10, cols. 1125–40.

Freis, H. (1967) "Die Cohortes Urbanae" (*Epigraphische Studien* **2** = *Beihefte der Bonner Jahrbücher* **21**). Böhlau Verlag, Köln Graz.

Frere, S. S. (1967). "Britannia, A History of Roman Britain". Routledge and Kegan Paul, London.

Grimes, W. F. (1930). "Holt, Denbighshire: The Works Depôt of the Twentieth Legion at Castle Lyons". (*Y Cymmrodor* **41**). The Society of Cymmrodorion, London.

Grimes, W. F. (1968). "The Excavations of Roman and Medieval London". Routledge and Kegan Paul, London.

Jarrett, M. G. (1969). *In* "The Roman Frontier in Wales". (V. E. Nash-Williams, 2nd edn revised, M. G. Jarrett, ed.). pp. 150–2. University of Wales Press, Cardiff.

Jones, A. H. M. (1960). *In* "Studies in Roman Government and Law." (Collected papers). pp. 151–75. Blackwell, Oxford.

Mattingly, H. (1967). "Roman Coins". (2nd edn revised). Methuen, London.

Merrifield, R. (1969). "Roman London". Ernest Benn Ltd., London.

Speidel, M. (1965). "Die Equites Singulares Augusti", Antiquitas Reihe **1**, Band, Bonn, 110.

Stein, E. (1932). "Die kaiserlichen Beamte und Truppenkörper in römischen Deutschland unter dem Prinzipat". L. W. Seidel und Sohn, Vienna.

Thomasson, B. E. (1960). "Die Statthalter der römischen Provinzen Nord-Afrikas, II" C.W.K. Gleerup, Lund.

Todd, M. (1966). *Numismatic Chronicle* (7th series), **6**, pp. 147–53.

Wages and Prices

R. REECE

IT IS A CHASTENING experience for someone who has spent a large portion of his archaeological working time on the study of Roman coins to have to think of a contribution that he can properly make to a volume intended for Peter Grimes. There is no difficulty in the Roman part of the subject – that (together with most other periods of British archaeology) fits easily into the Grimes interests, and Roman coins he has excavated by the hundred; the trouble comes in the uses to which Roman coins can be put. They are useful for dating, they sometimes have an artistic or historical design on them, they sometimes reflect high economic policy; but I fear that the Grimes' interest in Roman coins is exactly the same as in most other artefacts that he has excavated – "What did they mean to the living people who used them?". This paper will therefore look at Roman wages, money and prices around the year AD 300 in an attempt to suggest lines of thought on the most fundamental subject since coins were invented, the household budget.

The materials available for study are the wealth of wages, taxes, loans and receipts recorded on papyri mainly in the province of Egypt from the first century AD onwards, the coinage which Diocletian struck after a great reform of mints and currency in 294, the edict of maximum prices by which Diocletian attempted to check an inflationary spiral of prices and wages in 301, and, since its publication at the end of 1971, a piece of a further edict of 301 from Aphrodisias in which Diocletian seems to have been retarriffing the coins already in circulation.

A first important step is to establish the system into which the coins fitted so that we know their relationship one to another. The coins consist of gold pieces struck at the rate of sixty to the Roman pound (libra) of gold, and silver, this time ninety six to the libra; both these fractions are certain because not only do their weights today agree with them, but they are marked firmly on the reverses of many of the coins. Three bronze coins, none of whose proper names we now know, all containing an amount of silver, complete the list. The largest, now called the follis, has a diameter of about 26 mm, a smaller coin of about 20 mm has a portrait of the emperor wearing a crown of rays, therefore called radiate, and the smallest coin of about 14 mm has a laureate portrait. The new inscription from Aphrodisias suggests that after 301 the silver piece, or argenteus, was worth a hundred denarii, and the radiate piece, five; this leaves the follis at twenty which agrees well with its marking of XX to I, and the laureate small coin must be somewhere below five.

If we look at the edict of maximum prices we can guess that the smallest coin was probably meant to be a two denarius piece, because the only commodity with a price lower than that is "six pounds of grass". There are 23 items at 2 denarii; one, uncertain, at 3 (the wage per libra for unravelling raw silk); 87 prices at four denarii; but only one again at five (a prod or whip – turned).

It may be objected that since the edict gives maximum prices we ought to make all calculations at values lower than those quoted, on the assumption that prices should have stopped rising before the maximum was reached. A glance at the Imperial preamble to the edict shows that the Emperors were far more realistic than this, and knew that when human nature was given a maximum price, there was little hope of constantly buying or selling for less.

> Aroused justly and rightfully by all the facts which are detailed above . . . we have decreed that there be established, not the prices of articles for sale—for such an act would be unjust when many provinces occasionally rejoice in the good fortune of wished for low prices . . . but a maximum, so that when the violence of high prices appears anywhere—which calamity may the gods avert!— avarice might be checked by the limits of our statute . . .

Although only the "prod or whip – turned" is priced at a maximum of five denarii there are the higher values of 10 (17 items) and 15 denarii (four items) which could well be impractical if the radiate coin was worth any other number between two and twenty other than 5.

Picking our examples at random we therefore have the laureate two denarius piece which could purchase an ounce of pork sausage, a pint of Egyptian beer, or gain entry to a privately run bath; the radiate five denarius piece which would buy fifty olives in brine, five eggs, a fine sewing needle, or the charge for carrying one person for two and a half miles. The follis which is nearly the maximum daily wage for an agricultural worker or sewer cleaner would buy nearly 3 pints of ordinary wine, half a modius (i.e. about half a bucketful) of wheat, a large untanned sheepskin, or a sow's udder. The silver piece, which a carpenter or stone-mason would get for two or three days work, could buy a good weekend supply of wheat for bread, meat, wine, oil, vegetables and honey, or pay a month's fees for a boy learning under a teacher of architecture, or it would buy a pair of sandals each for the man and his wife, a plough with a yoke, or a pound of wool from Asturia. What would a gold piece buy?

The Aphrodisias inscription does not give any help on the relation of gold coinage to the rest, so, in order to complete our practical survey it is necessary to move briefly into the realms of theory. Diocletian's edict gives a value for the maximum price of a libra of gold; unfortunately only one copy has this value and that is badly worn or weathered. We know that the value is a multiple of ten thousand and it was first read as five times 10 000 (ε) or fifty thousand denarii. A further reading suggested nine times ten thousand (θ) with the right-hand half of the letter missing, and a last emendation pointed out that if the right-hand half of the ten thousand unit was missing, then digits in the thousands which would have come after it would also be missing, so that the true value might lie anywhere between 90 000 and 99 000 denarii for a libra of gold. The values for a libra of silver are completely missing, so that we do not know the ratio of the value of gold to silver at this date.

There are two ways round this impasse; we know rough limits for the ratio of gold to silver in the ancient world at large, so we can apply these to give a rough idea of the ratio in 301; more sensitive is the price of wheat which varied widely at times of shortage, but if prices are taken over a length of time, kept a remarkably constant relationship to gold. The importance of wheat to the majority of people in the Empire can be judged from its position in the maximum price edict – item 1 in the first section.

The normal values known for the relative prices of gold and silver lie between 1 : 10 and 1 : 15, that is, a libra of gold was always at least ten times and sometimes 15 times the value of a libra of silver. We can calculate the likely relationship of gold and silver coins if we remember that the libra of gold produced 60 coins, of silver 96.

1 libra of gold	equals from 10 librae of silver to 15 librae
1 gold coin	equals from 10/60 lib. of silver to 15/60 lib.
	equals from 1/6 lib. of silver to 1/4 lib.
1 gold coin	equals from 1/6 $\times$ 96 silver coins to 1/4 $\times$ 96
	equals from 16 to 24 silver coins

Although the price of wheat could double, or even treble, in times of famine there is a fairly constant stream of values from the first century AD to the fifth, centring on 30 to 33 modii (a modern bucket holds much the same as a Roman modius) for a gold piece. True, the

I

gold piece changed its weight just as wheat changed its price, but it would be over scrupulous to take this into our calculations when the price of wheat is subject to at least 30% doubt (i.e. 20 to 40 modii per gold piece would cover most of the known prices).

The maximum price edict gives 100 as the highest allowable price for wheat, measured in a double modius. With a price of fifty denarii for a single modius the gold piece ought to be worth 30×50 to 33×50 denarii, that is, from 1500 to 1650 denarii.

If we combine the two calculations, which admittedly are subject to errors, but should at least give a rough guide, remembering that a silver piece is worth 100 denarii, we have :

1 gold coin equals from 1600 to 2400 denarii

1 gold coin equals from 1500 to 1650 denarii.

Three conclusions seem likely : that the gold coin was worth about 1600 denarii or 16 silver coins; that the ratio of silver to gold was at its lowest likely value of around 10 to 1; and that the price of a pound of gold was around 96 000 denarii.

To return to the man in the Forum, and this time he will have to be a skilled painter of figures for the interior decoration of living rooms (150 denarii a day) who has saved a quarter of his income for two months, his gold piece may pay for an advocate to open and plead a case in the courts, or buy a tanned sealskin, or six twenty foot lengths of oak nearly 18 inches square, but if he were looking for a winter cloak complete with hood (byrrus) he would not be able to afford the British variety at 6000 denarii and would have to make do with the lowest grade, the African, at 1500 denarii.

There remain two subjects of daily importance which will serve to complete this very brief essay in relating the theory of coins to their actual use. We have written records to relate the wages of a labourer in the supposed "storm and stress" of the third century to his ancestor in Egypt in the supposed golden age of the mid-second century; and we have the coins which were struck and lost in the third century, and they can tell us something about the coinage in circulation at the time.

The usual historical picture of the second century is one of peace and prosperity with wars safely far away on the frontiers, able emperors, and a reassuringly rigid status quo. The picture of the third century, culled mainly from later civil and ecclesiastical historians, and rare contemporary comments, is one of violent upset, widespread misery, and financial ruin and loss. West made some interesting calculations on wages and the price of wheat in Egypt in the second and third centuries and came up with the surprising result that the peasant was able to buy more wheat in the third century than earlier.

His reaction was to question the reliability of his evidence. This seems unfortunate because the suggestion that the peasant might be better off in an age of change is capable of a satisfactory, and topical, explanation.

In the "golden age" of stability society was ordered, and wages and prices only seem to have risen gently. If the predominantly upper class writers about whom we know most, and from whom most of our history is derived, say that it was a golden age this means that inflation was slow enough not to upset the carefully graded status quo. In the third century we know that prices and wages rocketed up. It seems quite feasible that in this leap-frogging process the peasant might, at least temporarily, be better off, for his economics are simply the receiving and spending of a wage in a period of less than a month. His patron, or employer, might be more likely to suffer, for his economics and investments were often regulated on a longer term, and inflation could hit him by temporarily devaluing his holdings. But such set-backs can seldom have lasted long.

Inflation in terms of accounting was very real; the second century labourer might earn about 60 denarii a year in 155, while the fortunate labourer in 301 might earn up to 7000 denarii a year (maximum daily wage, 25). In terms of gold the second century wage is about 17 gm. (2 and 2/5 gold pieces, each of about 7·3 gm.), in 301, about 19 gm. (3 and 3/5 gold pieces, each of about 5·4 gm.). If we compare the wages in terms of food, that of the second century would buy 100 modii of wheat; in 301 a wage of 20 denarii a day – just less than the maximum, is equivalent to just under 100 modii of wheat a year. Whatever the economic events of the third century, and whatever the viewpoint the labourer seems to be in exactly the same situation in 155 and 301, a conclusion already reached by A. H. M. Jones.

Our final question must be how the gold, silver, and three bronze denominations of coins issued from 294 to 305 relate to the evidence of wages and prices already discussed. Gold and silver coins are today so rare that nothing useful may be said about their circulation and use. The three denominations of silvered bronze must be considered in two parts : the follis had a respectable amount of silver in it – often up to 3% – and would probably have retained a silvery appearance while in circulation; the radiate and laureate smaller coins contained less than 1% of silver, but could have had a temporary silver coating. Folles are commonly found on sites throughout Britain, France and Italy, and they seem to be common in the East, the radiate coins turn up more commonly in the Eastern provinces than in the West, and they are distinctly rare in Britain. The small laureate coins are very rarely found on sites anywhere.

I

Taken in isolation this evidence conflicts violently with the discussion so far, for both the price edict, and the wages known, suggest that if the large bulk of the population handled money at all they wanted to buy and sell at prices much less than 20 denarii, or one follis. In other words, the majority of money transactions of the majority of coin using citizens, took place at lower values than that of the commonly minted coin. The simple explanation comes from the phrase "taken in isolation". Diocletian's issue of new denominations in 294, re-organized by his putative coin edict of 301, of which the Aphrodisias inscription is presumably a part, did not set out to provide an empty world with coinage. The remains of mint production from both the Greek and Latin coining parts of the Empire for the past hundred years still provided the provinces with the bulk of their coinage. When Diocletian's new coins had been in production for seven years, i.e. in 301, they probably formed less than 5% of the total volume of coins in circulation. In the east Mediterranean area the tetradrachms struck at Alexandria in great number continued in circulation for some time. These coins had always been officially equal in value to the imperial denarii, but physically they were always heavier, and lower in silver content. The denarius ceased to be a commonly produced coin in 244, but rare issues are known from later in the third century. Tetradrachms continued to be struck right up to the reform of 294, and by that time they seem to have contained very little silver indeed. As they continued in circulation alongside the new coinage the simplest explanation seems to be that they continued as one denarius pieces, and thus fitted admirably into the reformed pattern.

In the western part of the Empire and the Balkans the bulk of the coinage consisted of the radiate coins which had been issued after the reform of Aurelian in 274. These were very similar in size, design and weight to Diocletian's new radiates, but they contained more silver, sometimes having up to 2 or 3%. Nothing would have been lost, and much gained, by allowing these coins to continue as five denarius pieces; they might already have held this value in circulation for they are marked XX to I and this could well mean 20 sestertii to one coin, or five denarii (1 denarius = 4 sestertii). Coins struck before 274 in the Italian mints and the Gallic mints of north-west Europe are ideal candidates for the value of two denarii, and if a rather doubtful attempt is made to cram every known coin into our system, the barbarous copies of such coins could be valued at one denarius.

All our evidence hangs neatly together. We know something of likely wages and maximum prices, we have money in Egypt ranging from gold coins at 1600 denarii or so down to tetradrachms of one denarius, and we have the same range in Britain if we include the very common radiate and barbarous radiate issues of the third century.

The neatness of the conclusions requires a special warning about the evidence on which they are built. While there is no reason at the moment to doubt the published interpretation of the Aphrodisias inscription it must remain hypothesis and be used as such, for not one of the vital phrases is complete. The evidence from papyri is a selection at random from an uncontrolled series of data but until these are reworked little progress can be made. The evidence of coins that have been found on sites is not at all as firm as it might seem, for such arguments as are advanced here should only properly be made on groups of coins associated one with another in an archaeological context. Very few such groups of coins are yet published in Britain, and are more or less unknown elsewhere; I hope that the supply of information will soon catch up with the theory which should be based on it.

References

Erim, K., Reynolds, J. M. and Crawford, M. *J.R.S.* (1971). **61**, pp. 171–7.

Frank, T. (1936–1940). "An Economic Survey of Ancient Rome", Vols. II and V, John Hopkins Press, Baltimore.

Lauffer, S. (1971). "Diocletians Preisedikt," Walter De Gruyter and Co., Berlin.

West, L. C. (1951). *In* "Studies in Roman Economic and Social History", (Coleman-Norton ed.), Princeton.

Sutherland, C. H. V. (1967). "Roman Imperial Coinage", Vol. VI London.

Jones, A. H. M. (1953). *Economic History Review* **5**, pp. 293–318.

Roman Museums

D. E. STRONG

MY PAPER, PETER, is about the collections of works of art and other objects in Roman public and religious buildings, which became, in effect, the museums and art galleries of ancient Rome, and with the way in which they were administered and conserved. I like to call them museums, though the modern type of museum is unthinkable in the Roman world. The Shorter OED says: "a museum is a building used for storing and exhibiting objects illustrative of antiquity, natural history, fine and industrial art" and records its first use in 1683. The main motivation for this kind of museum was educational. Its origins lie in the activities of rulers and powerful ministers in Europe in the eighteenth century, and of private individuals in England, who, inspired by educational zeal, gave their collections to form the basis of the great public collections which were intended as instruments of popular education*.

The ancient "museum", while it did approximate to certain kinds of modern art gallery, arose for different reasons, the chief factors in its growth being religious dedication and public benefaction. Public temples in the ancient world had long ago become full of miscellaneous objects acquired and dedicated in various ways, apart from the actual temple treasures of coin and metal. The Parthenon had Xerxes throne (Herodotus ix, 20); Lindos had a linen tunic dedicated by Amasis of Egypt (Herodotus ii, 182). Public buildings had battle pictures and trophies, and already by Hellenistic times many sightseers visited famous places to see the antiquities and the works of art. They wandered about in the interiors of temples and were overwhelmed by some of the things they saw, as were the two ladies in Herodas' Fourth Mimiambos†. If you went to Thespiae, you went to see the Cupid, because, as Cicero said, there was no other reason for going (Cicero *Verr.* II, 4, 4). By this time art collect-

---

* Cf. Dr Johnson's remark about the purchase of Lord Orford's pictures and Sir Ashton Lever's Museum ("Boswell's Life of Johnson", The Globe Edition, p. 654).

† Herodas *Mimiambi* (ed. Cunningham, 1971).

ing by private individuals was also well established. The Hellenistic kings were ardent collectors – the Ptolemies of books, and the Attalids of Pergamon of books and works of art of all kinds.

The Romans inherited this taste for collecting and greatly developed it. In the earliest times the collecting of statues, pictures and other objets d'art by the Romans had been a rather haphazard affair. The opportunity of acquiring booty on a large scale came to them at an early date and there were substantial acquisitions of Etruscan statues after the conquest of Veii (Livy 5, 22, 3–7) and of Praeneste (Livy 6, 29, 8–9); Livy disarmingly defines the Roman motives at Veii as *colentium magis quam recipientium*. The gods of the conquered city were to serve new masters; their statues were taken as part of the process known as *evocatio* and not as "objets d'art" taken by right of conquest. In the very different atmosphere of the second century BC Cato in his speech *uti praeda in publicum referatur* still expressed indignation that statues of gods were set up in private houses like furniture (H. Jordan *Orationum Reliquiae* lxxi). Of course there was always looting for looting's sake; Pausanias (8, 46) gives a short history of it to justify the Emperor Augustus in "acquiring" the tusks of the Calydonian Boar.

If originally in Rome religious dedication was the only acceptable method of dealing with captured works of art, public display soon became a powerful motive and, indeed, very much a part of Roman public life at least from the Second Punic War onwards. The catalogue of acquisitions from S. Italy, Sicily, Greece and Asia Minor was enormous. The loot was brought back, as Plutarch comments (*Marcellus* 21), primarily to be eye-catching in the triumph, and to decorate the city later. Sculpture had the chief appeal, especially large-scale sculpture because it was particularly appropriate for religious dedications. The *viri triumphales* made their dedications at first in temples and sanctuaries with accompanying inscriptions defining them as *monumenta rerum gestarum*. But in the course of the second century they were building commemorative monuments which gave an increasingly important place to statues, paintings and other objects captured from the enemy. A significant development came with the building of the Porticus Metelli by Q. Metellus Macedonicus in the 140's; this seems to have been the first building designed specifically with a view to exhibiting a profane work of art, in this case the toweringly vast bronze group by Lysippus of Alexander (Velleius 1, 11, 3) at the Granikos.

The Porticus Metelli set the stage for the last century of the Republic. In both the public and private sectors, works of art became the essential furnishing of architectural monuments and in some cases dominated their setting. Cicero (*Verr.* II, 4) lists three buildings, the Porticus Metelli, Porticus Catuli, and the Temple of Felicitas, which contained a big collection of Mummius' treasures, as the outstanding "museums" of his day. All three of them were triumphal buildings, paid for *ex manubiis*, one a *monumentum deorum immortalium* and the other *ornamenta urbis* (Cicero *de lege agraria* 2, 61). The result of the activities of the *triumphales* was that many buildings had rich and very miscellaneous collections of art works, often known by the names of famous dedicants (Pliny *N.H.* 34, 77). The chief dedications in temples generally bore some relation to the cult, though blatantly profane works were now getting into temple interiors (Plutarch *Pompey* 28).

In the first century BC no major building would be planned without suitable works of art to furnish it. Pompey created a museum (Pliny *N.H.* 7, 34) in the porticoes of his theatre almost as a matter of course, and not so much later C. Asinius Pollio who filled his Atrium Libertatis with Hellenistic sculpture (Pliny *N.H.* 36, 33), clearly believed that if you wanted to create an impressive building that would be looked at, you had to have plenty of eye-catching statuary of that kind. Around the same time Agrippa, taking a leaf from Cato's book, is said to have published a memorandum advocating nationalization of works of art (Pliny *N.H.* 35, 26), but without much success apparently, in view of the large number of very old and very fine statues that Caius Domitius Tullus (Pliny *Letters* 8, 18, 11), in Pliny the Younger's time, is supposed to have had stored away and never looked at.

But Agrippa's motives are clear enough. The last 75 years or so of the first century BC had been a period of indiscriminate looting which produced an inevitable reaction, and in the time of Augustus some notable works were actually returned to their original homes (Bowersock, 1967). As a result it was becoming more and more difficult to find suitable works for the new public buildings that were constantly being erected and for a number of old and now redundant buildings, such as the Saepta Julia, which were in effect turned into museums. Even, so, throughout the Empire, temples, public buildings and public places continued to be richly endowed with works of art of various origin and kind. One of the most magnificent museums of all, the Forum Pacis (Procopius *Gallic War* 8, 21), housed much of Nero's looted masterpieces from the *sellaria* of the Domus Aurea, as well as the temple treasures of Jerusalem (Josephus *Jewish War* 7, 158–62).

A number of public buildings developed as "museums" during the years of the Empire. One of these was the Forum of Augustus which became a kind of National Portrait Gallery, only to be surpassed in time by the more spacious Forum of Trajan, where the collections continued to be added to until the fourth century.* From the first the big imperial *thermae* were decorated with famous works of art and in the Late Empire statues and other works of art were frequently transferred to them from pagan sanctuaries and other *sordentia loca* as in AD 331–3, when the urban prefect, Sex. Anicius Paulinus, set up statues in the Baths of Decius and Sura on the Aventine, or in AD 365 when the Emperor ordered the urban prefect to decorate the Baths of Caracalla.†

How were the collections looked after and preserved when many fine and precious things were on display, often at the mercy of hooliganism, fire, weather and the rest? The *curia* of Pompey's theatre became a WC (Dio Cassius 47, 19, 1), an acceptable *damnatio memoriae*, no doubt, and one suspects that several other Roman public buildings may have served the same purpose without necessarily being intended for it.‡ Pliny (*N.H.* 36, 27) says that works of art in Rome were neglected because everyone was too busy and you needed quiet and space to enjoy them, and there must be some truth in this statement. Yet we know for certain that some famous works were very highly regarded by the people, as for example, the Apoxyomenos of Lysippus, and there is certainly no need to take such a totally cynical view as Friedländer (1923) does, for example, of the Romans' appreciation of works of art in general. It may be possible to throw more light on Roman attitudes by considering the machinery for administration and care of public works of art.

The Republic had a notoriously inefficient machinery for dealing with public works. Censorial contracting§ was cumbersome and lacked continuity, and there were times when things became chaotic. The day to day work of the second arm of the administration, the *aediles*, went more smoothly, but many of them were more concerned with obvious political returns than with dedication to their duties. As far as works of art are concerned, it is highly unlikely that a really efficient system can ever have been established. The contents of the old shrines of the city and the public buildings were, like the buildings themselves, the responsibility of the censors and *aediles*. There was no essential difference between sacred and profane

---

* Cf. Dessau *I.L.S.* 2948, 2949.

† *C.I.L.* VI, 1651, 1167, 1159 (Baths of Decius and Sura), *C.I.L.* VI, 794 1170–3 (Baths of Caracalla).

‡ For irreverent and corrosive acts against statues in public places, Juvenal i, 131; vi, 301.

§ For this see *B.I.C.S.* 15, 1967, 97ff.

buildings. The censors were certainly responsible for the cataloguing and distribution of the *res sacrae*. We find them distributing gold vases of King Antiochus to various temples (Livy 42, 6). They also removed statues from temples in certain circumstances and Sp. Cassius, for example, got removed from near the Temple of Tellus and melted down (Pliny *N.H.* 34, 30). Although it does not seem to be explicitly stated anywhere, it is clearly implied that the censors prepared lists of the contents of buildings; during the Second Punic War in the absence of censors and for other pressing reasons special triumvirs were appointed by plebiscite to carry out this work – the formula is *sacris conquirendis donisque persignandis* (Livy 25, 7).

By the end of the Republic the duty of cataloguing the often very miscellaneous contents was a major task. According to Pliny, the Temple of Venus Genetrix had a statue of Cleopatra, a collection of coins and jewels, as well as paintings by Greek masters inside and out (Pliny *N.H.* 35, 136). Collections of intaglios and cameos (Pliny *N.H.* 37, 1) were dedicated in temples together with glassware and other objects. Objects of natural history seem to have been rare; a rather exceptional case was a tusk of the Calydonian Boar, which for some reason or other finished up in a Sanctuary of Bacchus in the Gardens of Caesar (Pausanias 8, 46). Unfortunately we know almost nothing about Roman methods of arranging and cataloguing antiquities. P. Servilius (Cicero *Verr.* ii, 1, 21) is known to have prepared careful inventories of booty with dimensions, description and state of preservation of the objects. Inventories were presumably similar to those from Greek sources, such as the Delos inventories (*inscriptiones Graecae* xi, 2, nos. 135ff.), parts of which sometimes have the authentic ring of modern museum registers: a gold statuette with no arms and legs, a bronze jug with no bottom, footbowls, two of which were not sound, and a cow lacking its left horn.

The *aediles* had a general supervision of public buildings which seems to have been concerned chiefly with the day to day maintenance both of temples and secular buildings and with the supervision of the custodians, the *aeditui*, who were the guardians of the temples and their contents. Varro (*de r. r.* 1, 2, 2) records an encounter with the custodian of the Temple of Tellus who had been summoned by the *aedile* responsible. These *aeditui* were usually public slaves and, according to Mommsen (Marquardt, 1957), they were of two classes – those who merely opened and closed the doors and those who had more responsible duties. The *aediles* by virtue of their general *procuratio urbis* also had responsibility for dedications in public places. The Hercules in a tunic by the Rostra, which had been moved around quite a lot, had three inscriptions, the last of which

I*

recorded that the *curule aedile*, T. Septimius Sabinus, had returned it to public view (Pliny *N.H.* 34, 93).

Between them, the *aediles* and the censors under the Republic looked after all the public collections with help sometimes from other regular magistrates and extraordinary appointments. The exceptions were certain triumphal monuments whose buildings and contents remained the hereditary responsibility of the family. The Temple of Bellona and the Basilica Aemilia are examples. As far as the booty in them is concerned there should have been, and sometimes were, careful lists prepared at the time of the triumph and these would be preserved in the censors' records.

Towards the end of the Republic when the normal administration was breaking down, when censors had not been appointed for some years and the office of *aedile* had been neglected, the administration of works of art must have become very chaotic. At this point Octavian made himself responsible for a major programme of improvement, persuading Agrippa to assume, through the office of aedile, various duties including the supervision of works of art. It was he who seems to have turned the Saepta Julia into a sort of museum and in his enthusiasm published his famous memorandum. Augustus' long-term solution to the problem of public works was, of course, the appointment of curatorial boards, the third of which, established quite late in his reign somewhere between 11 BC and AD 14, was the Board of Public Buildings and Sacred Shrines which took over the role of both the censors and the *aediles* in the maintenance of public buildings.

We know precious little about the work of the *curatores*;* most of what we do concerns the assigning of land for public dedications and other purposes. A glimpse into the work of the office comes from the series of letters about the procurator of the Antonine Column who was a freedman in the office of the *curatores*. In one letter, the Emperor's accountants ask the curator to assign land for a dwelling to be built by the procurator in the vicinity of the column (*C.I.L.* VI, 1585). In general terms, the curators, of whom there were two, must have taken over the censors' and *aediles'* duties concerning care and maintenance of works of art. Vitellius (Suetonius *Vitellius* 5) held the office and is said to have behaved very badly in it in connection with temple treasures, substituting lead and oricalchum for the gold and silver. It is generally believed that the two *curatores* divided the duties, one being concerned with sacred shrines, the other with

---

* See A. E. Gordon in *University of California Publications in Classical Archaeology* ii, 1934–52, 279ff.

public buildings; in that case Vitellius' duties were those of curator of shrines.

There was a substantial staff attached to the office of the curators; we hear of sub-curators, of *procuratores operum publicorum* (one of whom is addressed in another of the letters of 193) and the procurators of individual buildings presumably came under the curators; we know of a *procurator operis theatri Pompeiani*, a freedman who, having followed Septimius Severus to Rome, got himself a nice job with the responsibility for the fabric of Pompey's theatre (*I.L.S.* 1430). By this time the office of curator which began as a senatorial appointment working *ex decreto senatus* had come under the control of the Emperor. Titus after the fire of AD 80 seems to have taken over the task of redecorating the temples (Suetonius *Titus* 8), and Domitian probably took the whole organization into his hands. We know the names of a number of curators, but not much about them or their previous experience of public works. T. Clodius Papirius Pulcher Maximus who was curator in 238 had at least performed the functions of the office on an earlier occasion.

There is a very involved and at present insoluble problem concerning the division which is known to have taken place between the Imperial works administration dealing with major Imperial buildings and the public works administration in general – between the *opera Caesaris* and the *opera publica*. However the division worked, there was presumably a similar division in respect of the art collections. Minor officials of whom we hear in inscriptions are generally closely connected with the emperor. Under Antoninus Pius we have an imperial freedman who is procurator of statues and paintings; under Marcus and Commodus an official known as an *adiutor rationis statuarum*; we also know of a *procurator a pinacothecis* (*C.I.L.VI,* 9007, 31053, 1708 (=*I.L.S.* 1222)). This was a period when very great interest was being taken in the national collections generally, as can be seen in the coinage and elsewhere. The majority of subordinate officers in the Public Works Department were imperial freedmen, but it is difficult to say whether this reflects tight imperial control over the whole of public works or whether the surviving inscriptions, which are not very many, happen to refer to the emperor's side of the administration.

The re-organization carried out in the early fourth century throws some light on what had gone before. A *curator statuarum* is first mentioned in 335–7 as a subordinate of the *praefectus urbi* and it has been suggested (Chastagnol, 1960) that this office was created in 331 when the office of *curator aedium sacrarum* was suppressed by Constantine and his duties divided between a *consularis operum maximorum* and a *curator statuarum*. The reform would then be connected with Constantine's order for a final inventory of the temple treasures to be prepared by the last curator who then gave up office; in future years the *praefectus urbi* working through the curator of statues was responsible for the re-organization and preservation of the national collections. It is quite revealing that the only really new official to come out of the reform is the *curator statuarum*. This demonstrates the dominance of statuary over other art forms from the Roman point of view.

In 331–3, when Sextus Anicius Paulinus was prefect, we have the earliest references to the transfer of statues from pagan sanctuaries to public baths and other public places (Lanciani, 1899). This man especially decorated the baths on the Aventine. The practice became increasingly common and in the Later Empire we have many references* to objects being moved *ex sordentibus locis* to other places. In 365 the Baths of Caracalla got a large number of statues by order of the emperor working through the *praefectus urbi*†. Very soon, the whole *sacra urbs* itself became a kind of museum and conservation became the theme of several imperial edicts – a very different attitude from that which produced, not so long before, the Arch of Constantine (de Franciscis, 1954–5).

To summarize what little we know about the administration of the art collections under the Empire, the general responsibility lay with the curators of public works, one of whom may have been responsible for public buildings and the other for sacred shrines. These curators operated under increasingly tight imperial control, while the very big imperial collections like those of the Forum of Augustus or the Forum Pacis were separately administered. There is a suggestion that larger specialist staffs were built up over the years. As far as we know, the whole system had worked efficiently except in times of crisis. Such a crisis came during and after Nero's reign. Nero's depredations, and the fire, and the Vitellians, left a chaotic situation for the Flavian emperors, which convinced Vespasian to take office as censor in AD 73 and interrupt the normal procedures. Pliny the Elder (*N.H.* 3, 5) preserves some of the statistics of that censorship and it has been argued that he also used the official inventories of the year as a source for his descriptions of works of art. On other occasions, circumstances were such that special measures were needed to catalogue and examine the treasure; Agricola was appointed to an office of this kind – *ad dona templorum recognoscenda* (Tacitus *Agricola* 6).

* E.g. *C.I.L.* XIV, Suppl., 4721 (Ostia); *I.L.S.* 5482, 5477, 5478.
† *C.I.L* VI, 794, 1170–1173a

In all this little has been said about the care and preservation of the objects. The existence of a moderately efficient machinery implies that the general supervision of the collections was reasonably satisfactory. There were quite stout locks on the doors, and there were curators who took their jobs seriously. The problem is to discover how much genuine interest there was in the collections and what expertise was available to those responsible for them. These two factors are the basis of good conservation. We want to know ideally how much knowledge of artistic theory there was, and what practical skills to conserve works of art. We also need to know how far the Romans concerned themselves with questions of display, museum conditions and so on. None of these are easy questions, but all are worth considering.

Firstly, general expertise. Among the Romans a knowledge of classical art in general developed quite steadily in the last two centuries BC Livy (25, 40)* defines the sack of Syracuse as the *initium mirandi graecarum artium opera,* and this means, of course, that, from then on, religious motives took second place to artistic ones. In the next two centuries the Romans were able to collect some of the very best works of classical art including statues by Pheidias himself (Pliny *N.H.* 34, 54). There is no doubt that people like the Scipios and Aemilius Paullus not only knew what they liked, but knew a good deal about it. Some of their contemporaries, on the other hand, were ignorant and boorish. Dio of Prusa (Favorinus 37, 42) refers to dedications by Mummius in which he inscribed Zeus on statues of Philip, son of Amyntas, and Nestor and Priam on two Arcadian youths from Pheneus; and this is not the only aspersion cast on Mummius' knowledge of ancient art†. In defence of such men it must be said that the textbook tradition about Greek art was distinctly thin, though many artists had written on their work since Polykleitos. Xenocrates‡ seems to have been the Romans' favourite art critic because he also had a sound practical knowledge of art; Pasiteles' five-volume work on *Nobilia opera,* which also seems to have been an essentially practical manual (Pliny *N.H.* 36, 39), was written in the last century of the Republic.

The artistic advisor, generally of Greek origin, is a phenomenon of that period, and a very important influence on the development of Roman taste. Already in the second century BC Greek artists and

---

* Contrast the earlier attitude, cf. Juvenal xi, 10.
† Yet Mummius was one of the great "collectors" (*C.I.L.* I, 627–31, 541).
‡ On him see K. Jex-Blake and E. Sellers, *The Elder Pliny's Chapters on the History of Art* xvi, ff.

craftsmen were being brought to Rome, and in the next century this immigration became a flood. It coincided with a phase in the thinking of educated Romans which saw collecting of a selective kind as an essential part of the cultivation of *humanitas* (cf. Cicero *ad Q.f.* 3, 1, 5). Looking back, this was the really creative period in the history of Roman taste. The objects collected (Schefold 1972) had to be appropriate to the atmosphere of the place for intellectual and aesthetic reasons. The Roman patron set problems of design and choice, not new problems but on a new scale; Crassus wanted a philosopher's garden, Cicero an Academy, Hortensius a building designed suitably for a picture of the Argonauts (Pliny *N.H.* 35, 130)*. The Greeks were able to cope, and circumstances threw up one or two very able and versatile characters; the Roman patron grew to rely on his advisors to stock, arrange and maintain his collections. His own attitude, publicly at least, was rather equivocal; he would rather not seem too enthusiastic nor too well informed.

In this atmosphere problems of display, conservation, repair and so on were bound to come up and we would very much like to know how they were handled. As far as acquisition is concerned, the situation has changed very little. In acquiring works of art you always have to rely more or less on the experts. Who were the experts? Originally they were mostly practical men like the S. Italian Pasiteles who not only wrote about art but worked himself in bronze, precious metal and stone, and indeed founded a school of sculptors (Borda, 1953). Two typical characters were Tlepolemos and Hieron from Cibyra in Caria, Verres' "hunting dogs", as Cicero calls them. One was a bronze worker and the other a painter, so they made a good team (Cicero *Verr.* ii, iv, 13). A very interesting man, whom one would like to know more about, was C. Avianius Evander who had a long career as art-agent and restorer†. He was apparently brought to Rome by Augustus in 25 BC, but he is referred to by Cicero much earlier as an agent or art dealer.

Another developing class of art-experts were the copyists. Quintilian (*Instit. Orat.* x, ii, 6) comments scathingly on those who simply make drawings with measurements of large pictures – *quemadmodum quidam pictores in id solum student ut describere tabulas mensuris ac lineis sciant.* We, of course, have every reason to be grateful to them because they must be the producers of the famous copy-books, through which, indirectly, copies of masterpieces have come down to us. They must have acquired in the process a very

---

* For Roman picture galleries *M.A.A.R.* xv, 1938, 70ff.
† *R.E.* II 2 (1896) 2372, VI 1 (1907) 843.

considerable knowledge of style and technique, both of painting and sculpture. The dealers too sometimes knew a lot. Dealers, if not generally notable for vast expertise, are always very shrewd, if successful. The learned Damasippus who is referred to by Horace (*Sat.* ii, 3, 16ff.) and is perhaps the same man as the Damasippus mentioned by Cicero (*Ad fam* vii, 23, 2; xii, 29, 2; xii, 33, 1) on a number of occasions, obviously knew a lot about all the things the collectors liked to get. The dealers and art experts could, as they do today, manufacture taste. Vitruvius (iii, introd. 2) reminds us how fickle taste can be and gives us the names of a few artists whom he thinks were men of great ability, but never quite made it with the cognoscenti. Vastly inflated prices then as now were paid for the works of fashionable people; a sketch by Arcesilaos would cost more than a finished picture by one of his contemporaries. Another man whose preliminary sketches (*rudimenta*) were highly prized was Protogenes, obviously a superb draughtsman (Petronius *Satyricon* 83; Quintilian xii, 10, 6).

The gentleman art-expert is a rather later phenomenon, but he does exist already in the first century BC. Even Cicero (*Tusc. Disp.* iv, 14, 32) has an understanding reference to bronze disease in Corinthian bronzes. In the first century AD Novius Vindex (Statius *Silvae* iv, 6) was a much admired cognoscente, very able at attributing works of art, and there may of course have been more to Mamurra (Martial, ix, 59, 1ff) than his reputed ability to tell Corinthian bronzes by their smell. By this time the gentlemen of leisure knew quite a bit about objets d'art. The Younger Pliny's (*Letters* iii, 6) episode with a Corinthian bronze of an old man is revealing; he can tell that the patina is old and he has firm views on how it should be mounted and displayed. His uncle may have been right that no one had time to study art in Rome, but a lot of people seem to have spent time looking at it. The Digest (xxi, 1, 65) calls to notice idle slaves who spent too much time looking at pictures and there is no doubt that there were a lot of idle people in Rome. Art expertise had, in fact, become reasonably respectable so that the Stoic Epictetus rather grandly admits that you do have to be skilled to look at statues intelligently (*Dissert* ii, 24.7).

Once having acquired your collection you were concerned to display it. Before the second century BC works of art were generally rather haphazardly placed in temples and other buildings without much thought being given to their best arrangement, but the monuments of the *viri triumphales* developed, as we saw, into places in which to dedicate works of art, and, inevitably, the architecture was adapted or specifically designed to receive them. In the private sector, the activities of the "humanists" strongly influenced the development of ideas about display. Private picture galleries or arrangements of statuary in villas and gardens were commissioned from the architects of the day with two aims, often rather conflicting ones, in mind. The first was to forge a close link between the architecture and the objects, and the second to display the objects themselves as well as possible. The architectural settings would certainly have been too elaborate for modern taste; a good parallel to the Roman approach is provided by the Villa Albani, designed by Winckelmann and Alessandro Albani, where each room or group of rooms is set around a pivotal work (Leppmann, 1971); the effect has been described as "a living museum organized from a scholarly view point", and this is very much the attitude of mind that appears in Cicero's correspondence with Atticus (cf. Cicero *ad. Att.* i, 15).

The wish to combine architecture, sculpture and painting in an organic scheme was not the sole deciding factor, nor was it necessarily incompatible with a wish to display the objects well. It was generally recognized that some pictures needed to be looked at from a distance and others from close up; a bad light, Seneca reminds us (*Epist.* vii, 65, 17; *De Beneficiis* ii, 33.2), can ruin a picture, and Vitruvius gives very precise recommendations for lighting (vi, 4, 2; vi, 7, 3). There should, he says, be a north light for picture galleries because it is steady and does not alter with the course of the sun. One is reminded of the care obviously taken by many Roman interior decorators to make the apparent and actual sources of light correspond in their pictures (von Blanckenhagen and Alexander, 1962). The needs of display are clearly of first consideration in the development of rooms as especially suitable for exhibition of works of art. The classic, and very simple, case is the *exedra*, or *schola* as it also seems to have been called, opening off a porticus (Pliny *N.H.* 36, 29; 36, 22). There are several references to the *scholae* of the Porticus of Octavia, and all the tapestries and pictures in Pompey's gardens were arranged in exedras. The reason for the *schola* is that the porticus itself is often narrow and crowded* and the *exeda* gives an opportunity both to stand away from the object and if necessary protect it by rope or barrier. In all ancient display there was also a strong tendency to arrange things symmetrically with one work balancing another. K. Lehmann (*Hesperia* 14, 1945, 259ff.) produced an ingenious argument for a museum layout in the *pronaos* in the Temple of Augustus which he based on the thirteen art-epigrams of Martial,

---

* For the difficulties of looking at works of art in some Roman public places see Juvenal vi, 153.

Book 14. The temple is known to have been rich in art-works and Lehmann thought that Martial was describing a series of objects in gold, silver, bronze and marble arranged as pendants, partly by subject matter and style and partly for their decorative qualities. The evidence is slight and the hypothesis a little over-ingenious, although it accords with Roman practice.

There is, however, no doubt that a good deal of thought went into the display of works of art. Many lessons were probably learnt also from the temporary exhibitions which became common in the Late Republic. C. Claudius, when *aedile*, got the famous Cupid of Thespiae (Cicero *Verr*. ii, 4, 6–7) to decorate the Forum prominently during a festival. This was obviously quite something of an achievement in view of Cicero's comment (see p. 247). C. Claudius Pulcher (Cicero *Verr*. ii, 4, 6–7) put on a big show of objects acquired by various means, while the *aediles* of 59 BC, Varro and Murena, brought back a series of frescoes from Sparta which they had had cut out of the walls, and put in wooden frames to arrange in the Comitium (Pliny *N.H.* 35, 173). Domitius Calvinus is supposed to have borrowed statues from Octavian, ostensibly for a temporary show in his new and shining Regia (Dio 48, 42), and then refused to return them to Octavian who was somehow of the opinion that it was sacrilege to move them. These temporary shows must have depended very largely on good display techniques, and some must have been influential in the development of ideas, especially on open-air display.

The public collections, as we have seen, were warded by custodians who were generally slaves or freedmen, and responsible for security and cleanliness. Their main concern obviously was safety, and the task of looking after the collections was a very responsible one, sometimes dangerous. There is no difficulty in believing that if the famous dog in the Cella Junonis of the Capitolium had been stolen, the custodians would have paid for it with their lives, and it is clear that they bore very considerable responsibility*. The dangers ranged from the removal of gilding from statues (Juvenal xiii, 150) to major thefts such as the helmet of Mars Ultor. But temples are generally thought of as safe as banks. Their doors were stoutly locked and you had to be ruthless to break in, as Verres was when he robbed the Temple of Herakles at Akragas by wrenching off the bolt and removing the statues from their blocks. The guard dogs were also a formidable safe-guard making exceptions only for such as Scipio Africanus (Aulus Gellius vi, 1, 6).

* For the suicide of the *aedituus* of the Capitoline Temple, Pliny *N.H.* 33, 15.

The traditional sideline of custodians is guiding the public, and it is clear that in this respect ancient guides were essentially no different from the modern. They had their invariable patter. In the Temple of Diana at Ephesus the guide told you to shade your eyes when looking at the Herakles and Hecate group by Menestratus otherwise you would be blinded (Pliny *N.H.* 36, 32). There is an echo perhaps of a guided tour in Pliny's references to the Domus Aurea (*N.H.* 35, 120), part of which may have become a sort of museum. We hear of the Minerva whose eyes follow you as you go past, and there is the epigram about Fabullus which has the same ring. The guides had a fixed itinerary, always stopping to comment on the same things, hence the confusion among the guides of Syracuse who had to describe things as they were before Verres' sack (Cicero *Verr.* ii, iv, 59). I had a not entirely dissimilar dilemma described to me at length by the Director of an open-air museum in the USA, whose itinerary explaining the typological and chronological development of the New England mill-village had been reversed when the access bridge was destroyed in the autumn floods. As always the guides invented a good deal and were particularly fond of inventing previous owners, because the Romans obviously shared with us a curiosity about things belonging to famous people. A good story usually increased the value (Juvenal vi, 156). Novius Vindex (Statius *Silvae* iv, 6, 59), so he said, had a Herakles which belonged to Alexander, Hannibal and Sulla. When there was doubt about the attribution of a particular work of art, as there often was (cf. Pliny *N.H.* 36, 29; 36, 28), the guides were no doubt only too glad to offer an opinion, and we may judge they were not slow to give a snap answer to a question: "Why was there only one tusk of the Calydonian Boar?"

Doubts about attribution, about previous owners and so on, were frequent because of the primitive nature of "labelling" if one may call it such. Statues were often brought to Rome without their original bases, old bases might be used for new statues, or statues might be altered and so on. The sculptor Tisicrates of the third century Lysippic School seems to have been particularly accident-prone. At Oropos (Siedentopf, 1968) a Tisicrates statue base was used for an equestrian statue of Sulla. According to Pliny (*N.H.* 34, 89) a certain Piston added a figure of a lady to a chariot by Tisicrates, and the Pentelic marble base with the inscription CORNELIA AFRICANI/GRACCHORVM from near the site of the Porticus Metelli has a later (3rd century?) inscription OPVS TISICRATIS (Mustilli 1939). The best "labelling" would be on portrait figures and busts where an inscription probably in epigrammatic form described each character. We have one surviving from the portrait gallery in the Temple of Apollo Palatinus (Dessau *I.L.S.* 1, 61) – greater permanency than modern Italian museum labels.

The *aeditui* may have been able to guard the collections successfully and show them proudly to the visitors, but can have done little to preserve them. The climate of Rome is good and the atmosphere was still comparatively clean, but inevitably statues and paintings suffered in the course of time. Petronius describes an imaginary picture gallery where the works of Zeuxis can be seen *nondum vetustatis iniuria victas* (*Satyricon* 83). Some works, of course, did age gracefully to justify Quintilian's comments on the inimitable patina of age. Statius (*Silvae* 1, 190) says that the Horse of Domitian will never suffer from weather, lightning, wind and time as other statues do. When we consider that a great deal of Roman display was in the open air, or almost open air, and subject to damage of all kinds, we must expect deterioration over the years. One wonders, for example, how the paintings which Caesar dedicated in front of his Temple of Venus Genetrix, fared with the years, and it would be interesting to know how many of the works of art listed by Pliny survived, say, into the fourth century.

Fire, of course, was the chief destroyer; in 191 it overwhelmed the Forum Pacis, and both the Forum of Caesar and the Theatre of Pompey were badly damaged in the third century. Obviously very little was known about conservation and restoration. Pausanias has one or two interesting references; he tells us that the ivory parts of the Olympian Zeus were treated with oil (5, 11, 5) to prevent damp while the ivory of the Athena Parthenos was deliberately kept damp. He also mentions the treatment of the bronze shields in the Stoa Poekile by covering them with pitch (8, 42, 7), and it is particularly interesting that one of these shields has survived until the present day. It is not quite clear whether this was done to preserve them or to produce a patina; the whole question of ancient patination, whether it was artificial or natural, is of course a difficult one. We have a reference in Pliny (*N.H.* 35, 97) to Apelles' varnish which protected pictures *pulvere ac sordibus*, but this did not prevent the picture of Aphrodite which was displayed in front of the Temple of Divus Julius from rapid decay.

When a picture had decayed in this way nothing much could be done; the Aphrodite was replaced by Nero. According to Pliny when Marcus Junius wanted to have Aristides' picture of a tragic actor and a boy in the temple of Apollo cleaned for the Ludi Apollinares, he commissioned a restorer who promptly ruined it (*N.H.* 35, 100). But as time went on expertise in this field must have increased. We know that the copyists carefully studied the style and technique of the old

masters and we get echoes of informed opinion in Pliny and elsewhere, as, for example, when we are told that Protogenes' Ialysus
(*N.H.* 35, 102) in the Templum Pacis had four coats of colour. The
restorer became quite skilful at removing frescoes from the wall. They
were able to do this in the case of the Temple of Ceres when it was
restored by Augustus, but they were defeated by the composition of
the stucco in the case of old paintings from Ardea and Lanuvium
which Caligula coveted (*N.H.* 35, 154). The removal of the paintings
from Sparta (see above p. 259) must have required a good deal of skill.
Painters were always being called upon to adapt old masters, to replace Alexander with Augustus, for example, and they must have
learnt a lot about technique in the process. Still, no one could be
found capable of restoring Apelles' Aphrodite, and successful
restorers were often richly rewarded (Suetonius *Vespasian* 18).

   With sculpture it was often easier and even though the famous
statues, unlike those which came into the possession of eighteenth
century English gentlemen, were not generally "headless and lame",
as Horace Walpole described the collection at Wilton House*, a lot
of restoration work had to be carried out. The repolishing of marble
statuary with wax must have been a regular activity for art restorers
(Juvenal xii, 86), and there are references to more ambitious
restoration work. We hear that Avianius Evander, the successful art
dealer and advisor, put the head back on Timotheus' statue of Diana
in the Palatine Temple of Apollo (Pliny *N.H.* 36, 32); this was a
skilled job, but there were certainly plenty of people who could have
done it, because statues were always being adapted by changing
heads or details, or making various additions (Blanck 1963). Some
damage was more difficult; Nero had a statue of Alexander as a boy
gilded and this was thought to spoil its effect, but although the
restorer removed most of the gold, he could not get it out of the
cavities and blemishes and it was never the same again. There was a
positive mania for this irreversible process in the Late Empire
(*Panegyrici Latini* iv (x), 35, 4). We have an interesting inscription
which refers to a highly specialized kind of restorer in the tombstone of M. Rapilius Serapio (*C.I.L.* VI, 9403) who made a good living
putting eyes back in statues. From surviving statues we know a
certain amount about the work of ancient restorers, although the
subject seems never to have been studied in detail. The statue of a
youth from the Villa of Nero at Subiaco (Lippold, 1922) had a restored
hand and the Ares Borghese, when it was re-used in the second

---

* On the other hand, they were often "earless and noseless", Juvenal viii. 2ff.

century for a portrait, had a very elaborate restoration which involved cutting out a large piece of the base to let in a new piece consisting of the feet and lower legs of the figure which had been broken off. This particular restorer was obviously reluctant to use metal fixings. The restoration of pottery, silver and other small objects was often rather heavy-handed because of the lack of good adhesives.

In a brief paper it is not possible to give more than an aerial view of the subject, but it seems clear that considerable attention was indeed paid to the problems of maintaining a large national art-collection in Rome. Almost all that collection has now been destroyed, but it is probably due to the expertise built up in the first four centuries of the Empire that it survived as long as it did. When in the fourth and fifth centuries Roman emperors were making last desperate efforts to preserve the national heritage – the monuments of the pagan world – against all kinds of depredation, this body of expertise still existed and could be organized* Deliberate destruction and looting account for the ultimate disappearance of the *populus copiosissimus statuarum* (Cassiodorus *Varia* vii, 13) from Rome, however much the emperors of the late fourth century tried to reverse the destructive acts of the earlier years (de Franciscis 1954–5). Nothing, for example, could effectively combat the widespread belief that pagan statues were inhabited by demons. One recalls the story of the Aphrodite of Gaza† which broke into pieces at the sight of Christian crosses, and Mango's (1963) comment that: "We may doubt that the collapse of the statue was altogether spontaneous". In Rome, denuded as it was by now of many of its finest collections, the struggle to preserve the classical past continued. As late as the year 483 (*I.L.S.* 3132) an inscription records the restoration of a statue of Minerva, the protector against fires, which had been badly damaged by fire in a *tumultus civilis*.

References

Blanck, H. (1963). "Wiederverwendung alter Statuen", Cologne.
von Blanckenhagen, P. H. and Alexander, C. (1962). "The Paintings from Boscotrecase". (Mitteilungen des D.A.I., Ergänzungsheft 6).
Borda, M. (1953). "La Scuola di Pasiteles". Bari.

* E.g. the picturae professores of Cod. Theod. 13, 4, 4.
† Marcus Diaconus, *Vita Porphyrii*, chaps. 59–61 (ed. Grégoire and Kugener, Paris, 1930, 47ff.).

Bowersock, G. (1967). "Augustus and the Greek World". University Press, Oxford.

Chastagnol, A. (1960). "La préfecture urbaine à Rome sous le Bas-Empire". Paris.

de Franciscis, P. (1954–5). Rendiconti Pontificia Accademia Romana di Archeologia, 28.

Friedländer, L. (1923). "Darstellungen aus der Sittengeschichte Roms", 10th edition, Vienna.

Lanciani, R. (1899). "The Destruction of Ancient Rome". London.

Leppmann, W. (1971). "Winckelmann". London.

Lippold, G. (1922). "Kopien und Umbildungen grieschischen Statuen'. Munich.

Mango, C. (1963). *Dumbarton Oaks Papers*, **17**, p. 55ff.

Marquardt, J. (1957). "Römische Staatsverwaltung", (3rd edition by G. Wissowa), reprint, Darmstadt.

Mustilli, D. (1939). "Il Museo Mussolini". Rome.

Schefold, K. (1972). "La peinture pompéienne", Brussels.

Siedentopf (1968). "Dass hellenistische Reiterdenkmal", Waldsassen.

Archaeology and the History of Mediaeval Technology

H. W. M. HODGES

THE DEVELOPMENT of technology in the mediaeval period in Europe differs from that of all preceding periods in one marked respect, for throughout the whole of the Middle Ages not a single important new raw material was introduced. Thus the craftsman of 1500 AD was still using precisely the same range of raw materials as his forebears had inherited from the Ancient World a millennium earlier. Hence, the history of mediaeval technology is very largely the study of the development of a number of mechanical devices, and it follows that one of the more useful methods of archaeological investigation, the analysis of materials, has little bearing on the subject. To a large extent, therefore, one has to rely upon traditional historical evidence, and it might seem reasonable to expect that, with the far greater number of written sources upon which to draw than is available for earlier periods, a fairly clear picture of the development of mediaeval technology could be drawn. Unfortunately this is not true, and attempts to write a history of mediaeval technology are usually unconvincing, and not infrequently absurd. This sad state of affairs is due only partly to the nature of the evidence itself, for historians are as much to blame for the manner in which the documents have been treated.

The main sources of evidence are either the written word, often no more than a passing reference to some device in a legal document; and illustrations, normally from illuminated manuscripts. As far as the legal documents of the Middle Ages are concerned it must be clearly understood that the earliest surviving mention of any device shows only the earliest point in time at which that piece of equipment was recognized in law. In all probability for most mechanical innovations of the mediaeval period there was a considerable time lag, far longer than would be the case today, between their invention and diffusion on the one hand, and the moment at which they first received legal recognition on the other hand. Until the function of a device had been clearly demonstrated and understood it is unlikely that it was either taxed or even included in a list of property. Thus the legal document of the Middle Ages is an exceedingly poor indication of the place and time at which a new device was introduced, and in a study which necessarily considers origins this creates obvious difficulties.

One is faced with a similar problem when one considers the function of the mediaeval artist. The illuminations of a manuscript were a means of adding to the text, and as often as not illustrated the written word using contemporary life as the model. Hence in most mediaeval manuscripts a machine would not be used in an illustration until it had become almost a part of everyday life, otherwise it would merely subtract from the text by diverting the reader's attention. The same general rule can be applied to other sources of illustration such as coloured glass windows and carvings whose function, equally, was to depict the workaday world. Seen in this light one might reasonably expect illustrations of machines to appear no earlier than references to them in legal documents, and in fact one normally finds that illustrations of mechanical devices first appear far later than the earliest written records in cases where both occur.

Standing somewhat apart from these written and illustrated sources are the few craftsmen's handbooks which require special consideration. Many of them are recipe books in which the various entries were copied from previous similar compilations, and one can trace the same recipes and the same fabulous stories being handed down throughout the whole of the Middle Ages, but there are other works which do not fall into this category. By far the most outstanding of these is the notebook of the Cistercian engineer, Villard de Honnecourt, who was active in the middle of the thirteenth century. Amongst other things he illustrated and described a screw-jack and a water-driven saw-mill in which the timbers were automatically fed against the saw-blade (Gille, 1956). Generally he has received a bad press from historians who have considered many of his machines to have been too advanced to have been adopted in his time. The possibility that de Honnecourt was simply recording machines, some perhaps novel in his day, all of which were in restricted use is seldom considered. Indeed, one has the uncomfortable feeling that de Honnecourt's notebooks are dealt with in this way because, were one to take them at face value, then the rest of the history of mediaeval technology would have to be rewritten. Possibly this is precisely what should be done.

The difficulties that one runs into by accepting the traditional historical evidence can be seen only too clearly when one compares what has been said about the introduction and development of two basic pieces of equipment whose function was to rotate a tool or workpiece, the simple crank handle and the treadle-and-spring drive (Gille, 1956; White, 1962). The crank handle is first known in the early ninth century as an illustration in the Utrecht Psalter where it is depicted for turning a rotary grind-stone. A century later it is described as a means of operating a kind of hurdy-gurdy, a device not illustrated until the twelfth century. From the twelfth century, too, comes the first of a series of illustrations of Fortuna turning her wheel of destiny by means of a crank handle. Early in the fourteenth century, in a coloured glass window at York Minster, is shown the mould core for a bell being rotated by a workman by means of a crank handle, and it is not until the fifteenth century that the crank handle, both single and compound, appears, to judge from illustrations, to have been widely applied to other machines. The impression is thus gained that the crank handle was only slowly put to use in the Middle Ages.

By contrast, treated at face value, the combination of treadle and overhead sapling-spring seems to have found a number of uses within a very short period of time. The treadle-operated loom was first described by Alexander Neckham at the end of the twelfth century: within the thirteenth century it is depicted as, too, are lathes and vertical saws operated by means of treadles-and-springs. The inferences that have been drawn from these very limited data are, first, that the treadle-and-spring was one aspect of a kind of miniature industrial revolution of the thirteenth century, and, secondly, that the mediaeval engineer was unbelievably slow in his adoption of the crank handle and, subsequently, the crank shaft.

Leaving aside for the moment the question of dating upon which the first of these inferences depends, it is fairly self evident that the crank handle and treadle-and-spring could have been complementary to one another, and the reason that the former found so few applications was that in many cases the work was better done by the latter. Thus, the crank-handle had an obvious advantage where slow, steady, continuous rotation was required over a short period of time, but its use often demanded two people rather than a single crafts-man. The treadle-and-spring on the other hand could be operated by a single person and was less tiring to use than a manually operated drive. It is certainly no accident that the pole-lathe was used for turning wood, a long operation, while the crank was employed to rotate the mould core for a bell, presumably not a major factor in the whole process of casting bells. Seen in this light, the treadle-and-spring, and later the cam-and-spring, inhibited the adoption of the crank-handle and crank-shaft, and the limited number of uses to which the crank was put becomes more credible.

As for the late twelfth century origin of the treadle-and-spring one must voice some reservations. There is, for example, another device incorporating the treadle-and-spring, the oliver, about which the origins are far too little known. In this machine a heavy hammer, usually a blacksmith's forging hammer, is raised by means of a sapling-spring, while a treadle is used to bring it down when striking. There seems to be no mention of this machine until 1686, by which time it is the origin of the word "oliver" which is under discussion. That the device was in use before 1686 is certain, but how long before, and by whom it was initially used are matters of pure conjecture.

On the rare occasions in which it is possible to check the historical dating for an innovation against archaeological data one finds the historical evidence totally misleading. Thus, the potter's wheel is known only from illustrations which show there to have been the two types of wheel in use in mediaeval Europe (Jope, 1956; Reith, 1960; Husa, 1967). The first type is known only in the thirteenth century manuscripts from France; the second type known from a carving in the north transept of Reims Cathedral of thirteenth century date is far more commonly found as a detail of manuscript illumination in fifteenth century Southern Germany and Bohemia. The first type was a flat, spoked wheel in which the hub served as the wheel-head on which the pots were thrown. It seems to have been mounted on a low bench, and the potter gave it momentum by pushing at the perimeter with a stick. The second type was roughly cylindrical, the wheel-head being connected to the fly-wheel by a series of vertical spokes, while the potter made it rotate by kicking the fly-wheel. It is not until the Renaissance that one comes across illustrations of the kick-wheel as one understands it today, with the wheel-head and fly-wheel connected by a vertical iron shaft.

Taken on its own, and applying the same kinds of criteria as were employed when discussing the crank-handle or treadle-and-spring, one could use this evidence to provide a number of postulates such as the thirteenth century appearance of the potter's wheel in Europe, or the very late, fifteenth century, acceptance of the kick-wheel in Central Europe. Mercifully in this case we have the archaeological evidence of the pottery itself to set the record straight, for most of western Europe by a matter of some centuries. Had one only the manuscript illustrations of the pottery by which to judge rather than the pottery itself, then the lamentably lop-sided manner in which mediaeval vessels are so commonly depicted might well be put forward as further evidence of the lack of any form of potter's wheel during the greater part of the Middle Ages. Furthermore, this view could be upheld by the total lack of any reference to the potter's wheel in contemporary craftsmen's handbooks such as those of Eraclius and Theophilus (Merrifield, 1849; Hendrie, 1847).

A similar disparity appears if one considers the historical references to glazed pottery. Thus Theophilus speaks only of fritted Byzantine glazes, while Eraclius, who also mentions this type of glaze, gives no hint of the use of lead glazes until the Third Book which is generally believed to have been compiled in the twelfth century. That is to say, the first literary references to lead glazes do not occur until a clear two centuries after they had become fairly common in Western Europe; and an even longer period after their initial appearance as shown by the archaeological material.

Unhappily although the archaeological data tells one that the historical evidence falls very far wide of the mark, it does not complete the picture. In this case too much remains unexplained, for the pottery does not help to determine whether one wheel was a development from the other, for example, or whether the two were separate introductions or inventions. It may even seem ingenious to raise the question of independent invention in this context, but there are instances in which quite different devices that appeared during the Middle Ages have been hopelessly confused merely because both have been given the same name. The wheelbarrow is one such device. Sinophiles seem to derive considerable pleasure in pointing out that while the wheelbarrow first appeared in China during the Han dynasty (Goodrich, 1948), it was unknown in Europe until the thirteenth century so failing to recognize that one is dealing with two different contraptions, of different design, performing different functions, and probably evolved as the result of different sets of circumstances. Thus the Chinese wheelbarrow had a very large wheel set between the shafts at some considerable distance from the front end of the barrow. The top half of the wheel was boxed in, or had a platform set above it, and on this the goods were stowed. It is invariably, in the early illustrations, depicted as being used during agricultural operations, and it has been suggested that it was an adaptation of a two-wheeled hand-cart designed to move freely down the narrow Chinese footpaths and field boundaries. The European wheelbarrow is depicted with a small wheel set between the shafts at the very front end, while the burden was placed in a hod set between the shafts. It is always shown in early illustrations being used during building work, and was clearly derived from the two-man hand-barrow in which the leading carrier had been replaced by a wheel. Indeed the wheelbarrow and hand-barrow are not infrequently shown in the same illustration, making the connection between the two patently clear (Husa, 1967).

All the problems of interpretation so far discussed have bedevilled the study of the windmill which must be seen as one of the outstanding achievements of mediaeval technicians. Most historians of mediaeval technology would probably agree that the Middle Ages saw the development of two quite distinct types of windmill, and that in all probability there was no connection between their separate origins (Wailes, 1956). The first, the vertical-axled windmill was evolved in Persia where, in a modified form, it still exists today (Wulff, 1965). Its presence was first recorded by the tenth century geographers al Istakhri and al Mas'udi, while its spread into Samarkand is noted by a Chinese author in the early thirteenth century, although no illustration exists until the end of that century. This type of windmill was, in all probability, an adaptation of the vertical-axled watermill, in which the turbine-wheel was replaced by a sail-wheel, the lower part of the mud-brick building being designed with apertures that allowed the wind to impinge upon one half of the sail-wheel only. As in the vertical-axled water-mill there was a direct drive from the sail-wheel to the mill-stone.

The European windmill, as first depicted, was of totally different construction. The mill-house was a wooden, gabled building mounted on a single substantial vertical post, about which it could rotate, and is thus referred to as a post-mill. The sails drove a horizontal axle which, through a crown-and-pinion gearing, turned the millstone. The two revolutionary features of the design were the house that could be turned into wind and the sails which were cloth-covered lattice structures set at an angle to the main arms or sweeps. The mediaeval craftsman was, however, no novice in the art of constructing large, mobile, wooden structures such as siege-towers, while the principle of rotating a heavy load on a vertical timber was also a feature of the slewing cranes often depicted in use on mediaeval building sites (Husa, 1967). Equally the cloth-covered lattice may be seen in many contexts – window coverings, wagon tilts and stall awnings, to mention the most obvious. A valid case could be made, therefore for the independent invention of the European post-mill.

Illustrations of post-mills do not appear until the end of the thirteenth century, and thereafter become relatively common showing a remarkably uniform design across the greater part of temperate Europe. However, the earlier existence of the windmill in Europe is known from references to it in legal documents, mostly dating from the end of the twelfth century onwards. The assumption is thus made that the early documentary references apply to post-mills, which although probable, is far from demonstrable, and it could be argued that the earliest references may well apply to some less developed form of windmill, perhaps one that could not be made to face into wind.

In discussing the early documentary evidence of windmills Lynn White (1962, 1969) goes to considerable lengths to demonstrate that "the horizontal-axle windmill appeared in Yorkshire in 1185 as an independent invention." This opinion is arrived at by dismissing any earlier, admittedly dubious, references to windmills on the familiar grounds that the documents are later forgeries, contain interpolations, or marginal glosses, or cannot be closely dated. The gist of White's argument seems to be to demonstrate that the windmill came, so as to speak, straight off the drawing-board, and within a matter of a decade or so was diffused, and being taxed, throughout a large part of Europe. A scrutiny of the document of 1185, however, only tells one that an agreed rent of eight shillings a year was to be paid to a Yorkshire landlord. In other words, by 1185 the potential output of a windmill was sufficiently well understood to allow a tenant and landlord in Yorkshire to agree upon a fair rent. The document gives no hint of the windmill being a novel device. A more rational interpretation of this document, and others slightly later than it, would be that by the end of the twelfth century the windmill was already beginning to become a fairly common device in Northern France and England from whence most of the documents referring to windmills come, be they considered genuine or false.

The independent development of the windmill in Europe, however probable, cannot be allowed to pass unquestioned. Little is known about the second major type of windmill that appeared in Europe during the Middle Ages, the tower mill, it being first illustrated in the late fourteenth century (Wailes, 1956). It differed from the post-mill in that the major part of the building was a cylindrical stone tower upon the top of which was a conical roof, or cap, carrying the sweeps and shaft, and which could be turned into wind. The sails and internal workings of the tower-mill were identical to those of the post-mill. This type of mill is still quite common in Iberia and other countries bordering the Mediterranean, and it is from this region that it is generally supposed to have been introduced into temperate Europe. In the Mediterranean lands, however, there is a sorry lack of any reference to, or illustration of the tower-mill prior to the fifteenth century. In the face of such a void the assumption is usually made that, if anything, the tower-mill was initially an adaption of the post-mill rather than vice versa. However the possibility that the tower-mill may have existed long before one has any records of it cannot be lightly dismissed, for save for a few oblique references one might not know that mills driven by animal traction were, if not common, at least used in the Middle Ages. Thus the late thirteenth century *Vocabulista in arabico* equates the word *tahuna* with *molendinium bestie, sine aqua*, while a French cartuary of the same century mentions specifically a horse-operated mill (Delisle, 1851), although no illustrations of such a mill seem to have survived*.

The possible origins of the post-mill can now be seen to be almost limitless. If one hazards a wild guess that the post-mill was being developed not at the end of the twelfth century, but rather at the end of the eleventh, then a whole series of unanswerable questions come to mind. Was the post-mill stimulated by someone, perhaps a member of the Varangian guard or the ubiquitous Crusader, who had seen the Persian windmill, or heard of it first hand in the Orient? Was it the brain-child of some European scholar of Arab writing who had read the geography of al Istakhri? Or was it the outcome of years of patient work by Europe's leading school of engineers, the Cistercian monks?

One will probably never know the answer to these and many similar questions raised by the study of mediaeval technology, but of one thing one may be sure: were the number of historical sources doubled, or miraculously multiplied many times, the principal objections to them as evidence would remain. They do not and cannot provide the kind of information that the study requires. For the future the only information that will help will have to come from archaeological excavations. Unfamiliar with the niceties of marginal glosses, suspect manuscripts and interpolations, archaeologists as a rule tend to be over-awed by historical discussion. They should not be, at least as far as the history of mediaeval technology is concerned, for demonstrably the traditional historical sources provide a chronological framework that is very considerably retarded, and as a concommittant a history that is patently false.

References

Delisle, L. (1851). *J.B.A.A.* **6**, 405–8.
Forbes, R. J. (1955). "Studies in Ancient Technology", Vol. 2. Leiden.

* In parenthesis it is interesting to note that the presence of a substantial mill-stone in a mediaeval building does not, therefore, necessarily imply that it came from either a wind- or water-mill.

Forbes, R. J. (1956). *In* "A History of Technology". (C. Singer, E. J. Holmyard, A. R. Hall and T. I. Williams, eds), Vol. 2, pp. 589–622. Oxford University Press, Oxford.

Gille, B. (1956). *In* "A History of Technology". (C. Singer, E. J. Holmyard, A. R. Hall and T. I. Williams, eds), Vol. 2, pp. 629–65. Oxford University Press, Oxford.

Goodrich, L. C. (1948). "A Short History of the Chinese People". George Allen & Unwin, London.

Hendrie, R. (1847). "An Essay upon Various Arts in Three Books by Theophilus". John Murray, London.

Husa, V. (1967). "Traditional Crafts and Skills". Hamlyn, London.

Jope, E. M. (1956). *In* "A History of Technology" (C. Singer, E. J. Holmyard, A. R. Hall and T. I. Williams, eds), Vol. 2, pp. 284–310. Oxford University Press, Oxford.

Merrifield, M. P. (1849). "Original Treatises on the Arts of Painting". John Murray, London.

Rieth, A. (1960). "5,000 Jahre Töpferscheibe". Thorbebecke, Konstanze.

Wailes, R. (1956). *In* "A History of Technology". (C. Singer, E. J. Holmyard, A. R. Hall and T. I. Williams, eds), Vol. 2, pp. 623–28. Oxford University Press, Oxford.

White, L. (1962). "Medieval Technology and Social Change". Oxford University Press, Oxford.

White, L. (1969). *In* "The Fontana Economic History of Europe". (C. M. Cipolla, ed), Vol. 1. Fontana.

Wulff, H. (1965). "The Traditional Crafts of Persia". Philadelphia University Press, Philadelphia.

Photogrammetry in Archaeology

H. M. STEWART

PHOTOGRAMMETRY, the science of extracting dimensional information from photographs and of making scale drawings from them, has obvious possibilities in archaeology. Exploration of these, however, is discouraged by the high cost of special equipment and services and by the rather complicated technicalities. In the following account* the economics are considered, and enough elementary theory is given to show what is feasible both with simple equipment and with commercial help. The instrumental operation is described briefly to illustrate the principles only, and will have to be amplified in practice by reference to the Bibliography or to the instrument manuals. This treatment is justified by the reader's need to know, preferably before he becomes deeply involved, whether the techniques are likely to be useful in his own case.

A photograph is a perspective projection in which the scale varies with the distance from the camera. Although in theory the scale may be calculated from the proportion focal length: lens-to-subject distance, it is simpler, especially in the case of aerial photographs, to obtain it by comparing the distances between points in the photograph and on the ground. This involves a small amount of ordinary surveying or comparison with an existing map of the area.

The need for such measurement, however, goes further. Since it is difficult to maintain strict verticality in an aerial camera, a slight tilt will occur, which must be corrected in plotting by the use of surveyed control points as described below. In addition the presence of surface relief will require vertical control by means of levelling. Photogrammetry cannot, therefore, entirely supplant traditional methods of surveying.

The decision whether to complete the work by ground methods or by photogrammetry will depend on the size, complexity and accessibility of the site, and also on the relative expense. Some

* The writer is indebted to Mr K. B. Atkinson and Mr E. H. Wickens of the Department of Photogrammetry and Surveying, University College London, for much valuable advice.

commercial firms which offer photogrammetric services recommend ordinary ground survey for areas of less than about 5 hectares. Flying involves certain fixed charges which are independent of and usually greater than the cost of photography. Their effect on the individual price of photographs is, however, offset as the number of these increases. Unfortunately, the archaeologist rarely deals with areas large enough to be economic in this respect, and in the absence of existing photographs his best hope is that the work may be combined commercially with some other project on the same route. This may mean some delay. Because of several variable factors charges are difficult to quote in general, but the minimum figure is likely to exceed £100.

Vertical photographs are taken in parallel runs from an aircraft in level flight, continuity of the cover being ensured by overlaps of about 60% between successive frames and about 30% between runs. The 60% overlap provides also for the plotting techniques described below and for stereoscopic examination of pairs of photographs. Paper prints are of contact size, normally 230 mm. square, and may contain in the margin the serial number, the date, the focal length, and the flying height (approximate only) obtained from the altimeter. This information is present on the negative, but is not always printed unless requested.

Since the scales of archaeological plans are usually at least 1:1 000, those of the photographs would have to be no smaller than 1:5 000 and preferably much larger. Because of the minimum flying-height of 1 500 feet imposed on fixed-winged aircraft an upper scale-limit of 1:3 000 is likely to be exceeded only by the use of helicopters, in which case 1:500 is possible.

Existing aerial photographs, available from the sources listed at the end of this paper, are mostly in the range 1:20 000 to 1:3 000. Cover at the larger scales must obviously be very sparse.

As an alternative method of photography cameras have been mounted in kites (Addison, 1949), balloons (Walton, 1969; Whittlesey, 1967, 1968) and model aircraft, all of which, however, require special weather conditions, and are difficult to control with any precision.

Work at larger scales is possible with ground-based equipment such as high tripods or masts (Cooke and Wacher, 1970; McFadgen, 1971; Nylén, 1963; Whittlesey, 1966). The maximum size of square that can be covered by a vertical camera is equal to the shorter dimension of the negative $\times \dfrac{\text{height of camera}}{\text{focal length}}$. This means that in order to cover a 3-m. square with a 35 mm. camera one would need to use a normal 50-mm. lens at a height of about 6·5 m. or a 38-mm. (wide-angle) lens at about 5 m. (Lenses of shorter focal length might introduce too much distortion.) In order to allow a margin in photographing a grid square it would be advisable to increase these heights somewhat.

Where the detail is fairly compact, the camera may be mounted on a horizontal bracket fixed to the top of a levelling staff, the shutter being operated by a pneumatic cable release. With a 4-m. staff the area covered by a 50-mm. lens is just under 3×2 m. so that the bracket need not be longer than 1 m. to reach the middle from one of the longer sides. This technique is useful in conjunction with a marked-out grid of 1-m. squares.

Surveying with Single Photographs

The methods described below relate specifically to vertical photographs, but may be used also with horizontal ones of vertical features.

There are two main forms of distortion in an aerial photograph, one of which, namely tilt, has already been mentioned. The other is produced by ground relief, which causes variations in scale at different levels, thus affecting the relative positions of points in plan.

Where the relief is negligible, camera tilt alone may be corrected by optical means. If a photographic enlarger with a tilting head is adjusted so as to reproduce the angle of the camera at the moment of exposure, the image projected on to a horizontal surface will under certain conditions approximate to a true plan. The optics are in practice upset by the difference in the camera and the enlarger lenses, and would present considerable difficulty in the case of a very oblique photograph. Here, however, we are concerned only with slight departures from the vertical.

The angle of the camera is reproduced by causing four widely separated points of detail in the negative to project on to their plotted positions on the plan, the rectified image being obtained by adjusting first the shape and then the scale. (In an enlarger with fixed head the paper instead of the negative may be tilted.) Should no suitable points occur on the ground, they must be established by means of prominent markers such as white-painted boards before the photographs are taken.

Another instrument which may be used for rectifying photographs is the camera lucida, in which the image of the print is seen super-

*

imposed on paper by means of a glass prism. The print, which is mounted on a tilting easel, is adjusted so that four control points coincide with their plotted positions, and the other details are then traced. Because of its different optical system the instrument may be used to correct obliquities rather greater than is possible with the enlarger. Surface relief may be dealt with by dividing the photograph into areas which lie in separate planes, each of which must have its own set of control points. The camera lucida is made in several forms, two of which are manufactured by Zeiss (Jena) and Zeiss (Oberkochen).

Graphical methods of rectification are also possible, but more laborious; see Crone (1963), Kilford (1970), and Williams (1969).

Surveying with Overlapping Photographs

Although a single vertical photograph may be used for mapping ground which is virtually flat or which may be divided easily into separate planes, it becomes very unreliable where there is much relief. The top of a flag-staff, while coinciding with its base when in the middle of a vertical photograph, will elsewhere appear to lean outward. It is evident, therefore, that any high point away from the centre will be similarly displaced from its true plan position.

The fact that the displacement is radial, however, enables us to determine at least the direction of a required point from the centre, and if we know its directions from the centres of two overlapping photographs, correctly oriented in relation to each other, we may find its plan position by intersection as on the plane table.

In photographs taken with a survey camera the centre or *principal point* (the intersection of the camera axis with the focal plane) is indicated on the negative either directly by a small cross or indirectly by collimation marks in the middle of each margin. Because of the 60% overlap each photograph has in addition to its own principal point the ground position of the principal point of the next photograph. A line joining these points on each print is known as the *base line*, and represents the distance travelled by the aircraft between exposures.

Although it would be possible to plot points by tracing the angles between their radial directions and the base line, this would be very laborious. Instead the plotting may be done mechanically on an instrument such as the Radial Line Plotter (manufactured by Rank Precision Industries Ltd.), in which intersecting cursor arms rotating about the principal points of the two photographs, viewed through a stereoscope, are moved over the surface to trace features at the required scale by means of a mechanical linkage. This instrument does not, of course, correct for tilt.

The Measurement of Height

If we look through a horizontal sheet of glass at a point some distance below it, the position of the point as seen by the left and the right eyes may be marked on the glass by two separate spots. In the case of a slightly higher point, involving greater convergence of the eyes, the spots will be marked closer together on the glass. There is, therefore, a relationship between the height of a point and the separation of its images in the picture plane.

On the substitution of two co-planar photographs for the optical fields of view the same conditions apply. When these photographs are placed side by side and oriented with reference to each other under a mirror stereoscope, the separation of identical points of detail may be measured with a stereometer. This instrument consists of a rod bearing two sliding glass plates with index marks in the form of spots as in the example described above. One of the plates is set roughly by a clamp and the other precisely by a micrometer screw. Although the measurements of separation so obtained will depend on the initial rough setting (common for all subsequent readings), it is the *differences* in reading which are important.

From two given spot heights and their micrometer readings it is possible to find the heights of other points proportionally from their readings by means of a graph. This graph is, in fact, very slightly curved, but for the present purpose it may be considered as a straight line. In order to avoid large extrapolations the given spot heights should be widely separated vertically.

Many of the points of which the heights are required will not, however, be represented by precise points of detail in the photographs. Here use is made of the principle of stereoscopy. If the two spots marked on the glass in the earlier example above are viewed through two tubes so that each eye sees only its respective spot, a fused image will be obtained, apparently floating in space at the same height as the original point. The same result is produced by the index spots in the stereometer, these being adjusted in separation by means of the micrometer screw until their combined image, seen through the stereoscope, appears to rest on the ground. A skilled operator should be able to make this adjustment consistently to within 0·03 mm.

Because of tilt in the photographs heights obtained by stereometer are reliable only near the given spot heights. Since calculation elsewhere is complicated by the fact that both photographs in an overlap are differently tilted, a mechanical solution is preferable.

Various types of plotting machine have been devised in order to combine the planning and heighting processes described above. Although because of the high cost of these instruments the work would have to be done commercially, it is important to understand the conditions required for their operation.

Two stereoscopic photographs are adjusted in the instrument so that they are in correct relative orientation. This is done by matching six points in the overlapping portion – the two principal points and one point in each corner of the overlap. The resulting stereoscopic "model" is subsequently adjusted in scale and made horizontal, the latter operation requiring at least three widely separated control points.

Although the plotting scale may on some instruments be considerably larger than that of the photographs, it is best kept within the ratio 5 : 1. The contour interval possible varies with the height of the camera, and the type of plotting equipment. Generally, it ranges from about H/350 to H/1 000 or less.

What has been said about the measurement of height in vertical photographs applies equally to the measurement of depth in horizontal ones. For recording architectural elevations, sculptured relief, etc (Atkinson, 1968, 1969) twin stereometric cameras are available, mounted on a bar of fixed length, usually 1–2 m., in such a way that the negatives are co-planar. The photographs may be taken horizontally and also at various inclinations. If the camera-to-subject distance is more than about eight times the length of the bar, the stereoscopic effect is too weak and the base length must be increased by separating the cameras. Alternatively, a phototheodolite, consisting of a theodolite with camera incorporated, may be set up at the ends of a measured base-line and directed perpendicularly to it so that the photographs are co-planar. Since these instruments are expensive and need some skill to operate, it will be necessary in many cases to place the work in the hands of a commercial firm.

When commercial help is obtained for the photography, it would be well to have the plotting done also, since the cost of this is relatively small.

In general, plotting with overlapping photographs is best suited to large sites, to architectural and other features which are difficult of access, and to sculptural detail (Hallert, 1971). On the average small site photographs, possibly in mosaic form, might be used for filling in the more complicated details only. This would avoid the delay which might result if facilities for stereo plotting were not readily available. Some form of working plan is usually essential for the conduct of an excavation.

Sources of Air Photographs

Official photographs of Britain, chiefly at a scale of 1 : 10 000, may be obtained from the Air Photographs Officer, Central Register of Air Photography, Department of the Environment, Whitehall, London, SW1, or from the Scottish Development Department, York Buildings, Queen Street, Edinburgh. The Ordnance Survey, Romsey Road, Maybush, Southampton, SO9 4DH, can also supply photography of large areas of Great Britain. The area required should be indicated by a map reference, preferably accompanied by a tracing from the 1 : 63 360 ("One-Inch") map.

Several commercial firms (see below) also have print libraries from which copies may be purchased.

Wartime aerial cover of those parts of Europe, excluding Britain, which were involved in the Second World War is held by the Air Photograph Library, Department of Geography, University of Keele, Staffordshire. Parts of Africa and Asia are also represented.

The Library of Air Photographs, University of Cambridge, covering British archaeological sites, and the Allen Collection, Ashmolean Museum, Oxford, relating chiefly to the Oxford area, are also available. These, however, consist largely of oblique photographs, which are not usually well suited to map-making.

Commercial Services

The following firms undertake air and ground survey, cartography and various types of photogrammetric work. They also have libraries of air photographs, chiefly of Britain, but including in most cases some overseas material.

B.K.S. Air Survey Ltd., Cleeve Road, Leatherhead, Surrey.

Cartographical Services (Southampton) Ltd., Landford Manor, Salisbury, Wilts.

Fairey Surveys Ltd., Reform Road, Maidenhead, Berks.

Hunting Surveys Ltd., Elstree Way, Boreham Wood, Herts.

Meridian Airmaps Ltd., Marlborough Road, Lancing, Sussex.

References

General

Crone, D. R. (1963). "Elementary Photogrammetry". Arnold, London.
Kilford, W. K. (1970). "Elementary Air Survey" (2nd edn). Pitman, London.

Archaeological

Addison, F. (1949). "Jebel Moya" I, 6; II, pls. 16–18, Wellcome Excavations in the Sudan, Oxford University Press.
Atkinson, K. B. (1968). *Photogrammetric Record* **6**(31), 24–31.
Atkinson, K. B. (1969). *Photogrammetric Record* **6**(34), 357–78.
Cooke, F. B. M. and Simpson, D. D. A. (1967). *Antiquity* **41**, 220–21.
Cooke, F. B. M. and Wacher, J. S. (1970). *Antiquity* **44**, 214–16.
Hallert, B. (1971). *Norwegian Archaeological Review* **4**(1), 28–36.
    Comments on the above: Nordbladh, J. and Rosvall, J. *ibid.* **4**(2), 69–74; Christensen, A. E. *ibid.* **4**(2), 75–76.
McFadgen, B. G. (1971). *Archaeometry* **13**, 71–81.
Nylén, E. (1963). *Antikvariskt Arkiv* **24**, Stockholm.
Walton, M. G. (1969). *In* Throckmorton *et al.* "Surveying in Archaeology Underwater". Colt Archaeological Institute, Monograph Series 5, 66–71, Quaritch, London.
Whittlesey, J. (1966). *Archaeology* **19**, 273–76, New York.
Whittlesey, J. (1967). *Archaeology* **20**, 67–68, New York.
Whittlesey, J. (1968). *Archaeology* **21**, 66–67, New York.
Williams, J. C. C. (1969). "Simple Photogrammetry". Academic Press, London & New York.

Specialized Photographic Techniques

V. M. CONLON

AFTER THE DEATH of Mr Cookson, who for many years was photographer to the Institute of Archaeology, Professor Grimes, the Director, recommended that I should carry on as principal of the Photographic Department. After a lifetime in the profession, my ambition was to develop photographic techniques that were adapted to the special needs of archaeologists. The Director also felt that there was a need for a more scientific approach to archaeological photography. With the support of his enthusiasm and interest in student research, I thus had the opportunity to carry out both his and my own wishes by tackling whatever problems arose.

The rapid advance of photography during the last twenty years requires in any practitioner an understanding of photographic theory. This may involve archaeologists in the use of fairly advanced physics for the understanding of scientific research techniques. One such important case is the use of invisible radiations which may reveal details which, if photographed by visible light, would remain invisible.

For instance: infra-red and ultra-violet radiations lie just beyond the limits of the light-spectrum visible to man. They are of wavelengths approximately between 700 nm.* and 12000 nm. (infra-red) and from 200 nm. to 400 nm. (ultra-violet). On occasion, either may be used to give valuable information not otherwise obtainable.

Infra-Red

Infra-red waves have powers of penetration far beyond those of

* The kilometre (Km), metre (m), millimetre (mm), micrometre (μm), and nanometre (nm) are the only permissible measurements of length on the S.I. system, each being $\frac{1}{1000}$ of the former. 1 nm is $\frac{1}{1,000,000,000}$ ($10-9$) of 1 m. The Ångstrom Unit (Å) $\frac{1}{100,000,000}$ ($10-8$ m) has been abandoned.

the shorter rays of visible light and so offer a means of recording what may otherwise be invisible. They can be used by archaeologists in the field or in the studio. It is a fact that objects which absorb certain colours of visible light may reflect infra-red rays to a marked degree. Thus the green pigment, chlorophyll in vegetation, absorbs most of the visible light but reflects the infra-red.

Colours of soils, rocks and sand often render differently on infra-red sensitive material from their appearance on ordinary panchromatic film, and the effects obtainable by this means make a subject worthy of study. Writings on papyrus quite invisible to the eye may often clearly be read in an infra-red photograph. Paintings in carbon on pottery or wall paintings almost obliterated by contact with soil or by weathering might be seen in relative completeness by infra-red illumination. Burial photographs by infra-red show contrast in certain features which in panchromatic material tend to be flattened.

Any camera can be used for infra-red photography providing that it is opaque to infra-red rays, i.e. non-metallic and so non-conducting of heat, otherwise fogging may easily occur.

The miniature camera is more or less foolproof. It is more often in using the field camera, where bellows and slides are vulnerable, that fogging may occur. Special non-conducting dark-slides are designed for the use of infra-red material.

Radiations of wavelengths longer than 700 nm., the upper limit of the visible spectrum, can be produced by artificial means, as by a 500-watt photoflood lamp, or strong sunlight.

Black-and-white infra-red films or plates are specially coated with an emulsion sensitive to violet blue and red light as well as to the infra-red. This can be obtained in the larger formats or in 35 mm. cassettes (Kodak's serial no. at present is 4143; this is mentioned as the firm recently replaced a previous grade of emulsion which is no longer obtainable). The new emulsion is of a higher speed, but is rather less contrasty than the old. Good results can, nevertheless, be obtained by using a contrasty developer. Coarse grain is a disadvantage in all infra-red emulsions, but careful control of exposure, temperature and the use of a developer of special formula will overcome this.

To block out unwanted visible light rays a filter must be used either on the camera-lens or the light source. For working by artificial light, the 88A filter is most satisfactory, giving the necessary selected transmission. For exterior work either the 25 or the 88A filter may be used: the latter for deeper penetration of mist or haze. Both these filters absorb the blue light to which the film is also sensitive. Visual focusing through a red filter, which transmits visible rays

Fig. 1. Kodachrome II.

Fig. 2. Infra-red colour. (by courtesy of John Dayton.)

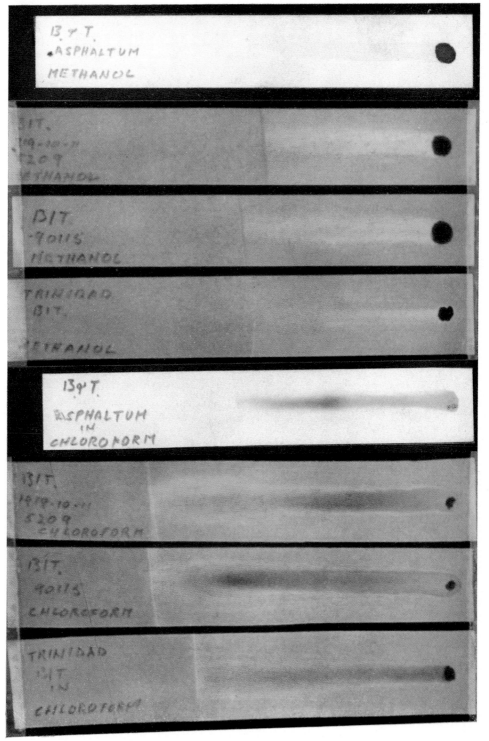

Fig. 4. Substances that fluoresce were photographed in ultra-violet light, using high speed ektachrome film with a deep yellow filter, No. 12. A Bitumen eluted in chloroform. B and D Samples of paper test strips, as seen in daylight. C Bitumen eluted in methanol. (by courtesy of John C. Bateman.)

nearest in length to the infra-red, is necessary, as no image is visible through the 88A filter. Once the image has been focused in red light, the distance between lens and emulsion should be further increased by approximately 1/250th part of the focal length of the lens. By using a small aperture such as F32, any slight error in adjustment will be compensated for by the increased depth of field.

A special *infra-red colour emulsion* is now available and the unusual characteristics of this film will be an asset in many photographic situations. It is sometimes called "false colour" film, because objects are reproduced in colours so different from those which the human eye sees in the subject. It is nevertheless capable of distinguishing dramatically qualities in the subject which are imperceptible to the naked eye or to ordinary colour film and so provides a new and powerful tool for archaeologists and other scientists.

Recently we did some experiments in which comparative aerial photographs were taken in black-and-white, infra-red, Ektachrome colour film and Ektachrome infra-red. The last proved its value, for although the infra-red colour was incorrect, through the use of a wrong filter, a survey of the country's contours was made possible, although only by the outline. Penetration of the atmosphere by infra-red enabled the features of importance in this particular case to be recorded in just the right degree of contrast. On the ordinary colour-film they were inevitably confused by varying colours of soil and vegetation.

John Dayton, a higher-degree student at the Institute of Archaeology, first experimented with black-and-white infra-red sensitive film. He then tried Kodachrome II (plate 1) with an exposure of 125 secs at F11, and finally infra-red colour (plate 2) exposed for 60 secs at F2·8. Both shots were made from an altitude of 4000 feet. The overall blue colour of the picture is due to the fact that the filter used did not absorb all the blue light to which the emulsion is extremely sensitive. A Kodak no. 12 filter would have been better. His perseverance in carrying out experiments under difficult conditons has provided preliminary evidence as to methods which might be used eventually by archaeologists for surveying wide areas of country. The same precautions as to the type of camera and slides used are necessary, as in the use of black-and-white infra-red film. Loading in darkness will prevent any premature fogging and, for this purpose, the valuable loading bag can be covered by an extra cloth.

Kodak infra-red Ektachrome film has good latitude if the proper filters are used. Recording is necessary of apertures, shutter speeds,

K*

etc. used in each shot, so that successes may be repeated on subsequent occasions and fault corrected.

Normal colour emulsions have three light sensitive emulsion layers, these being sensitized respectively to the blue, green and red of the visible spectrum.

In the infra-red colour emulsion the blue sensitive layer is replaced by one sensitized to infra-red radiations. This lies above the two layers which are sensitive one to green and the other to red radiation. The yellow no. 12 filter over the lens absorbs any blue light. The

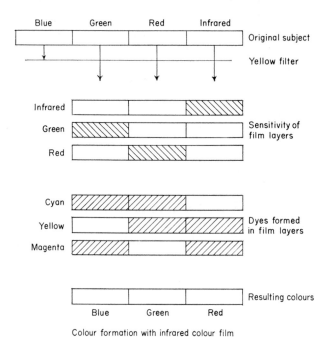

Colour formation with infrared colour film

Fig. 4.

Visual appearance of object	Infra-red strongly absorbed	Infra-red strongly reflected
Red	Green	Yellow
Green	Blue	Magenta
Blue	Grey to Black	Red
Cyan	Blue	Magenta
Magenta	Green	Yellow
Yellow	Cyan	Grey to White
Grey	Cyan	Grey

so-called "false colour" given by the infra-red film is summarized by the following chart and explanation.

For interpretation of infra-red colour pictures, it is evident that one has thoroughly to understand the special colours yielded. As in reading a map, the various arbitrary colours all convey particular information, so, in infra-red colour pictures, the colours will be as easy to read as on a map, when experience has perfected the use of the emulsion, and practice has been obtained in interpretation.

For indoor infra-red colour photography, the no. 12 filter is again used. Electronic flash gives the artificial illumination nearest to daylight in quality and this is recommended for good colour rendering.

By keeping detailed notes of exposures and lighting used in particular situations and for particular subjects, results should not vary greatly, and one would gradually learn by experience how to interpret the results.

Ultra-Violet

Photography by ultra-violet radiation is another scientific technique rarely used by archaeologists which, like infra-red, might reveal important evidence not visible when using ordinary emulsions. The band of ultra-violet radiation consists of a long waveband, 320 to 400 nanometres, middle ultra-violet, 280 to 320 nm., and a short waveband, 200 to 280 nm.

Ultra-violet radiation is generated by specially screened lamps adjustable to produce particular bands of wavelengths for the use of the photographer. Such lamps are mostly of the mercury-discharge blacklamp type provided with 125w mercury discharge tubes contained in Woods glass outer envelope. All visible lighting must be cut out so that excited fluorescence in a subject or reflected ultra-violet can become visible in the darkness, although visible light is filtered out at the lamps, filters on the lens are also needed for both these methods. For photographing fluorescence only, the 2B or a 12 filter will give satisfactory results. These are so designed that only the desired visible radiation is recorded by the film. For the method using reflection, the 18A is often recommended.

For photography by ultra-violet in the field it is necessary to have a folding light-tight tent, the size of which is governed by the necessity to work in reasonable comfort with whatever type of camera is used or for covering the whole area required, which might be a grave, skeleton, mosaic or wall plaster.

For fieldwork battery-powered lamps have been designed to provide a source of the long wave, ultra-violet, 320 to 400 nm. They have a universal type of battery, so that these may be replaced in most parts of the world, making it possible to use this technique in (for instance) caves or tombs where it would perhaps be impossible to get power from a generator. The lamps are not powerful enough to cover a large area, but this difficulty can be overcome by working over it in sections.

An emulsion which is sensitive to the blue end of the visible spectrum is recommended if high contrast is needed, but the slow speed of this emulsion restricts its use, unless time is not a consideration, as in studio work. Experience will decide a choice; for the larger format, Ilford Zenith plate or Kodak Ortho Royal; for the 35 mm. camera, Kodak recording film (speed 1000 Weston) gives excellent results and avoids the necessity for a prolonged exposure.

In developing films or plates which tend to have coarse grain, dilution and prolonged development will reduce this.

Most lenses are suitable for ultra-violet except when using the short waveband, 200 to 280 nm. In that case, because of the absorption of ultra-violet by ordinary glass and fluorescence of cement between compound lenses, it is essential to use a quartz lens. If photographing a subject in sections, it is inadvisable to use a wide-angle lens. Because of excessive distortion at the edges of the field, difficulty will be encountered in piecing together several prints to represent the whole subject, owing to differing degrees of error at the joins.

It is gradually becoming clear that there are many uses for this technique in archaeology, after some preliminary experiment in most cases.

In the studio we may have to work on painted pottery in which the patterns are worn, faded writing on papyrus, coloured designs on ancient wall plaster, or old vellum or paper documents. In most of these subjects the pigments or inks are metallic compounds. If an ultra-violet photograph shows little beyond what is already visible to the eye, it may be guessed that the colouring is a carbon ink, and this would better be photographed by infra-red.

When re-assembling broken bones, missing pieces still in the matrix in which the bones were buried can be found by viewing it under the ultra-violet lamps. In this way important small fragments often become readily visible owing to their fluorescence when excited by specific radiations.

In the field, photography by ultra-violet illumination has been used on sections in cave earths (consisting mainly of non-fluorescent clays) to identify fossiliferous layers and show the positions of any bones embedded in them.

In the case of skeletal remains in sand soils, these may be badly decayed and if moved from their matrix will break up. If, before they are touched a photograph by ultra-violet is taken, the outlines of the bones will fluoresce and show the excavator the position of each part before it is cleaned or lifted. If bone shows a white fluorescence under ultra-violet this proves the presence of organic matter. No such fluorescence will be obtained from cremated bone, so that the reaction of any piece to ultra-violet radiation will distinguish it at once as part of an inhumation or a cremation.

Even the soil in which a skeleton has been buried will sometimes retain the outline after the bones have been removed, owing to the presence of particles of bone dust or organic matter which will fluoresce.

For painted pottery, any parts spoiled or blurred by contact with soil, or, in the case of objects buried in caves or wall-paintings, where the atmosphere has affected and partly destroyed the paint, photography can now be carried out on the site, with the ultra-violet battery lamps. Records can thus often be made of lay-out and materials which it may not be possible to remove to base.

Recording fluorescence in colour. Since different minerals and organic materials fluoresce in different colours under ultra-violet excitation, it may be useful to distinguish them by colour photography. Total darkness is required for this, as in the case of black-and-white emulsions. The location and nature of mineral deposits in rocks may be shown, and also fossil bones, human or animal skeletons, and the presence of many organic and mineral substances in wall-paintings, woven textiles and overpainted works of art.

The radiation is generated by the same ultra-violet mercury discharge blacklamp or the battery lamp if in the field. With photographic emulsions being inherently sensitive to ultra-violet and blue, a barrier filter must be used to absorb the blue rays that would affect coloured fluorescences.

Kodak filters 2B, 12 or 15, are blue and ultra-violet absorbers. In the illustrated example (plate 2) of an experiment by paper chromatography, the no. 12 filter gave a satisfactory result, using Kodak High-speed Ektachrome daylight film. Daylight-type colour film is generally to be recommended, for with it yellows and reds are rendered well, while films designed for artificial light accentuate the blues. It is only by experimenting, however, that one can obtain the colour result approaching most nearly to the actuality, as the fluorescence of different materials varies widely.

Any camera may be used or a lens of any focal length suitable for the actual distances between camera, object and light source. These may have to be rather short, since the low energy of colour fluorescences often requires long exposures. For the experiment described below a Schacht M Travenar 1. 28/50 R lens, a macrotype, was used, and is often found satisfactory for close-up work at various low magnifications, bordering on those used in microscope work. There was no need in this case of a quartz lens. To make positive distinctions between different fluorescence-colours, separate tests must first be made.

If colour developing is to be carried out by a professional, one must find a dependable processor or the results might be rendered useless by variations in development.

The subject of this research, by Mr John Bateman, as a photographic project at the University of London in the Photographic Department, is a method for distinguishing mineral bitumen from vegetable tar or pitch. Paper chromatography is used to separate from bitumen and wood tar, or wood tar pitch, and coal tar or coal tar pitch, substances that fluoresce characteristically in ultra-violet light.

A particle of the unknown material is dissolved in a minimum quality of chloroform. A drop of the solution is placed 1 cm. from the lower end of a Whatman filter paper strip (10 cm. × 1½ cm.). The bottom of the paper dips into a trough of a suitable solvent which is drawn by capillarity up the paper, carrying with it at different rates some different constituents of the material in question.

When seen under ultra-violet light, the separate fronts of these are seen as streaks of different fluorescent colours, which may distinguish one constituent from another.

The coloured illustrations were made on Ektachrome high-speed daylight film, using a 35 mm. camera fitted with the Schacht M Travenar 1. 28/50 R lens and a Kodak 12 filter, at an aperture of F2.8 and 8 seconds exposure.

The result shows the characteristic colours given by bitumen dissolved in chloroform with methanol as the running solvent. The characteristic chromatogram of each material will make a positive distinction possible between it and any similar material run under the same conditions.

The photographic problem was to give a meaningful reproduction of the chromatograms which in daylight appear only in black-and-white as illustrated.

The Photography of Flints

P. G. DORRELL

MANY ARCHAEOLOGISTS consider the photography of flint tools to be more or less a waste of time, the results being rarely as accurate and never as informative as those obtained from a good drawing. There are several grounds for complaint. Against a light background the edges of even slightly translucent flints are lost, while a dark background will cause darker flint to become virtually invisible. No matter how carefully the lighting may be arranged, reflections will cause some faces of the flint to be emphasized more than others – an emphasis having little relationship to natural shape or to working. The colour of the material may be so marked, or so variegated, that the face-intersections are partly or wholly obscured. Another, and perhaps subtler, drawback is that if a group of tools, or indeed of any other artifacts, is photographed so as to fill the picture-area of a short focal length of lens, those towards the edges of the frame will not present a strictly plan view, and may indeed suffer distortion of their dimensions, the ratios of which may well be of importance in analysis. Unfortunately when the objects are of irregular shape it is rarely possible to detect this fault in the finished print.

It might seem then that it would be wiser to abandon flint photography altogether and to trust that the time and skill will be available to draw whatever flints are significant both in the field and in the study of collections. But time is almost always at a premium on an excavation, especially overseas, and skilled draughtsmanship is not always available – the more so as the only hand that many flint specialists trust is their own. This problem becomes critical of course in countries which will not allow finds to be exported. So it may be worthwhile to explore briefly the drawbacks in photography and to try to provide answers at least to some of them.

The first objection quoted above is easily dealt with. If the underside of the flint is painted with any opaque, water-soluble medium, it will appear as completely opaque and the edges will be recorded (Figs. 1 and 2). The colour of the paint seems to be of little import-

Fig. 1.   Fig. 2.

ance unless the photograph is to be in colour and the flint is very thin, when white or a light grey is preferable.

Problems of the unequal emphasis of different surfaces, and of variegated colour, are far more difficult to overcome and may often prove to be insurmountable. Direct, intense reflections can usually be eliminated by diffusing the light-source with gauze or with translucent plastic (a large, white plastic bottle halved lengthwise makes an excellent and easily obtainable diffuser). A similar result may sometimes be obtained by means of polarizing filters or by using a dulling spray. Whatever is done in this direction however is likely to be to some extent self-defeating. If the incident light is so diffused, or the artifact so treated, that all surfaces reflect equal amounts of light, then none may be distinguishable at all. It would be invidious to cite examples, but several standard works contain flint photographs in which the lighting is so subtle that even the outline of the artifact has been lost.

A great improvement may often be attained by treating the flint itself with a thin, opaque, non-reflecting coating. Details of this technique are given in Ives (1941), and in Weide and Webster (1967). A commonly used method is to deposit a layer of ammonium chloride over the artefact, thin enough not to obscure any three-dimensional detail, but opaque enough to mask the colour of the flint, and to present a uniform white surface. This technique has been used successfully in the past but when it was tried recently at the Institute a number of snags emerged. The bottoms of deeply conchoidal facets were inclined to fill up, the powder slid off steep faces, and the process had to be carefully watched and controlled throughout.

Although, in laboratory terms, the apparatus is simple in the extreme – a hot-plate, and flasks of ammonia and of hydrocholoric acid connected by tubes and a y-junction to a bell-jar or desiccator – even this equipment might not be readily available on an excavation, nor might quantities of ammonia and hydrochloric acid be welcome in a

Fig. 3.

Fig. 4.

field headquarters. Various paints, sprays and powders have now been tried in the Institute as alternatives and it has been found that ordinary commercial light grey poster paint, thinly applied, is as effective as any, and can be easily washed off afterwards.

It can be seen by comparing Figs. 3 and 4 that the worked faces of this flint, admittedly an extreme example of colour and texture variation, can be reasonably well recorded by this method. Obviously this delineation of surfaces is at the expense of any record of the material itself, in fact the tool appears to be cut from meringue or something similar. The result is clearly not ideal, but at least a page of such flints would give a reasonably faithful rendering of shapes and surfaces, and the eye could distinguish and compare the more important features.

Based on this method another technique, widely used in technical drawing, suggests itself which might be useful at times. If a negative of a painted-out flint is printed on non-glossy paper, preferably to

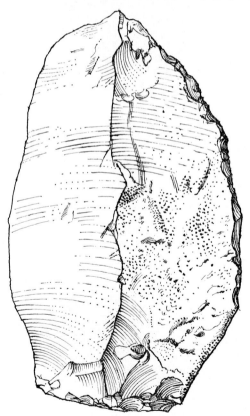

Fig. 5.

give a rather pale image, it can be used as a guide for drawing and the image then bleached away to leave a line drawing (Fig. 6). For a proficient flint draughtsman any such complication is superfluous, but for anyone less competent it might offer advantages of accuracy and of time saved. In particular when finds cannot be brought home, and when time is short it might provide a way of recording large quantities of material. The painting-out and photography is relatively quick and simple, and the more time-consuming operations of printing, drawing and bleaching can be reserved for later. It is true that most draughtsmen dislike drawing from anything but the original object, with obvious reason, but the choice may not be between degrees of accuracy, but between recording and not recording finds.

In order to test this method Mr Terry Ball, who is a professional surveyor and draughtsman but not a professional drawer of flints, very kindly offered to make two drawings of the flint pictured in

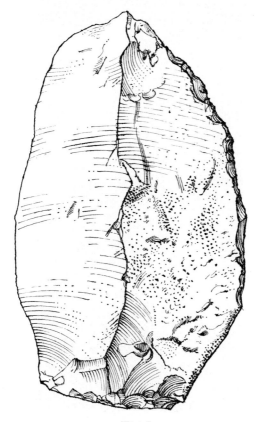

Fig. 6.

Fig. 3. One was made by the ordinary methods of measurement
(Fig. 5), and the other by the technique outlined above (Fig. 6). In
terms of accuracy the results are not very different. Details of the
exact shape and position of small surface features are shown more
clearly in Fig. 6, while the texture of the flint is rendered more
accurately in Fig. 5. However, it took Mr Ball nearly twice as long to
make the free-hand drawing as it did to work from the greyed print.
The time saved, moreover, was longer than the time taken to photo-

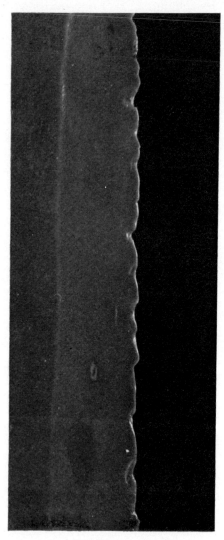

Fig. 7.

graph, print and finally to bleach-out the print. If a large number of drawings were in prospect the saving in time of skilled labour might well be worth the extra handling and organization involved in photography.

In one field of flint recording photography is certainly the most useful method, and often the only one possible. This is in the study of retouch or wear marks of such size that magnification of the artefact

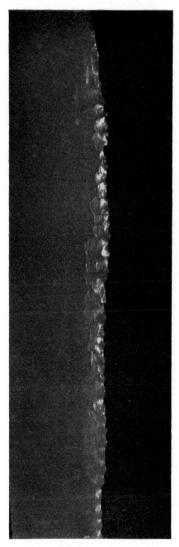
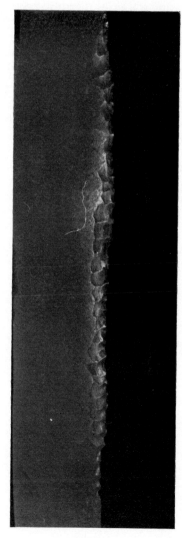

Fig. 8.   Fig. 9.

is necessary in the recording. Often such marks could be drawn only approximately, accurate measurement being almost impossible to attain. Fortunately it is usually possible to photograph such features without difficulty if attention is paid to the direction and diffusion of the lighting. Figure 7 shows the upper surface edge of a much worn and polished sickle blade. One light, its axis at right angles to, and slightly below the edge is sufficient to reveal the form and condition of the retouch (had this blade been made from any but the most opaque material it would have been necessary to paint out its under-surface, black background notwithstanding). Figures 8 and 9 show the edge of a finely retouched blade. In both photographs one light was used at right angles to, and slightly above, the edge. In Fig. 8 the light was direct, while in Fig. 9 it was diffused with translucent plastic. Not only are the retouch scars far more clearly defined in Fig. 9 and the distracting spots of reflection eliminated, but a band of gloss along the edge is revealed. It is not of much value to suggest general rules for the angles, distance, intensity and diffusion of lighting in such circumstances : far better to move the lights or the artefact while watching the effect through the camera viewfinder until an optimum position is reached. The process is time-consuming but calls for no special skill or equipment.

Studies of the microscopic striations and abrasion marks which result from tool-use are rather more specialized and call for more sophisticated methods and equipment. A general account of the techniques involved is given in Semenov.

The photographs illustrating this article were all taken with a medium-priced 35-mm. reflex camera, using a 55-mm. focal length lens and extension tubes. This type of camera, the sort in fact carried by most archaeologists, seems perfectly adequate for nearly all flint photography. If the lens is of this focal length or longer the dangers of wide-angle distortion, mentioned earlier, will be largely avoided. The lighting came from two desk-lamps fitted with 100 watt bulbs.

References

Ives, R. L. (1941). *American Antiquity*, **6**.
Semenov, S. A. (1964). "Prehistoric Technology". Cory, Adams and Mackay, London.
Weide, D. L. and Webster, G. D. (1967). *American Antiquity*, **32**.

Author Index

Subject Index